EU Payment Services

EU Payment Services

Regulation and Innovation

LOUISE DAMKJÆR CHRISTENSEN

Associate Professor of Financial Market Law, Department of Law, University of Southern Denmark, Odense, Denmark

OXFORD
UNIVERSITY PRESS

OXFORD
UNIVERSITY PRESS

Great Clarendon Street, Oxford, OX2 6DP,
United Kingdom

Oxford University Press is a department of the University of Oxford.
It furthers the University's objective of excellence in research, scholarship,
and education by publishing worldwide. Oxford is a registered trade mark of
Oxford University Press in the UK and in certain other countries

Published in the United States of America by Oxford University Press
198 Madison Avenue, New York, NY 10016, United States of America

British Library Cataloguing in Publication Data
Data available

Library of Congress Control Number: 2025931401

ISBN 9780198949053

DOI: 10.1093/9780198949084.001.0001

Printed and bound by
CPI Group (UK) Ltd, Croydon, CR0 4YY

The manufacturer's authorised representative in the EU for product safety is Oxford University Press España S.A. of El Parque Empresarial San Fernando de Henares, Avenida de Castilla, 2 – 28830 Madrid (www.oup.es/en or product.safety@oup.com). OUP España S.A. also acts as importer into Spain of products made by the manufacturer.

FSC
www.fsc.org
MIX
Paper | Supporting
responsible forestry
FSC® C013604

Preface

This book is a product of my PhD thesis which was titled 'Adapting to Financial Innovation in EU Payment Services Regulation' and submitted to the PhD School at the University of Southern Denmark on 20 December 2022. The oral defence took place in Odense, Denmark on 23 March 2023. Since then, the thesis has undergone revisions to transform it into this book. It is my hope that it will provide its readers with insights into the regulation of payment services in the EU and the interplay between regulation and innovation.

When writing this book, I sought to include in the final manuscript as much relevant material published before June 2024 as possible. The book includes the consideration of some economic elements. As the intended readership of the book is legal scholars and practitioners, the inclusion and treatment of the economic material has been chosen with this group in mind.

I am grateful to my excellent team of supervisors, Associate Professor Niels Skovmand Rasmussen (University of Southern Denmark), Professor Jesper Lau Hansen (University of Copenhagen), and Professor Andrea Minto (Ca'Foscari University of Venice), for their support and guidance throughout which has helped me greatly in producing this book.

I would also like to thank the PhD assessment committee, consisting of Professor Nina Dietz Legind (University of Southern Denmark), Professor Eva Micheler (London School of Economics), and Professor Henrik Lando (Copenhagen Business School), for challenging my work at the public defence, and for their valuable comments on my thesis which have helped me improve the quality of this book.

Thanks are also due to the Law Department at the University of Southern Denmark for making this work possible, as well as to my many great colleagues who have shown tireless support. I would also like to thank the Law School at the London School of Economics for hosting me as a visiting research student in the autumn of 2021. I have benefited from the discussions with the Law School's professors, researchers, and PhD candidates. Finally, the greatest appreciation will have to be given to my loving husband Dennis, who has supported me throughout this journey.

Louise Damkjær Christensen
Kolding, November 2024

Contents

Table of Cases

EUROPEAN UNION

NATIONAL

Denmark

Table of Legislation

EUROPEAN UNION: REGULATIONS AND DIRECTIVES

Communications from the Commission

Guidelines, opinions, and decisions from European Supervisory Authorities

NATIONAL LEGISLATION:

Denmark

UNITED KINGDOM

Abbreviations

AIS	Account Information Service
AISP	AIS provider
API	Application Programming Interface
CSC	common and secure open standards of communication
EBA	European Banking Authority
EC	European Community
ECJ	European Court of Justice/Court of Justice of the European Union
EIOPA	European Insurance and Occupational Pensions Authority
ESA	European Supervisory Authority
ESMA	European Securities and Markets Authority
EU	European Union
NCA	National Competent Authority
NTP	Normative Turned Positive theory
PIS	Payment Initiation Service
PISP	PIS provider
PSD1	Payment Services Directive (first)
PSD2	Payment Services Directive (second)
PSP	payment service provider
RTS	regulatory technical standard
SCA	strong customer authentication
TEU	Treaty on European Union
TFEU	Treaty on the Functioning of the European Union

1

INTRODUCING EU PAYMENT SERVICES

1 Introduction

Innovation in payment services has changed the regulatory landscape for more than a decade. The Payment Services Directive was adopted in 2007,[1] with the aim of harmonising payment services regulation across EU Member States. Afterwards, innovative developments caused that directive to be quickly revised and in 2015 the second Payment Services Directive (PSD2) was adopted.[2] Since then, entrepreneurs and incumbent institutions have not been taking it slow, as new forms and ways of payment and related services continue to grow. The question therefore becomes whether the regulatory framework, the PSD2, can keep up with the pace of the innovative development. The purpose of this book is to examine the PSD2's ability to regulate EU payment services while also accommodating innovation in payment services.

By now, there is no doubt that financial innovation in technological solutions is dominating most aspects of financial services.[3] This is also true for payment services, especially where the third-party payment service providers and the underlying infrastructure deliver something valuable for the industry, yet challenging from a regulatory perspective. This book examines how the EU, through the PSD2, attempts to address this regulatory challenge by adding a layer of economic theory to bring new perspectives as to the reasoning of regulatory choices.

As such, the book not only examines the PSD2 from a legal perspective but also explains current regulation through economic contributions, particularly market failure theory. With this combination, the analysis of critical

[1] Directive 2007/64/EC of the European Parliament and of the Council of 13 November 2007 on payment services in the internal market amending Directives 97/7/EC, 2002/65/EC, 2005/60/EC and 2006/48/EC and repealing Directive 97/5/EC [2007] OJ L 319/1.

[2] Directive (EU) 2015/2366 of the European Parliament and of the Council of 25 November 2015 on payment services in the internal market, amending Directives 2002/65/EC, 2009/110/EC and 2013/36/EU and Regulation (EU) No 1093/2010, and repealing Directive 2007/64/EC [2015] OJ L 337/35.

[3] For more on this and the consequences for competition on the market: Inna Romānova and others, 'The Payment Services Directive 2 and Competitiveness: The Perspective of European Fintech Companies' (2018) XXI European Research Studies Journal 5.

EU Payment Services. Louise Damkjær Christensen, Oxford University Press. © Louise Damkjær Christensen 2025.
DOI: 10.1093/9780198949084.003.0001

elements of payment services regulation goes deeper and presents the market in a wider context. By emphasising the practical coexistence of legal and economic elements in drafting regulation, the book contributes to a more holistic understanding of EU payment services regulation and how this manages to accommodate innovation in an increasingly digital world.

1.1 Why regulate payment services?

Why do we regulate? What purpose does legislation serve? Are decisions by private actors not sufficient? These questions are perhaps the most notable when doing law and economics research and should be given renewed consideration when dealing with the developments in financial technology (FinTech). Innovation in payment services, for example, has resulted in a new category of third-party payment service providers. Should government regulate this development? And if so, how should it be done?

The classic perception of the efficient, free market as we know it from economic theory is not entirely truthful.[4] The market does fail.[5] A natural companion to the free market is therefore the theory of market failure.[6] The theory explains how the free market might fail to deliver efficient outcomes such as competition and information symmetry. When the market fails, it serves as the justification for government intervention, an intervention which often consists of regulation.[7] Creating a perfect balance between the free market and necessary intervention would be near impossible, but, at the very least, regulators should aim to implement feasible opportunities for improvement of financial regulation. To enable this development, it is important to understand the functions and interactions of the financial system.[8] Furthermore, history has shown us that the relationship between politicians acting as legislators and the implemented regulation is often affected by times of crisis, resulting in too lax

[4] Notable mentions for the scope of this book are Francis M Bator, 'The Anatomy of Market Failure' (1958) 72 The Quarterly Journal of Economics 351, 353; Arthur Cecil Pigou, *The Economics of Welfare* (MacMillan and Co 1921) 111.

[5] This was already recognised in 1776 by Adam Smith, *An Inquiry into the Nature and Causes of the Wealth of Nations* (George Routledge and Sons 1890 (original 1776)) where he admits that the invisible hand is not always sufficient, calling for regulatory intervention when this is the case.

[6] Of the more notable contributions can be mentioned Bator, 'The Anatomy of Market Failure'; Charles Wolf Jr, '"Non-Market" Failures and Market Failures' (1978) The Rand Paper Series; Pigou, *The Economics of Welfare'* who was one of the early figures in the theory's development. He particularly favored taxation as a way to amend market failures.

[7] John Armour and others, *Principles of Financial Regulation* (OUP 2016) especially chapter 3.

[8] Armour and others, *Principles of Financial Regulation* 13.

regulation in good times and more intervention in bad times than market failures could possibly justify.

The term 'regulation' instead of 'legislation' is preferred, as regulation in its broad sense encompasses much more than just legislation. While the term 'legislation' covers purely the narrow and traditional understanding of legal sources, being acts and statutes, 'regulation' can take many more forms, such as soft law instruments, enforcement, supervision, and even social norms. Furthermore, regulation as a term is also grounded in the economic approach, where financial regulation can be conceived as measures imposed by government on the financial sector,[9] hence not limiting these terms to a pure legal, traditionalist understanding of legal sources.

And with this, we can begin to answer the questions posed initially, starting from the end and working back towards the beginning. First, the free market can not only be perceived as a state where no regulation exists but also as a market with regulation which enables private actors to make decisions. At times, it can be necessary to intervene in such markets as they are not always sufficient on their own to deliver efficiency for society.[10] The purpose of legislation, as well as regulation, is therefore to shape and secure a market that can deliver efficiency.[11] Strictly speaking, regulation can either be market-enabling or market-converse. Where market-enabling regulation tries to make the market work better or prevent market failures, market-converse regulation tries to achieve some other purpose than to enhance market transactions, for example social equality by redistribution.[12] It is particularly the market-enabling regulation which will be the focus of this book, although market-converse regulation will also be examined, for example when it serves to improve consumer protection.

The first question, why we regulate, is not simple. The answer to this question can be perceived as two-fold; on the one hand we have the traditional reason of using regulation to correct market failures,[13] while on the other we have public policy setting forth demands to the market. With the overarching

[9] Armour and others, *Principles of Financial Regulation* 12.

[10] James Crotty, 'The Realism of Assumptions does matter—Why Keynes-Minskey theory must replace efficient market theory as the guide to financial regulation policy' in Martin H Wolfson and Gerald A Epstein (eds), *The Handbook of the Political Economy of Financial Crises* (OUP 2013); Smith, *An Inquiry into the Nature and Causes of the Wealth of Nations*; John Maynard Keynes, *The General Theory of Employment, Interest, and Money* (Palgrave Macmillan 2018 (original 1936)).

[11] Armour and others, *Principles of Financial Regulation* ch 3.

[12] For example OECD, *Regulatory Policy and Governance* (2011) 10–11 shows a division of regulatory policies into market efficiency and societal goals.

[13] Armour and others, *Principles of Financial Regulation* 70; Tyler Cowen (ed), *The Theory of Market Failure—A Critical Examination* (George Mason University Press 1988) 209.

goal of benefitting society, public policy can induce a 'failure' of the market, and thereby justify regulatory intervention, often in the form of market-converse regulation.[14] The answer to the question is therefore more likely that we regulate to shape or restructure the market in a way that we believe to benefit society the most. This aim has been pursued in shaping the developments of FinTech in a manner that enables society to prosper.

The development of FinTech has long brought us innovative solutions.[15] Some products of FinTech are more novel than others, just as some have a greater disruptive impact on the financial sector than others. Though, one might also ask, what is FinTech? The Financial Stability Board (FSB) defines FinTech as '*technology-enabled innovation in financial services that could result in new business models, applications, processes, or products with an associated material effect on the provision of financial services.*'[16] In the 2018 FinTech Action Plan[17] the European Commission used the definition set by the FSB, and the European Supervisory Authorities (ESAs)—consisting of the European Banking Authority (EBA), the European Securities and Markets Authority (ESMA), and the European Insurance and Occupational Pensions Authority (EIOPA)—also refer to the definition of FinTech set by the FSB. The ESAs present this as the definition of FinTech at the EU and international standard-setting level,[18] which is stressed by the Basel Committee on Banking Supervision adopting the definition as well in their report on the implications of FinTech for banks and bank supervisors.[19] The definition set by the FSB is both versatile and outlines specific requirements for businesses pursuing FinTech projects, thus making it suitable as a working definition for this book as well. The fact that it is also accepted as the definition of FinTech at an international standard-setting level by the regulatory and supervisory authorities accentuates the value of the definition.

[14] Julian Le Grand, 'The Theory of Government Failure' (1991) 21 British Journal of Political Science 423.

[15] The most important innovation for payment services perhaps being the enabling of Open Banking where the underlying software developments deserves credit. Marta Barroso and Juan Laborda, 'Digital transformation and the emergence of the Fintech sector: Systematic literature review' (2022) 2 100028 provides a thorough literature review on the subject.

[16] Financial Stability Board, *Financial Stability Implications from FinTech: Supervisory and Regulatory Issues that Merit Authorities' Attention* (2017) 11.

[17] European Commission, *Communication from the Commission: FinTech Action plan: For a more competitive and innovative European financial sector* (COM(2018) 109 final, 2018) note 1.

[18] European Banking Authority, European Securities and Markets Authority and European Insurance and Occupational Pensions Authority, *Joint Report: FinTech: Regulatory sandboxes and innovation hubs* (2019) note 1.

[19] Basel Committee on Banking Supervision, *Sound Practices: Implications of fintech developments for banks and bank supervisors* (2018) 8.

What makes FinTech interesting for the payment services market is how the regulatory framework shows it has difficulties keeping up with the pace of innovation. The FSB definition of FinTech is broad enough to include all financial services enabled by technology by all market players and encompasses more than just services and products tangible to the customer. It also covers the technology enabling services and the new business models used. Considering the rapid development of FinTech and its impact on the financial sector, it is evident that this book should also evaluate the PSD2's ability to accommodate financial innovation development in the EU payment services market. It is therefore clear that we need to regulate payment services and particularly new innovations, but have the EU legislators gotten it right so far?

The focus of this book is EU payment services, how they are regulated, and whether this accounts for innovative developments in payment services. The relevant regulation is therefore the PSD2 which will be examined in relation to its management of market failures in light of financial innovation. Elements from economics and law are required in order to evaluate the regulatory framework of this area, which entails strong growth and extensive financial innovation, and which greatly impacts society every day.[20] This also situates the book solidly within the field of law and economics and approaches the topic of EU payment services from this perspective with a focus on regulation and innovation.

1.2 EU payment services regulation

With the adoption of the PSD1 in 2007, the work towards harmonising legislation with common rules for payments on the EU level officially started. The first Directive was later repealed and replaced after the Commission's impact assessment of 2013,[21] which concluded that a revision was necessary to correct the failures of the first Directive. This was partly due to the unfortunate decision during the preparation of the first Directive that rules related to third-party PSPs were not to be included.[22] Along with other issues, this was one of the primary reasons for the PSD1 becoming outdated so quickly after

[20] It might not be in the forefront of most people's mind but we do after all pay for goods everyday with payment services such as card or mobile solutions.

[21] European Commission, *Commission Staff Working Document Impact Assessment* (SWD(2013) 288 final, 2013).

[22] European Commission, *Commission Staff Working Document Impact Assessment* (SWD(2013) 288 final) 25; Mary Donnelly, 'Payments in the digital market: Evaluating the contribution of Payment Services Directive II' (2016) 32 Computer Law & Security Review 828.

its implementation.[23] The enactment of the PSD2 was therefore necessary to tackle the rising challenges of increasing market power for incumbents, ensuring enhanced consumer protection, and accommodating further financial innovation.

The PSD2, which was adopted in 2015 and transposed into national legislation by the 1st January 2018, aimed to improve the existing rules and to take new digital payment services into account.[24] Where the first Directive introduced the so-called payment services and increased competition and choice for consumers, the second Directive increases focus on consumer protection and promotion of innovation in mobile and internet payment services. This leaves the question of whether the adopted provisions in fact address the issues that existed prior to implementation.

The PSD2 is an excellent example of legislation that attempts to shape the existing market into a more desirable configuration.[25] The implementation of the PSD2 therefore constitutes an example of regulatory intervention where both market and non-market failures are present prior to the intervention. The scope of this book is the PSD2 as a measure of regulatory intervention to address market and non-market failures with the aim of improving competition, consumer protection, and innovation in financial services.

The purpose of this book is to examine how EU legislation addresses market and non-market failures in a financial market and adapts to innovative developments. A particular feature of the PSD2 is the widening of scope to cover third-party payment service providers. With this in mind, the book seeks to establish *what is,* and at the same time it looks towards the future suggesting *what ought to be.*

Market failures form the basis of the rationale to intervene in markets with regulation. One might ask why the effort of working with failures, goals, and strategies must be pursued, and the answer is quite simple: when doing preparatory work to draw up new legislation, it is essential to be aware of what gaps exist in the status quo (the failures), consider how we, as a society, want the market to function after the implementation of this legislation (the goals), and how we can best achieve this (the strategies). For the latter part, it is

[23] Innovation and technological developments also contributed to this, as is also emphasised by Alan Brener, 'Payment Service Directive II and Its Implications' in Theo Lynn and others (eds), *Disrupting Finance* (Palgrave Pivot, Cham. 2019) 109.

[24] European Commission, 'Payment Services' <https://finance.ec.europa.eu/consumer-finance-and-payments/payment-services/payment-services_en> accessed 10 February 2022

[25] Alan Brener, 'EU payment services regulation and international developments' in Iris H-Y Chiu and Gudula Deipenbrock (eds), *Routledge Handbook of Financial Technology and Law* (Routledge 2021) 159.

important to consider different regulatory strategies and the incentives they create towards achieving the goals formulated to address the existing failures.

Third-party payment service providers typically represent innovative developments within financial services, and hence the accommodation of these providers in the EU payment services market will be a specific focus and serve as a delimitation of the book's scope. A further delimitation is the setting out of specific cases of failures and how these have been addressed. The description of these cases and their selection criteria can be found in section 3 of this chapter. The cases delimit the parts of the PSD2 which will be examined thoroughly in this book, as the purpose of the book is not to be a commentary, but instead to examine the current regulation from a critical perspective, considering both the perspective of the regulator and the functioning of the market.

1.3 The impact of innovation on payment services literature

The legal literature about payment services has, in the light of FinTech development, experienced an increase in volume. The most comprehensive coverage of the PSD2 is perhaps Gimigliano and Beroš' 2021 Commentary.[26] The Commentary provides insights into the understanding and practicalities of the provisions of the PSD2. The Commentary also describes its central provisions and provides necessary insights into the contents of the Directive. However, the Commentary does fall short of asking critical questions which this book attempts to address, such as the Directive's management of market failures and accommodation of further financial innovation.

Another contribution to the field of payment services is a chapter in the book 'FinTech Law and Regulation', edited by Jelena Madir.[27] This chapter lightly touches upon the changes needed in the regulatory landscape for payment services due to the increasing impact of financial innovation. The contribution provides good insights and gives the reader an overview of the potential for changes in the regulatory landscape.

A further addition to the legal literature on payment services is the Routledge Handbook of Financial Technology and Law[28] which contains a

[26] Gabriella Gimigliano and Marta Bozina Beros (eds), *The Payment Services Directive II: A Commentary* (Elgar Commentaries in Financial Law, Edward Elgar Publishing 2021).

[27] Jelena Madir (ed), *FinTech Law and Regulation* (Elgar Financial Law and Practice, 2nd edn, Edward Elgar Publishing 2021).

[28] Iris H-Y Chiu and Gudula Deipenbrock (eds), *Routledge Handbook of Financial Technology and Law* (Routledge 2021).

section with two chapters treating issues related to payment services. The focus in the Routledge Handbook is on liability concepts and the development of the PSD2, including an international perspective. The first chapter on liability concepts provides the reader with a presentation of current regulation. In the other chapter of the Routledge Handbook,[29] Alan Brener makes an interesting contribution, stating in the introduction to the chapter that 'this Directive is a clear example of a conceptual approach to employing regulation to shape a market.'[30] This statement resonates with the topic of this book, as Brener is focused on the concepts, objectives, and background of current regulation and how to best shape the market to fulfil the desires of society. Furthermore, Brener specifically highlights consumer protection and security as requisite safeguards for liberalising the payments market. Unfortunately, the limited space of a single chapter in an edited book with a much broader focus is not sufficient to undertake an exhaustive analysis. The legal literature therefore still leaves a gap to be filled, although the general volume of literature on FinTech has been growing in recent years.

A recent addition to the legal literature on payment services is John Casanova and Max Savoie's edited book 'Payment Services Law and Practice'.[31] As the title reveals, the main purpose of the book is not to undertake extensive legal scholarship, but instead to provide the legal practitioner with an introduction to the regulation of payment services in the EU and the UK, and the practical aspects of legal practice in this area. The book also provides introductions to national regulation of payment services in countries such as the US and Hong Kong. Due to the focus on legal practice, the contribution holds similar value to the commentary, although the edited book does open up certain discussions which the Commentary does not.

Kern Alexander contributes with some notes on Open Banking and the PSD2 in his 2019 'Principles of Banking Regulation'.[32] Here Alexander argues that FinTech has created opportunities for non-banks to increase their respective market share through the digitisation of banking.[33] Alexander considers the development, especially driven by the regulatory initiatives in the PSD2, to have caused a permanent change in the bank-customer relationship, moving the customers' interface with their service provider to third-party

[29] Brener, 'EU payment services regulation and international developments'.
[30] Brener, 'EU payment services regulation and international developments' 159.
[31] John Casanova and Max Savoie (eds), *Payment Services—Law and Practice* (Edward Elgar Publishing 2022).
[32] Kern Alexander, *Principles of Banking Regulation* (CUP 2019) ch 12(2).
[33] Alexander, *Principles of Banking Regulation* 332.

providers instead of their account servicing PSP. An interesting question raised by Alexander is whether bank customers will consent to having their data accessed by third-party PSPs. While the willingness to consent is not investigated in this book, the consequences of giving access, the consumers' ability to understand these consequences, and the power-balance between banks and third-party PSPs will be treated in later chapters.

Zooming out to consider the wider regulatory landscape that is financial services law, the amount of legal literature is vast. For one, 'The Oxford Handbook on Financial Regulation'[34] provides a thorough examination of the various aspects of financial regulation in general. For example, the handbook dives into important topics such as consumer protection, financial stability, and the organisation of the financial system's regulation. Although the handbook treats the financial regulation subjects generally, the observations and discussions are valuable for the work contained in this book. The different contributions in the handbook can be transferred to specific issues in regulating the market for payment services.

Another important contribution on financial regulation generally is Armour and others' 'Principles of Financial Regulation'.[35] Here, the authors go into depth on various aspects of the financial market, the starting point being the foundations. Again, it becomes possible to transfer the observations and findings from the general level onto specific issues identified in examining the PSD2. Furthermore, the contribution is particularly interesting for this book's focus on market failures and regulatory goals, as Armour and the other authors treat this subject thoroughly.

When considering how to shape the regulatory framework, the contribution made by Kern Alexander[36] in 'Principles of Banking Regulation' resonates rather well with the scope of this book. Alexander argues that to keep pace with institutional and market innovations, a functional approach to banking regulation is necessary. This argument could also be applied to the market for payment services. Particularly when dealing with areas which are developing rapidly, it is important to apply the functional approach to avoid circumvention of regulation. The PSD2 addresses functions by defining the scope of application of payment services, having listed the functions which are covered in the Directive's Annex 1.

[34] Niamh Moloney, Eilís Ferran, and Jennifer Payne (eds), *The Oxford Handbook of Financial Regulation* (OUP 2015).

[35] Armour and others, *Principles of Financial Regulation.*

[36] Alexander, *Principles of Banking Regulation* 299.

Whether searching in payment services specific legal literature or in the more general contributions to financial regulation, the legal literature leaves a gap for this book to fill. It would seem that there have been no prior investigations into the PSD2's ability to address market failures, and while innovation is a hot topic in literature, there has not been any extensive examination as to whether the PSD2 accommodates this development in a way that is healthy for competition and safe for consumers. This book seeks to answer these questions, which necessitates some further definitions of key terms, which will be presented in the following section 2.

2 Payments and the actors on the market for payment services

In a book on the PSD2, defining key terms such as payment services and payment service providers is essential. The following subsections 2.1–2.6 will therefore provide a definition and an understanding of key terms and actors when dealing with the market for payment services. This includes the terms 'payments' and 'payment services', and the actors 'payment service providers', 'payment service users', and supervisory authorities. On top of these regulatory terms, 'Open Banking' will also be defined and explained, as it constitutes an enabler of many new innovations in payment services.

2.1 Payments

Since the dawn of time, people have traded with each other by exchanging one item for another. At some point money was invented as a measure of payment in trade. While the pure transaction of cash directly from the payer to the payee, without any intermediary intervention, is not covered by the PSD2,[37] the transaction of moving money from the payer to the payee via intermediaries is. The PSD2 does not define the term 'payment', but instead focuses on the terms 'payer', 'payee', and 'payment transaction'.

The payer and the payee are required participants in a payment transaction. The payer is the person, natural or legal, who holds a payment account and allows a payment order from that account, or, where there is no payment account, a natural or legal person who gives a payment order,[38] for example

[37] Directive (EU) 2015/2366 (PSD2) art. 3(1)(a).
[38] Directive (EU) 2015/2366 (PSD2) art. 4(1)(8).

using electronically stored money (e-money). The payee is the natural or legal person who is the intended recipient of the funds which have been the subject of a payment transaction.[39]

Having covered the definitions of the required participants to initiate a payment, the term 'payment transaction' deserves attention. The payer initiates the payment transaction, or the payee initiates it on the payer's behalf, for example a card transaction in a merchant's store. The transaction is the transfer or withdrawal of funds, irrespective of any underlying obligations between the payer and the payee.[40] The last part, the transaction being irrespective of any underlying obligation between the parties, is of importance when there is doubt or disagreement between the payer and the payee, whether this be about the amount owed, the object being traded for the transfer of funds, or something else. The underlying obligation has been disconnected from the obligations that can possibly be transferred to the provider of the payment service performing the payment transaction.

In the light of innovative developments, the Directive also defines 'remote payment transactions', which cover payment transactions initiated via the internet or through a device that can be used for distance communication,[41] for example a mobile phone. These transactions have become more influential as an ever-growing number of consumers have been born in the digital age.[42] Innovations in financial services also tend to utilise the fact that transactions can be performed remotely using mobile phones and utilise it as a selling feature by promoting accessibility and easy usage.

Another term in relation to the payment transaction to be defined is 'funds'. The Directive defines 'funds', as banknotes and coins, also known as fiat currency, scriptural money, namely current accounts in electronic or non-cash forms held with your bank, and electronic money.[43] Funds are essential to payments as they constitute the object being transferred from the payer to the payee. The presence of funds being transferred is also essential for a transaction to be covered by the PSD2. The Directive's scope is set out in article 2, with paragraph 1 stating that the Directive applies to payment services provided

[39] Directive (EU) 2015/2366 (PSD2) art. 4(1)(9).

[40] Directive (EU) 2015/2366 (PSD2) art. 4(1)(5).

[41] Directive (EU) 2015/2366 (PSD2) art. 4(1)(6).

[42] With the world being largely digital and having been so for a number of years now, every new-born child (at least in the western world) is born in the digital age.

[43] As defined in art. 2(2) of Directive 2009/110/EC of the European Parliament and of the Council of 16 September 2009 on the taking up, pursuit and prudential supervision of the business of electronic money institutions amending Directives 2005/60/EC and 2006/48/EC and repealing Directive 2000/46/EC [2009] OJ L 267/7.

within the EU. A 'payment service' is any business activity set out in Annex 1,[44] which will be described further in the following subsection 2.2, focusing solely on payment services.

2.2 Payment services

As the Directive's Annex 1 shows, a payment service can take multiple forms.[45] The Annex lists the different payment services which are covered by the PSD2. The Directive covers cash placements and withdrawals from payment accounts, the execution of transactions either using available funds or covered by a credit line, including direct debits, transactions through a payment card or similar device, and credit transfers. Furthermore, it covers the issuance of payment instruments and acquisition of payment transactions, money remittances, payment initiation services, and account information services.

The two latter functions, the Annex's points 7 and 8, the Payment Initiation Service (PIS) and the Account Information Service (AIS), are new additions introduced in the PSD2. These are often also referred to as third-party payment service providers, as they act as a third party to the payment service user and the account servicing payment service provider. The third-party payment service providers often contribute innovative solutions to improve current options for payment services. As these were left out of the scope of the regulatory framework of the PSD1, challenges could have arisen when incorporating them into the regulatory framework of the PSD2. These challenges could relate to, but are not limited to, matters such as competition and consumer protection. This also underlines why innovative third-party providers are key to assess the PSD2's ability to accommodate innovation in current regulation.

All payment services, except the AIS, share the common feature of partaking in the transfer of funds. The AIS stands out as it only provides the user with an overview of their deposits and spending data, depending on the configuration chosen by the individual AIS provider (AISP). The definition of AIS in the PSD2 does not limit the options for configuration significantly, which creates opportunities for the AISP, but also raises issues in terms of protecting consumers' financial data. The Directive defines the AIS as:

[44] Directive (EU) 2015/2366 (PSD2) art. 4(1)(3).
[45] Directive (EU) 2015/2366 (PSD2) art. 4(3).

> an online service to provide consolidated information on one or more payment accounts held by the payment service user with either another payment service provider or with more than one payment service provider.[46]

As the definition clearly shows, the AISP never touches, transfers, or initiates the movement of user funds. The AISP only accesses the user's payment accounts to provide consolidated information about the user's financial situation.

The other newcomer to the Directive, the PIS, is defined by the Directive as:

> a service to initiate a payment order at the request of the payment service user with respect to a payment account held at another payment service provider.[47]

Like the AISP, the PIS provider (PISP) never touches or transfers funds. The purpose of the service is to initiate the transaction. As such, the PISP becomes the only intermediary for both the payer and the payee, maintaining the connection to the parties' account servicing payment service providers who will have to execute the transaction.

2.3 Payment service providers

While the former section defined the payment services, the subject of this section is the payment service provider (PSP). The PSD2 defines in its article 4(1)(11) a payment service provider as:

> a body referred to in its art. 1(1) or a natural or legal person benefitting from an exemption pursuant to art. 32 or 33.

Article 1(1) states the Directive's subject matter as:

> establishing rules in accordance with which Member States shall distinguish between categories of payment service providers including credit institutions, electronic money institutions, post office giro institutions, payment institutions, the ECB and national central banks, and Member States or their regional or local authorities.

[46] Directive (EU) 2015/2366 (PSD2) art. 4(1)(16).
[47] Directive (EU) 2015/2366 (PSD2) art. 4(1)(15).

The focus of this book is primarily PSPs being either credit institutions, electronic money institutions, or payment institutions. The remaining categories will only be considered if they hold any intrinsic value in relation to the selected categories.

The most notable distinction among PSPs is between credit institutions and payment institutions only providing payment services. The credit institution often acts as account servicing PSP while the counterparty is the payment institution, only providing payment services such as a PISP or an AISP. Whereas the credit institution, with its much broader licence,[48] is allowed to deliver not only payment services but also to take deposits and provide credit for its own account, the third-party PSP does not provide a deposit account for their customers, but only enables them to use the services they provide, requiring access to their payment account held with a credit institution. When the third-party PSP does not provide payment accounts, but only the AIS, PIS, or another payment service, it can only be registered as a payment institution. As such, there exists an uneven relationship between the credit institution and the third-party PSP. This disparity will be seen, for example when addressing competition aspects in chapter 5, where provisions such as PSD2 articles 36, 66, and 67 place a heavy burden on the credit institution to accommodate payment institutions.

Anyone who wishes to provide payment services in the internal market of the EU will have to apply for authorisation as a payment institution in a Member State prior to any provision of payment services. This constitutes a legal entry barrier, ensuring that only approved providers are allowed access to the market. However, if a PSP is already authorised as a credit institution it does not need to apply for authorisation as a payment institution as well.[49] It should be clarified that, when using the term 'financial institutions', this covers both payment institutions and credit institutions.[50] When referring to incumbent institutions, this usually covers the more traditional PSPs being the credit institutions. New entrants are, generally speaking, third-party PSPs, but can also develop into PSPs that become authorised as credit institutions.[51]

[48] Licensed as a credit institution via the CRD regime in Directive 2013/36/EU of the European Parliament and of the Council of 26 June 2013 on access to the activity of credit institutions and the prudential supervision of credit institutions and investment firms, amending Directive 2002/87/EC and repealing Directives 2006/48/EC and 2006/49/EC [2013] OJ L 176/338.

[49] Directive (EU) 2015/2366 (PSD2) recital 24.

[50] This definition is also in line with art. 4(1)(26) of Regulation (EU) No 575/2013 of the European Parliament and of the Council of 26 June 2013 on prudential requirements for credit institutions and investment firms and amending Regulation (EU) No 648/2012 [2013] OJ L 176/1.

[51] This was, for example, the case with the Danish company Lunar which eventually in August 2020 obtained their banking license.

2.4 Payment service users

Having covered who the PSPs are, the next subject of definition is the payment service user. As touched upon above in relation to the payments, a payment transaction requires a payer and a payee. These parties are the payment service users. An important distinction when dealing with payment service users is the two different groups—consumers and merchants. The latter is often a payee receiving payment for a good or a service provided to the payer but can also constitute payers conducting payment transactions in their line of business. This group is, from a regulatory perspective, not granted any preferential treatment, as they are expected to be able to bargain sufficiently on their own. However, on occasion, the PSD2 does grant business payers, or at least SMEs, the same rights as consumers.

Consumers on the other hand, are a different matter. As the Directive states in the recitals,[52] the consumer group is considered less able to assess risks of fraud and take countervailing measures. Consumers are treated preferentially, which is in line with a goal of financial regulation, to protect consumers. As consumer protection is an important subject in relation to payment services, the definition of the term 'consumer' in the PSD2 should also be mentioned. The Directive treats a consumer as:

> a natural person who, in payment service contracts covered by this Directive, is acting for purposes other than his or her trade, business or profession.[53]

When using the term 'payment service user' throughout the book, unless otherwise stated, the primary subject is meant to be understood as the consumer, although this term will also frequently be used when treating matters related to consumer protection.

2.5 The supervisory authorities

Prior to the Global Financial Crisis of 2007–08, technological development was already challenging the way we approach financial supervision.[54] With the Global Financial Crisis and the liberalisation wave in mind, the regulatory

[52] Directive (EU) 2015/2366 (PSD2) recital 73.
[53] Directive (EU) 2015/2366 (PSD2) art. 4(1)(20).
[54] Charles A E Goodhart, *The Regulatory Response to the Financial Crisis* (Edward Elgar Publishing 2009) 38.

sine curve took its upswing into the wave of financial stability. This though has been challenged not only by an upbeat in digitalisation but also by a tendency towards decentralisation and globalisation. While the regulatory and supervisory authorities went all in on securing financial stability, the world developed, hastily. Technology is moving most financial service providers onto web-based solutions, if not app-based. Globalisation is blurring the lines of the nationality of companies and also making cross-border activity a success criterion, and a movement within tech-developers is favouring decentralisation to avoid centralised control.[55]

The favouring of decentralisation over centralisation is also seen in the EU supervisory framework. Here, the power that has been transferred to the ESAs compared to the National Competent Authorities (NCAs) is rather limited. This is very interesting, as one would presume that to achieve high levels of harmonisation, it would be more efficient to place most competence at the centralised level. Although we must also remember that this requires Member States to delegate such competence to the EU.

It is particularly important to introduce the ESAs here, as their work impacts the practical application of the PSD2. The ESAs have already done much in this respect, as their passing of soft law instruments such as guidelines, recommendations, and Q&As, and the adoption of these instruments in Member States, would seem to constitute an overture to centralisation in practice.

In the area of payment services, the most relevant ESA is the EBA. The EBA was created in 2010 by its founding regulation[56] and began its work in January 2011. The founding regulation describes the EBA's purpose, functions, and powers. For example, article 16 delegates the authority to issue guidelines in accordance with a delegation in a legislative act. The authority also monitors the activity in, among other markets, the market for payment services, in accordance with the obligations set out in the PSD2. When the EU Commission initiates a revision of legislation, for example the revision of the PSD2, the EBA is responsible for conducting public consultations and organising the findings. The EBA plays multiple roles, and its soft law instruments are of value to the analytical work of this book.[57]

[55] A great example of the latter is the Bitcoin movement, which started as an effort to be free of the control Central Banks have on monetary policy as manifested by Satoshi Nakamoto, *Bitcoin: A Peer-to-Peer Electronic Cash System* (White Paper 2008).

[56] Regulation (EU) No 1093/2010 of the European Parliament and of the Council of 24 November 2010 establishing a European Supervisory Authority (European Banking Authority), amending Decision No 716/2009/EC and repealing Commission Decision 2009/78/EC [2010] OJ L 331/12.

[57] In a similar, though much more extensive fashion, Niamh Moloney, *The Age of ESMA: Governing EU Financial Markets* (Hart Publishing 2018) goes to great lengths to describe the importance and value of the EBA's sister authority, the ESMA.

2.6 Open Banking

The term 'Open Banking' is often, in the EU, associated with the PSD2. Particularly relevant are the rights the Directive provides to consumers and other payment service users, to use third-party PSPs, under articles 66 and 67. These provisions are examined further in chapter 5. With Open Banking, the access to banking data is opened up to allow third parties to access and utilise the data in accordance with the consent given by the payment service user.[58]

Within the EU, the Open Banking movement is regulation-driven, led by the PSD2.[59] As such, in the EU the rights by law are focused solely on payment account data which might be supplemented in the future with the upcoming Open Finance initiative of the EU Commission in the form of the Financial Data Access Regulation.[60] For now, Open Banking in the EU is based on the free access to data which the PSD2 secures for payment service users.

Although the PSD2 establishes the legal rights, underneath a digital solution is needed to implement these rights in practice. Perhaps the best known standardisation supporting Open Banking is the UK's Open Banking Standard,[61] which seeks to standardise access to data within the UK across the entire ecosystem.[62] As chapters 5 and 6 also explore, standardisation is key to ensuring both efficient and secure access to payments data. This not only protects the rights of payment service users but also improves competition in the payment services market by lowering the practical entry barriers.

The topic of this book is EU payment services with a focus on their regulation and innovation. Open Banking no doubt fits into the latter category, but it is, in the EU at least, enabled through regulation. The focus moving forward will therefore be on regulation, in essence the PSD2, and how it enables

[58] Oscar Borgogno and Giuseppe Colangelo, 'Consumer Inertia and Competition-sensitive Data Governance: The Case of Open Banking' (2020) Journal of European Consumer and Market Law 143; Federico Ferretti, 'Open Banking: Gordian Legal Knots in the Uncomfortable Cohabitation between the PSD2 and the GDPR' (2022) 30 European Review of Private Law 73.

[59] Francesco De Pascalis, 'The Journey to Open Finance: Learning from the Open Banking Movement' (2022) 33 European Business Law Review 397; Sarah Lamont, *Open Banking Walked so Open Finance Could Run* (Fintech Prime Time 2024); Ferretti, 'Open Banking: Gordian Legal Knots in the Uncomfortable Cohabitation between the PSD2 and the GDPR'.

[60] 'Proposal for a Regulation of the European Parliament and of the Council on a framework for Financial Data Access and amending Regulations (EU) No 1093/2010, (EU) No 1094/2010, (EU) No 1095/2010 and (EU) 2022/2554' (COM(2023) 360 final, 2023).

[61] Open Banking Limited, 'The Open Banking Standard' (2024).<https://standards.openbanking.org.uk/> accessed 8 July 2024.

[62] Francesco De Pascalis and Alan Brener, *Open Banking—Global development and regulation* (Routledge International Studies in Money and Banking, Routledge 2024) provides a thorough examination of the Open Banking movement from a global perspective.

innovation, such as, but not limited to, Open Banking. The term Open Banking will only be further considered where relevant.

3 Notes on structure and content

While this chapter has provided the reader with information on payments, payment services, and the wider context of the EU payment services market, the following chapter 2 will introduce the reader to essential economic theory on market and non-market failures. These theories play a fundamental role in the understanding of payment services regulation and how the regulator manages to make room for innovation, now and in the future.

In chapter 3, the market and non-market failures related to EU payment services regulation will first be presented, followed by an overview of the goals of regulation in the area of payment services, including consideration of the applied regulatory strategies. This chapter also introduces the concept of evaluation, which is based on the preceding elements. The chapter also sets out the structure of the following chapters 4, 5, and 6, which provides the reader with easy access to, and separation of, the economic, legal, and public policy-based elements of the book.

As this book is not a commentary on the PSD2, only specific areas of the Directive have been selected for detailed examination. The material presented in chapter 3 has guided the criteria chosen to identify the areas that are of most interest. The criteria are (a) whether a problem can be explained by a market failure or a non-market failure, (b) whether the subject matter has a direct connection to either a PSD2 goal or a meta-goal, and (c) whether the subject matter entails an element of 'innovation' in payment services. The content of, and reflections on, these criteria will be further described in the following paragraphs.

a) 'can be explained by a market failure or a non-market failure'

The first criterion is whether the problem can be explained through market failure theory or non-market failure theory. It is possible that both market and non-market failures are present. This is essentially the first phase of the framework described in chapter 3, section 2. The failure or problem present in the market determines which regulatory steps and changes are considered necessary by the regulator to mitigate the problem and attempt to correct the failure. It is not possible to have an interesting, problematic area without either a market or non-market failure present.

b) 'have a direct connection to a PSD2 goal or a meta-goal'

The second criterion relates to the subject's link to either a Directive-specific goal or to a meta-goal. This can be expressed as a market failure or a non-market failure which can work against a regulatory goal, or in the regulatory measure applied to address the problem. As some PSD2 goals are also represented as meta-goals of financial regulation, it is possible that both levels of goals are present. The selection seeks to present at least one Directive-specific goal in each chapter but also considers meta-goals as particularly important for the financial system and hence for the stability of the payment services market. This criterion also mirrors the second step of the framework, presented in chapter 3, section 3, and essentially focuses on the regulatory measure applied to address or mitigate a failure or problem.

c) 'entail an element of 'innovation' in payment services'

The third and last criterion is the subject's relationship to an innovation or the general innovative development in payment services. This also corresponds with the book's focus on the PSD2's ability to adapt to, and address challenges arising from, innovative developments in financial services and specifically in the regulation of the EU payment services market. The element of 'innovation' can be expressed, for example, through new services or new providers, but the link does not have to be as specific as a new service. It can also be seen in changes in the regulatory picture, such as changes in risks. The innovation element can be implicitly or explicitly present in all three stages of the analytical framework and, given its natural connection to the developments in payment services, will constitute a natural element in the third stage of evaluation, which is described further in chapter 3, section 4.

Chapter 4 examines the licensing regime and its development from the PSD1 to the PSD2. A non-market failure of the PSD1 was the inconsistent application of the Directive and diverging licensing rules and practices across the

Member States.[63] Furthermore, the scope of the Directive left a vacuum for some PSPs, as they were not covered by the Directive and hence could not become authorised as payment institutions. This also left the market with a systemic stability issue as these out-of-scope providers could provide their services without complying with the standards set by the Directive, which authorised providers, their competitors, had to comply with. The chapter examines how the PSD2 attempts to correct this issue, aiming to improve the conditions for new innovative providers, while also raising new problems in relation to fair competition and consumer protection.

The exemption provisions in articles 32 and 33 make it possible for PSPs who do not fulfil the criteria for payment institutions, to become registered in their Member State, subject to conditions. The provisions set a different, lower legal entry barrier for some market participants, leading to a difference in PSPs' costs of achieving compliance. It could therefore be argued that such providers receive an unfair advantage, as they can spend more on product development, marketing, and other market enhancing activities. This potential issue will also be examined further in chapter 4.

Another issue raised by the exemption provisions relates to consumer protection. By lowering the requirements set for PSPs, the protection of consumers, and generally of the payment service users of the exempted provider, could be diminished. This calls for further examination of the exemption provisions' suitability in light of the Directive's goal of consumer protection, in contrast to its goal of increased innovation.

With the narrow scope of the PSD1 and the innovative developments in the market leading to new services and providers, the subject, the licensing regime, immediately meets criteria (a) and (c). The last criterion is met due to the legislator's intention of enabling fair competition, enhancing consumer protection, and expanding the regulatory framework to accommodate innovative development. The balancing of goals and the handling of failures in the market addressed by the PSD2's licensing regime will be examined and discussed further in chapter 4.

The focus in chapter 5 is on enabling competition on the EU payment services market. The Directive's articles 66 and 67 are an attempt to manage the market failure of imperfect competition. Prior to the PSD2's implementation, third-party PSPs were dependent on bilateral agreements with account servicing PSPs—which were often incumbent credit institutions and therefore

[63] As was repeatedly evidenced in European Commission, *Commission Staff Working Document Impact Assessment* (SWD(2013) 288 final).

also their direct competitors—to gain the crucial access to their customers' payment accounts. As the third-party PSPs depend on access to their users' payment accounts held with other institutions, this was a major flaw in the market which had to be addressed through regulatory intervention.

Although articles 66 and 67 relate directly to third-party PSPs, two other provisions also call for further examination. The Directive's article 35 provides access to payment systems for all payment institutions, and article 36 gives payment institutions the right to hold an account at a credit institution. These provisions are essential in order for third-party PSPs to be able to establish and conduct their business. Chapter 5 will initially examine these two provisions, before moving on to articles 66 and 67.

The chapter's subject can be explained by the market failure of market control and inefficient competition. The problem has partly emerged due to the innovative development in payment services resulting in new types of services, and the businesses providing them. The Directive has addressed this through the application of conduct of business rules to market participants, forcing them to give access upon a payment service user's request, to lower the entry barriers created by the market failure of market power. But do articles 66 and 67 of PSD2 help achieve the goals of the Directive, ie more competition, increased consumer protection, and financial innovation? Through an examination of the articles, the Directive's recitals, and other relevant legal sources, chapter 5 will investigate the handling of the market failure, and the correlation between the goals underlying the regulatory intervention and the choice of measure. This will provide context for a discussion of the potential issue of biased decision making among consumers which the Directive ought to address, to avoid any negative impact on consumer protection. Finally, the chapter evaluates the applied measure's ability to achieve the goal of increased financial innovation, and its overall impact on market efficiency.

Financial crime does not only pose an issue specifically for payment services but is a general problem in financial markets. The issue is a manifestation of the externality produced by activities on financial markets. Innovation in financial services, including payment services, increases the risk of financial crime. This means that innovation is both a factor which increases the risk of the externality, and an independent goal of the PSD2. Chapter 6 will examine the Directive's ability to curb the risks arising from increasing financial innovation.

Innovation can bring more competition to the market for payment services, but it can also create or illuminate methods for performing various forms of financial crime. This has been illustrated in the past by cryptocurrencies such as Bitcoin being used for terrorist financing.[64] Inventing intuitive and easy access, and especially mobile payment services, leads to an increased risk of criminal exploitation of service users. Provisions such as the PSD2's articles on strong customer authentication (SCA) are therefore crucial for protecting consumers in a continuously developing market and can contribute to identifying payment service users. Another problem for the Directive to handle is the increased production, use, and sharing of financial data. These can be exploited by market participants and be used to commit financial fraud against payment service users. The measures applied by the Directive to address this increased risk will also be investigated further.

The chapter differs from the previous two chapters by taking as its starting point the meta-goal of preventing financial crime. Financial crime is a problem which can be explained by market failures and addressed through legislative intervention. The chapter analyses the regulatory strategy applied and is particularly concerned with the relationship between the use of sanctions versus preventive measures. Finally, the chapter will also address the potential conflicts between the meta-goals of financial regulation and Directive-specific goals which are of particular interest when a Directive-specific goal like innovation comes into conflict with the meta-goal of preventing financial crime.

The last chapter, chapter 7, will summarise the findings. The findings will be presented and discussed to pose public policy recommendations. This last chapter looks towards the future, especially the expectations of the revisions to EU payment services regulation, particularly a third Payment Services Directive and a Payment Services Regulation, and the chapter takes stock of the accommodation for innovation in future EU payment services regulation.

[64] Ian McKendry, 'ISIL May Be Using Bitcon, Fincen's Calvery Says' American Banker (Law and Regulation) (16th November 2015) <https://www.americanbanker.com/news/isil-may-be-using-bitcoin-fincens-calvery-says> accessed 24th April 2022; Resty Woro Yuniar, 'Bitcoin, PayPal Used to Finance Terrorism, Indonesian Agency Says' The Wall Street Journal (World—Asia) (10th January 2017) <https://www.wsj.com/articles/bitcoin-paypal-used-to-finance-terrorism-indonesian-agency-says-1483964198> accessed 24th April 2022.

2

APPLYING ECONOMIC THEORY TO PAYMENT SERVICES REGULATION

1 Introduction

Law plays a fundamental role in the functioning of society,[1] although this does not indicate that law on its own can build a well-functioning society. Law needs the help of other disciplines to build strong societal frameworks. One of these disciplines is economics.[2] By adding economic theory and economic considerations to the legal framework, it becomes adapted to societal development on which it can have potentially a positive impact. For example, by using the right incentives when drafting legislation, the legislator can affect decisions made by the subjects of that legislation, but the legislator must also remember the spill-over effects created by the same piece of legislation and those same incentives. Spill-over effects can have both positive and negative consequences for businesses and for people who would otherwise not be directly affected by the specific legislation. Here, economics plays an essential role in aiding the understanding of the market, for example, through the use of non-market failure theory which includes the mentioned spill-over effect. By applying economic theoretical considerations to our legal approach when drafting legislation, it becomes possible to scientifically test the fitness of intended regulatory measures.

The ECJ has also combined economics and law in the reasoning of its judgments. In competition law cases, the ECJ has used economic theory in its reasoning as to whether companies have acted wrongfully. In *Hoffmann-La Roche v Commission*[3] the Court described substantial market power being understood as the ability to prevent effective competition being maintained

[1] Katharina Pistor, *The Code of Capital: How the Law Creates Wealth and Inequality* (Princeton University Press 2019).

[2] See Alf Ross, *Om ret og retfærdighed* (Nyt Nordisk Forlag 1953) 332, 422, on the need for another element in the legal discipline to fill the gap which socio-legal studies cannot cover.

[3] Case 85/76 *Hoffmann-La Roche & Co AG v Commission of the European Communities* [1979] ECR I-461 EU:C:1979:36.

EU Payment Services. Louise Damkjær Christensen, Oxford University Press. © Louise Damkjær Christensen 2025.
DOI: 10.1093/9780198949084.003.0002

on the relevant market.[4] And in *United Brands v Commission*[5] the Court described the market as failing to provide competition when an undertaking has the ability to behave to an appreciable extent independently of its competitors, customers, and ultimately its consumers.[6] The same tendency to apply economic theory to this area of law can be seen in the European Commission's Guidance on the Commission's Enforcement Priorities in Applying Article 82 of the EC Treaty' (now TFEU article 102) to abusive exclusionary conduct by dominant undertakings. Here, the Commission also described the market failure of imperfect competition as being present when an undertaking possesses the ability to profitably raise prices above competitive level for a significant period of time.[7] As such, in these examples, the ECJ applied market failure theory to reason their judgment, showing that the theory is useful in the application of law; hence the theory must also be applicable when trying to evaluate the fitness of existing law.

As illustrated by these ECJ decisions, economics contributes something valuable to the understanding and use of law. Combining law with economics contributes with thorough examination, argumentation, and evaluation of legal measures based on the application of economics, to a given area of law. The purpose is to optimise the legal framework to create efficiency and mould societal behaviour according to the desires expressed by public policy.

Market failures play a significant role in analysing where regulatory gaps exist in current regulation, but non-market failures can also be triggered by the growing presence of FinTech in the financial services range. By using a filter of economic terms in a legal context, it is possible to review the regulatory framework in a perspective which is aligned with real-world developments. Existing problems, such as information asymmetries, have high value when deciding how to address a regulatory challenge. This approach also allows us to evaluate current initiatives towards addressing challenges, and whether these have had any influence on the intended subjects. Such discussions are valuable when reviewing the regulatory framework.

The following sections of this chapter will explain the use of economic theory applied in chapters 4–6 of this book. First, general considerations relating to Normative Turned Positive (NTP) theory will be presented followed

[4] Case 85/76 *Hoffmann-La Roche & Co* para 38.

[5] Case 27/76 *United Brands Company and United Brands Continentaal BV v Commission of the European Communities* [1978] ECR I-207 EU:C:1978:22.

[6] Case 27/76 *United Brands v Commission* para 65.

[7] European Commission, Communication from the Commission — Guidance on the Commission's enforcement priorities in applying Article 82 of the EC Treaty to abusive exclusionary conduct by dominant undertakings (OJ C 45, 24.2.2009) 7–20, paras 10, 11.

by a thorough introduction to market failure theory, which can be perceived as the response to the flaws of the theory of efficient markets. A complementary element to market failure theory is non-market failure theory, which represents the potential implications of regulatory intervention based on the market's shortcomings. These theoretical contributions are then used to assemble a framework applicable to financial regulation, with the objective of evaluating financial regulation's ability to accommodate innovation in financial services and address pre-existing market shortcomings and problems deriving from prior regulatory intervention.

2 Making market failure theory applicable to law

In the field of financial services, economics serves as an inevitable component in creating efficient regulation. To figure out how financial regulation can help the market function better, it is necessary to know what the financial system does. This can best be explained through economic concepts, as the functioning of the financial system is an economic matter. Economic theory already embodies a developed understanding of the relationship between the market and the impact of regulation. It is therefore fundamental, and a necessity, to base any treatment of the regulatory framework of a specific section in the financial market on the economic theory explaining its functioning.

When explaining current regulation, it is important to have a sufficient understanding of the underlying economic theory. This is necessary because the theory explains the market to which the regulation is applied. Making efficient regulation therefore requires an understanding of the market. To evaluate current regulation's ability to address pre-existing problems and accommodate for future innovation, NTP[8] theory can be useful, as NTP can be used by applying market failure theory to explain regulation.

As will be elaborated on in the following subsections, the departure point theoretically is the one of market and non-market failure, as outlined by Charles Wolf Jr in his 1978 papers.[9] The reason for choosing this specific theoretical contribution as a starting point will be explained when Wolf's contribution is discussed. Wolf's version of the theory has been modified in accordance

[8] Cento Veljanovski, 'Economic Approaches to Regulation' in Robert Baldwin, Martin Cave and Martin Lodge (eds), *The Oxford Handbook of Regulation* (OUP 2010) 24.

[9] Charles Wolf Jr, 'A Theory of "Non-Market Failure": Framework for Implementation Analysis' (1978) The Rand Paper Series; Charles Wolf Jr, '"Non-Market" Failures and Market Failures' (1978) The Rand Paper Series.

with relevant developments of market, non-market, and government failure theory. Adjusting Wolf's theory to take account of these later theoretical developments, provides a strong basis to explain the current regulation of payment services in the EU. A selection of alternative expositions of market and non-market failure frameworks will therefore be presented to provide an understanding of the theoretical framework and its context.

2.1 The theory of market failure

The theory of market failure takes its departure point in the economic theory of the market's efficiency. The free market is theoretically the best system to ensure efficiency. Efficiency is essentially the effectiveness with which means are used to achieve ends.[10] Neo-classical economists consider the free market to be the most efficient mechanism to create production and allocate resources. The efficiency can be grouped into three types—productive, allocative, and dynamic—which can all be summed up as the market doing as well as possible.[11]

Productive efficiency is the optimisation of output from the available resources, whereas allocative efficiency is the optimal distribution of all goods and services among buyers in the market. The last type, dynamic efficiency, which is also a product of the first two, is essential to consider when discussing financial markets. The financial system is central to achieving dynamic efficiency, as financial markets aim to promote savings and investments over extended periods of time.[12] Since dynamic efficiency aims to allocate resources as efficiently as possible over time, as well as between activities and people, it would seem to be dependent on securing the best possible input for the financial system. This is where financial regulation becomes quintessential.

In a utopian world, the market would prove to be efficient in its distribution of welfare without any interference. This distribution of welfare is also known as the 'invisible hand',[13] which in the theory of market efficiency contributes to creating optimal market conditions. The idea of the market's invisible hand

[10] Paul Hayne, *The Economic Way of Thinking* (6th edn, Macmillan 1991) 129.

[11] Arthur Cecil Pigou, *The Economics of Welfare* (MacMillan and Co 1921) 111; Meir Kohn, *Financial Institutions and Markets* (2nd edn, OUP 2004) 44; on the conditions for allocative efficiency see Francis M Bator, 'The Anatomy of Market Failure' (1958) 72 The Quarterly Journal of Economics 351, 353.

[12] John Armour and others, *Principles of Financial Regulation* (OUP 2016) 53.

[13] David Begg, Stanley Fischer and Rudiger Dornbusch, *Economics* (6th edn, McGraw-Hill Publishing Company 2000) 625; Kohn, *Financial Institutions and Markets* 52.

dates back to Adam Smith's 1776 work 'The Wealth of Nations', where Smith argued that individuals pursuing their self-interest would be led 'as by an invisible hand' to do things that are in the interests of society as a whole.[14] Whether the free market is always efficient and the invisible hand works in the interests of society have been subject to many discussions.

Where supporters of the free-market theory believe government intervention should only concern itself with protecting private property, critics contest the efficiency of this, claiming that some market failures require government intervention. One of the most renowned critics of the free market is Karl Marx,[15] with his critique of the market's exploitation of labour. Marx was a front-runner against capitalism and advocated against leaving private actors in markets to act freely as he believed capitalists would exploit workers. John Maynard Keynes[16] was also critical of the market's laissez-faire approach, which he believed resulted in boom-and-bust cycles, as illustrated by the 'dotcom' bubble and the Global Financial Crisis.[17] From a more political perspective, Joseph Stiglitz[18] critiqued the market's fundamentalism, which assumes that free markets are always the best solution. Joseph Heath[19] and Charlie Blunden[20] perceive the market from a more ethical perspective, believing that businesses should abstain from exploiting market failures. This, however noble it might be, is unlikely to be the behaviour of the majority of businesses as is also illustrated by the entry barriers created by incumbents in the market for payment services prior to the adoption of the PSD2. Finally, in a more recent contribution to the discussion, James Crotty argues, that the theory set out by Keynes and later supported by Hyman Minskey, is superior and therefore a much better guide to regulation policy, because it is based on what he finds to be realistic assumptions.[21] In varying degrees, the critics all

[14] Adam Smith, *An Inquiry into the Nature and Causes of the Wealth of Nations* (George Routledge and Sons 1890 (original 1776)).

[15] Karl Marx, *Das Kapital* (Gustav Kiepenheuer Verlag AG 1932 (original 1867)).

[16] John Maynard Keynes, *The General Theory of Employment, Interest, and Money* (Palgrave Macmillan 2018 (original 1936)).

[17] Although, of course, Keynes himself was not influenced by these specific events but instead by the Great Depression and the Second World War.

[18] Bruce C Greenwald and Joseph E Stiglitz, 'Externalities in Economies with Imperfect Information and Incomplete Markets' (1986) 101 The Quarterly Journal of Economics 229.

[19] Joseph Heath, 'A Market Failures Approach to Business Ethics', *Morality, Competition, and the Firm: The Market Failures Approach to Business Ethics* (OUP 2014).

[20] Charlie Blunden, 'Between Market Failures and Justice Failures: Trade-Offs Between Efficiency and Equality in Business Ethics: JBE' (2022) 178 Journal of Business Ethics 647.

[21] James Crotty, 'The Realism of Assumptions does matter - Why Keynes-Minskey theory must replace efficient market theory as the guide to financial regulation policy' in Martin H Wolfson and Gerald A Epstein (eds), *The Handbook of the Political Economy of Financial Crises* (OUP 2013).

share an opposition to perceiving the market as capable of delivering optimal results.

On the opposite wing, supporting the theory of free market efficiency, we find economists like Ludwig von Mises, Friedrich von Hayek, Ronald Coase, and Milton Friedman. These views also reflect the perspectives of the Austrian School of Economics and the Chicago School. Their stance is that the market's robustness makes it able to adjust to or internalise market failures, making government intervention redundant.[22] But even supporters can admit that the conditions necessary to obtain the effects of the free market are hard to come by. For example, Pindyck and Rubinfield[23] argue that the free market is efficient if a specific list of conditions is fulfilled, but since these include difficult to achieve conditions such as full competition, the result is sometimes a market failure and a need for intervention.

The understanding of the free market whereby governments do not intervene, could be modified so as to provide an understanding of free markets as markets where private actors can act freely within a framework of what is legal and what is not legal set by the legislator. What is essential in order to consider a market free is its function, where it lets the invisible hand steer the market participants. This, in turn, is essential to understanding the theory of market failure. In financial markets, as in other markets, the invisible hand has been shown to be flawed. Free markets do not always result in efficient markets. When the free market fails to achieve efficiency a market failure is said to have occurred.[24] These failures can appear in different forms, such as information asymmetry, high entry barriers, or negative externalities like pollution. Subsection 2.1.1 will introduce a grouping of market failures relevant to the examination of the EU payment services market.

2.1.1 Market failures

When grouping the types of market failures, it is necessary to consider the different theoretical contributions to this field of economics. The most common division of market failures groups these into market power, or imperfect

[22] For example Friedrich A von Hayek, *The Road to Serfdom* (Routledge 1944); Friedrich A von Hayek, 'The Use of Knowledge in Society' (1945) 35 The American Economic Review 519; Friedrich A von Hayek, *Denationalisation of Money* (The Institute of Economic Affairs 1976); and also Pigou, *The Economics of Welfare* 298 on the justification for some government intervention.

[23] Robert S Pindyck and Daniel L Rubinfield, *Microeconomics* (8th edn, Pearson 2013) 623.

[24] Bator, 'The Anatomy of Market Failure'; Wolf Jr, '"Non-Market" Failures and Market Failures'; Brian Dollery and Joe Wallis, 'The Theory of Market Failure and Policy Making in Contemporary Local Government' (2001) 2001-6 Working Paper Series in Economics at University of New England 9; Begg, Fischer and Dornbusch, *Economics* 265.

markets, asymmetric information, externalities, and public goods.[25] Common to these is that each causes an inefficient distribution of goods and services in the free market. A free market that is not Pareto efficient will, in theory, lead to a net loss of economic value or welfare, which is undesirable for a society that wishes to maximise welfare. These shortcomings of the market are used as the rationale for government intervention,[26] which can be in the form of regulation, taxation and subsidies, or government provision. The intervention of interest here is intervention in the form of regulation. In the following, each market failure will be described and discussed, followed by a short presentation of other contributions to the field of market failure theory which have been given less attention in the selected framework.

The first category of market failure, which also plays a significant role in relation to the topic of EU payment services, is the failure of market power. In general, market power can appear as increasing returns, for example, when the marginal costs of production are declining but the price charged is not, which can also be described as causing prices to be above marginal cost. If there exists a (natural) monopoly, the producer will not have any incentive to lower the price of the product in line with the declining costs, which can be the result of economies of scale. This is a great disadvantage to consumers, who will be paying more for the product even though its production cost, and thereby economic value, has decreased. Although it can also be argued that the economic value of the good to the consumer depends on its utility to them, this is beside the point. Market power also fails when a market actor is neutral to pressure from competitors, i.e. although the competition is pushing prices down, the market actor controlling the market does not have to lower their prices to maintain the same market share.[27]

In the sphere of payment services, it can be illustrated how government intervention has tried to mitigate a market failure. The market for payment services prior to FinTech was highly influenced by powerful incumbent institutions who controlled most of the market.[28] To allow new entrants to enter with the rise of FinTech and create fair competition, government intervention

[25] Veljanovski, 'Economic Approaches to Regulation' who also refers to Bator's 1958 paper although it concerns itself primarily with allocative efficiency; Wolf Jr, '"Non-Market" Failures and Market Failures'; Pindyck and Rubinfield, *Microeconomics* 625; Dollery and Wallis, 'The Theory of Market Failure and Policy Making in Contemporary Local Government' 9.

[26] Armour and others, *Principles of Financial Regulation* 70; Tyler Cowen (ed), *The Theory of Market Failure - A Critical Examination* (George Mason University Press 1988) 209.

[27] This is also supported by decisions of the ECJ on competition matters see for example Case 27/76 *United Brands v Commission*; Case 85/76 *Hoffmann-La Roche*& Co.

[28] European Commission, *Commission Staff Working Document Impact Assessment* SWD (2013) 289 final (2013) 17.

in the form of the PSD2 was introduced. The provisions of articles 66 and 67 of the Directive meant that control of access to customers' payment accounts moved from dependence on bilateral agreements with banks into the hands of the customer. This creates a greater possibility of entering the market than if access relied entirely upon the goodwill of incumbent institutions. Otherwise, the incumbent institutions, with their market power, could hinder the entrance of new market players. This situation represents a market failure in the form of market power, where the control of incumbents results in entry barriers.

For an efficient market to function, it is assumed that all participants possess perfect information and will act rationally upon this information.[29] This is rarely the case. Imperfect, or asymmetric, information can be present both in the relationship between market participant and regulator, and between market participant and consumer. Asymmetric information describes the situation where one party to a transaction is better informed than the other.[30] Imperfect information as a type of market failure is therefore relevant when analysing government intervention and how this issue has been addressed. Imperfect information can also have a negative influence when trying to maintain, or create, a level playing field. Furthermore, asymmetric information also increases the risk of hazard among market participants.[31] Moral hazard exist when a party is inclined to take higher risks because that party is insured or protected against the consequences. A related term is adverse selection, where a better-informed party to a transaction is able to take advantage of the lesser informed party's position, for example by charging a higher price than the value of the product would be to the lesser informed party if that party possessed the same information as the first, better informed, party.[32] Moral hazard can particularly be a risk when market participants can take risks without consequences, for example, if consumers have no liability in the case of unauthorised payment transactions.

A sub-category to the market failure of imperfect information is the consumer's biased, individual decision-making. Consumers tend to not only possess asymmetric information, but also to have highly variating competences and biases in relation to their decisions. This means that even when all consumers receive the same information from service providers, their decision-making process will vary, as individual attributes lead to different information

[29] Pigou, *The Economics of Welfare* 131.

[30] Kohn, *Financial Institutions and Markets* 61.

[31] Pindyck and Rubinfield, *Microeconomics* 643.

[32] George A Akerlof, 'The Market for "Lemons": Quality Uncertainty and the Market Mechanism' (1970) 84 The Quarterly Journal of Economics 488.

processes and risk perception.[33] When dealing with a market where a large proportion of users are consumers, this is relevant when evaluating the management of imperfect information.

The third type of market failure, externalities, can be either negative or positive. Externalities are created when one's action influences the well-being of another person. These can vary greatly in nature and impact. The problem with externalities is that the market participant producing a good does not experience the impact of the externality, hence they do not take the externality into account when making decisions about a given product or service.[34] Governmental interference can therefore be desirable in introducing incentives for decision makers to create more positive externalities and less negative externalities. Within financial markets, externalities can include financial inclusion and innovation, as well as money laundering and terrorist financing. Obviously, society wishes to produce beneficial externalities such as financial inclusion, but wishes to reduce, if not eliminate, unwanted externalities such as money laundering and terrorist financing.

Related to externalities is the last type of market failure, the public good. This can be defined as goods or services that are non-excludable and non-rival.[35] This means that people cannot be prevented from enjoying them, and that one person's use does not diminish another person's use. This also means that there is a natural free-rider problem attached to public goods. A free-rider is someone who enjoys the good without contributing to the costs of producing it.[36] The public good can, in some cases, also be perceived as an extreme case of externalities.[37] In financial markets, financial stability is considered a public good, which regulators seek to incentivise financial institutions to maintain.[38]

One of the early contributions to the modern understanding of market failure theory is Francis Bator's 1958 paper 'The Anatomy of Market Failure'.[39] The paper provides an early take on the conditions necessary for sustaining an efficient market, and in relation to these turns its attention towards the market's failures. Bator generally divides the failures into three types: ownership

[33] Armour and others, *Principles of Financial Regulation* 60.

[34] Howell E Jackson and others, Analytical Methods for Lawyers (2011) Foundation Press 336.

[35] Jackson and others, Analytical Methods for Lawyers 344.

[36] George J Stigler, 'Free Riders and Collective Action: An Appendix to Theories of Economic Regulation' (1974) 5 The Bell Journal of Economics and Management Science 359; Mark A R Kleiman and Steven M Teles, 'Market and Non-Market Failures' in Michael Moran, Martin Rein and Robert E Goodin (eds), *The Oxford Handbook of Public Policy* (OUP 2006) 629.

[37] Bator, 'The Anatomy of Market Failure' 369.

[38] Rosa Lastra, 'Systemic Risk and Macro-Prudential Supervision' in Niamh Moloney, Eilís Ferran, and Jennifer Payne (eds), *The Oxford Handbook of Financial Regulation* (OUP 2015) 313.

[39] Bator, 'The Anatomy of Market Failure'.

externalities, technical externalities, and public good externalities.[40] The first two types are placed under the category of externalities, while the latter is more appropriately grouped as public goods. Bator also touches upon competition and information issues but does so in the context of the conditions required for an efficient market. Bator's contribution was foundational for the further development of market failure theory, but later developments have resulted in a grouping more suitable for the analytical work necessary when applying the theory to explain financial regulation.

Other contributors to the development of market failure theory list similar, but not the same, groupings of market failures. One example is David Begg,[41] who lists market failures as being imperfect competition, social priorities such as equity, externalities, and other missing markets such as future goods, risk, and information.[42] The inclusion of social priorities represents an interesting contribution to theoretical development. However, explaining a failure of the free market on the basis of politics and policy does not align with market failure theory since the basis of that theory lies in free market theory. Social priorities could rather be perceived as a causation of a market failure and not the failure itself. The grouping generally shows fewer pre-defined characteristics than the grouping presented above and hence is not optimal to work with as an analytical framework in financial regulation.

Although different models and categorisations of the theory of market failures exist and are acknowledged, the categorisation presented in this subsection has been found to best support the analytical work of explaining and evaluating EU payment services regulation. The categorisation into market control, asymmetric information, externalities, and public goods makes it possible to clearly delineate the types of market failure from each other and provides an easily comprehensible theoretical framework for the reader of this book.[43]

2.2 The theory of non-market failure

Only in a utopian world would there be a free market with no residue of prior intervention. The market failure theory calls for a counterpart that takes into

[40] Bator, 'The Anatomy of Market Failure' 363.
[41] Begg, Fischer and Dornbusch, *Economics*.
[42] Begg, Fischer and Dornbusch, *Economics* 265.
[43] This grouping is also used by Kleiman and Teles, 'Market and Non-Market Failures'; Veljanovski, 'Economic Approaches to Regulation'; Armour and others, *Principles of Financial Regulation*.

consideration the typical situations arising after intervention in a market. With his 1978 paper,[44] Charles Wolf expanded on the neo-classical economic theory of market failure by adding its counterparty, the non-market failure.[45] This type of failure encompasses situations where governmental or other authorities have intervened in the market, often with the purpose of amending or improving the functioning of the market. Governments tend to argue that a market failure is a sufficient rationale for intervention,[46]as the PSD2 also serves to illustrate. When intervention is executed, the chances are, as Wolf argues, that the measure applied to address the market failure is not a perfect fit. This results in the non-market failure.[47] In essence, it can be described as a market malfunction caused by government applying the visible hand.

The relevance of applying the theory can be explained first by the fact that the primary subject is the PSD2, i.e. the Directive also addresses issues relating to its predecessor, the PSD1. Secondly, the focus of government intervention in the PSD2 is through regulation. The Directive has applied measures and intervened in the market which could potentially have caused new non-market failures to arise or increased the impact of existing ones. Of course, it should also be noted that no piece of legislation can last forever. The subject-matter of legislation is bound to develop and hence calls for revision continually arise over time. Nonetheless, these points are important to note when testing the suitability of a theoretical framework. Starting from a utopian perspective would be out of tune with the continuous development in the market for payment services and would reduce the scientific value of the legal examination of EU Payment Services.

2.2.1 Non-market failures

To access and evaluate the current regulatory framework and its ability to accommodate innovation, it is essential to identify where and how government has intervened to address a market failure. Non-market failures have a significant importance in relation to the regulation of EU Payment Services. Government intervention can take many forms and can be undertaken by national governments, the EU, or any other authority.[48] Government could

[44] Wolf Jr, 'A Theory of "Non-Market Failure": Framework for Implementation Analysis'.

[45] Kohn, *Financial Institutions and Markets* also referred to as government failure, though the term non-market failure seems more appropriate as it covers a wider range of cases than the quite narrow fixation on government.

[46] Armour and others, *Principles of Financial Regulation* 70.

[47] Sock-Yong Phang, 'Market Failures', *Housing Finance Systems: Market Failures and Government Failures* (Palgrave Macmillan UK 2013) also finds it likely that government intervention can result in a(nother) failure despite aiming for enhancing market efficiency.

[48] Julian Le Grand, 'The Theory of Government Failure' (1991) 21 British Journal of Political Science 423, 431.

decide to produce the goods itself creating a legal monopoly, or decide to intervene through a mixed oligopoly where the public provider competes with private companies. This form of intervention is less frequent within the area of financial markets but it is the sole source of the supply of coins and bank notes, and within the Eurozone Target 2 has been established to support large value payments.

Another form of government intervention is regulation. Again, this can come in many shapes and forms, for example by requiring disclosure of information, or imposing restrictions through licensing, standards, antitrust legislation, and so forth. These regulatory mechanisms are often used in markets of financial services. Other forms of intervention can include taxes and subsidies to incentivise market actors to behave according to societal goals, but the focus here will be on regulatory intervention.

If a market failure has occurred and cannot be corrected by the market itself, government intervention can be said to be in the public's interest. This is true if intervention increases the total surplus or contributes to a specific goal,[49] although this presumes that government possesses accurate information and can provide appropriate incentives. As this is not always true, a non-market failure might occur. A non-market failure happens when the government intervention to correct a market failure, either does not remedy the initial failure or creates new problems. If the expected market behaviour is not realised this might be due to the intervention remedy not being fit for purpose or the market might evolve so quickly that the remedy becomes outdated prior to implementation.

Non-market failures can be categorised as redundant and rising costs, internalities, derived externalities, and distributional inequities.[50] Due to the missing market link, where production is made to fit revenues so that benefits exceed costs, non-market initiatives are prone to producing redundant and rising costs without considering efficiency or balancing benefits and costs. Internalities are closely related to the rising and redundant costs as these can be explained as the organisational goals that guide, regulate, and evaluate agency performance instead of the traditional performance indicators available to market organisations. These goals can be used to justify rising budgets, as they can be included in the calculation of created surplus even though they cannot easily be measured.

[49] Charles Wolf Jr, 'Market and Non-Market Failures' (1987) vol 7 (issue 1) Journal of Public Policy 53.

[50] Wolf Jr, 'Market and Non-Market Failures' 63f.

Internalities often consist of budget growth, technological advances, and information acquisition and control.[51] Technological advances are particularly a returning issue as the advancement has evidently outpaced the staggering pace of EU legislation, including the legislation in Member States. Acquiring information can also prove difficult for one centralised authority compared to the collected workings of the market. On top of this comes the trouble with controlling developments and keeping pace with advancements and information on market behaviour, all elements that are necessary when tailoring a regulatory measure to address a market failure.

Derived externalities of government intervention can be defined as unanticipated side effects, or spill-overs, either in the intervention area or in other areas. Government often operates through large organisations using blunt instruments, the consequences of which can be difficult to anticipate. Furthermore, the short time horizon of politicians predisposes them to overlook potential externalities. This tendency is also strengthened by political pressure for intervention, where action might be taken without adequate analysis, especially combined with the internalities and organisational goals.[52] For example, consumer losses in financial services might create political pressure to intervene with the goal of balancing asymmetric information between supplier and consumer. If this were done through a strict liability scheme, moral hazard among consumers would most likely occur as they would have insufficient incentive to take efficient precautions. If, instead, a disclosure regime were enforced, the problem of asymmetric information could be handled without creating consumer moral hazard, though the issue of biased consumer decision making would still be present, as would potential information overload.

The last category of non-market failure is distributional inequity, which can arise from redistribution of power. Government intervention is based on the exercise of power which can redistribute income or use other redistributive mechanisms. This can happen when public policy measures put authority in the hands of some, to be exercised over others, or change who the holder of that authority is. Public policy measures will seek to increase specific activities, affecting the demand for some skills, services, or products, while limiting the demand for others.[53]

Another contribution to the theory of non-market failure, or in this case called government failures, is the 1991 journal paper by Julian Le Grand.[54]

[51] Wolf Jr, '"Non-Market" Failures and Market Failures'.
[52] Wolf Jr, '"Non-Market" Failures and Market Failures'.
[53] Wolf Jr, '"Non-Market" Failures and Market Failures'.
[54] Le Grand, 'The Theory of Government Failure'.

Le Grand approaches the framework from a different perspective than Wolf. Instead of categorising market failures, Le Grand describes the failures which can arise based on the three types of government intervention. When government intervenes with regulation, Le Grand argues that this can be done in four ways, either to regulate quantity, quality, and price, or the structure of the market. For all types of regulation, the main concern is information, and whether government is able to both collect and process this information in a manner which does not result in allocative or dynamic inefficiency.[55] Although the paper contributes some interesting points, it does not establish the same kind of manageable categorisation as Wolf's theory. This means that Wolf's categorisation of non-market failures is more suitable for the purpose of evaluating the EU Payment Services regulation and will be used for the analytical framework presented in chapter 3.

3 Applying market and non-market failure theory to payment services regulation

When examining the ability of a regulatory framework to address failures and accommodate innovation, an alternative approach to the traditional legal doctrinal methodology is called for. This is because the aim of the analysis is not to determine what the existing law is but to evaluate what it does, why it does it, and what effect that will have. Here, economic theory is particularly useful. There exists a natural beneficial relationship in the combination of economic theory, legal tools, and public policy considerations. This combination enables us to identify problems in an existing market, propose one or more possible legal solutions, and develop thorough argumentation whose solution is most optimal considering societal goals and efficiency. Applying the theory of market failure and the theory of non-market failure to the market for payment services in the EU, it becomes possible to assess the current regulatory framework and evaluate its ability to accommodate the rapidly evolving innovations in the market.

With the combination of the two complementary economic theories, the failures of the market's function are reviewed as well as the failures resulting from intervening in the market. This creates an ideal basis to examine and evaluate the regulation applied to address existing failures. As outlined above, the theory of market failures is well-established and has attracted both critics

[55] Le Grand, 'The Theory of Government Failure' 438.

and followers. The theory of non-market failure, or government failure as some call it, has been a little slower to gain attention but is still acknowledged as necessary to guide government intervention in order to avoid inefficiency. The categorisations made in section 2 of this chapter, will be appropriate for examining and evaluating legal measures applied to this area which will be discussed further in chapter 3. Applying an economic theory to a market subject to regulation calls for further definition of some crucial elements. This will be addressed in subsection 3.1, followed by a definition of the understanding of regulatory intervention when the subject is part of the EU Common Market.

3.1 Defining market and non-market failures in a legal setting

Before applying an economic theory to the payment services market, it is necessary to define crucial elements of the theory to establish a common understanding. It is necessary to define when a market failure has occurred and when a non-market failure has occurred. Although Wolf touches upon this question to some extent, some further considerations will be discussed here, as this question is crucial to an understanding of the theoretical framework, and hence the examination of the payment services market.

Fundamentally, market failure can be defined as occurring when there exists imperfect competition, imperfect information, too many negative, and too few positive, externalities, or an insufficient amount of public goods. This is the classical version of market failure theory as is also described in section 2.1. In these cases, market failure can be decided based on efficiency as a measurable fact, although society as a whole is not concerned only with efficiency. This creates the exception to the classical version, which is market failure induced by public policy.[56]

Public policy induced market failure is per definition a human creation.[57] Here, public policy or politics define when a market failure has occurred. This happens through the idealisation of society, where goals are created stating which outputs the market ought to produce and how these outputs ought to be distributed. To stay with the visible/invisible hand terminology, one could

[56] This type of market failure has similarities to the second form of distributional inequity briefly touched upon by Charles Wolf in his 1978 paper '"Non-Market Failures" and Market Failures'. On p 5, Wolf notes that this form is not market failure in the strict sense but fails to put another label on it. The similarity ends when Wolf does not go all the way and conclude that it is in fact a market failure induced by public policy or social desire.

[57] For a similar line of thought also see Bator, 'The Anatomy of Market Failure' 377.

say that society applies the visible hand to direct the invisible hand. In this situation, it is no longer the classical market imperfections that are to blame, but rather societal demands on the market which are not in line with the original function of the market. The invisible hand cannot be controlled by the visible, and the invisible hand would then no longer exist in its original, intended form.

In any case, it is of course possible that elements of both situations of market failure are present in a specific case, where the public policy can be the deciding factor of whether government interferes. It will also be expected that the topics being examined will entail both market and non-market failures at the same time. To qualify the discussion of whether regulatory intervention adequately addresses relevant market failures, or whether these failures merely exist because of current public policy, the identified market failures will be categorised in accordance with these two types.

These definitions of when market failures occur contribute but with a twist on the traditional economic perception of the rationale for regulation. In the traditional view, it is the classical economic market failure that is the rationale for government intervention. When drafting and implementing regulation to address these market failures, government also forms regulatory goals. But if it is these goals that define the moment that a given market failure occurs, then the rationale presents itself before the market failure has occurred and the failure is created by government. Although this makes the theoretical picture more muddy than is desired, it does not change the essential value of the relationship between failures, goals, and regulatory strategies, which will be explained in depth for the market of payment services in chapter 3.

3.2 Defining regulatory intervention in the payment services market

As the term ‘regulation’ has already been used, and will continue to be used repeatedly, we turn our attention to defining its intended meaning.[58] The understanding of regulation here is based on an economic approach, though it also connects naturally with the legal perspective applied. Regulation is to be understood as measures imposed by governments or other authoritative bodies with competence to impose such measures on the subject. This also results in a wider understanding of the term ‘regulation’ than just statutory legislation. It also comprises the body of legal sources constituting the legal

[58] Armour and others, *Principles of Financial Regulation* 12.

framework for the subject matter. This includes, but is not limited to, national acts, EU directives and regulations, and soft law instruments from both national and EU institutions such as guidelines, recommendations, and Q&As.

For the EU common market, particularly the financial services sector, there is an abundance of non-binding soft law measures. These are often based on the delegation of power in the founding regulations,[59] of the ESAs which empower the ESAs to issue various soft law instruments as well as decide cases involving a breach of Union law when national competent authorities (NCAs) do not apply the prescribed acts or apply them in a way which appears to breach Union law.[60] Furthermore, under article 17(6), the ESA may address the financial institution directly if necessary to maintain or restore neutral conditions in the market or to ensure the orderly functioning and integrity of the financial system. Article 18 provides authorisation for ESAs to act in cases of emergency, including in the case of adverse developments which could seriously jeopardise the orderly functioning and integrity of financial markets or systemic stability. When NCAs disagree in cross-border situations, the ESAs have the power to decide these disagreements.[61] Governing these articles are the provisions in article 39, which seek to impose specific processual rules for the decision-making procedure. Although decisions made by the ESAs are not final, they are to be considered regulatory interventions.

The soft law instruments issued by the ESAs are also considered regulatory intervention despite their non-binding nature. The value of these instruments as legal sources was recently sought to be established in *Fédération bancaire francaise (FBF)*.[62] The case concerned whether a French credit institution could bring an action under TFEU article 263 for annulment of guidelines issued by the EBA. The issued guidelines were based on the powers conferred on the EBA by article 16 of its founding regulation.[63] The Court set as a prerequisite for any decision regarding annulment of soft law instruments a determination as to whether an act produces binding legal effects.

To examine the binding legal effects of an act its substance and effects must be assessed on the basis of objective criteria.[64] The Court opined that the

[59] Regulation (EU) No 1093/2010 (EBA Regulation); Regulation (EU) No 1094/2010 (EIOPA Regulation); Regulation (EU) No 1095/2010 (ESMA Regulation).

[60] founding regulations art 17.

[61] founding regulations art 19.

[62] Case C-911/19 *Fédération bancaire francaise (FBF) v Autorité de contrôle prudentiel et de résolution (ACPR)* [2021] EU:C:2021:599.

[63] Regulation (EU) No 1093/2010 of the European Parliament and of the Council of 24 November 2010 establishing a European Supervisory Authority (European Banking Authority), amending Decision No 716/2009/EC and repealing Commission Decision 2009/78/EC [2010] OJ L 331/12.

[64] Case C-911/19 *FBF* para 38.

guidelines in question were subject to the same rules of law as were recommendations issued by the EBA. Such recommendations are not binding upon those to whom they are addressed, hence they do not in principle have any binding force.[65] The Court also referred to article 16(3) of the EBA Regulation which states the comply or explain principle. This does not, according to the Court, trigger an obligation to comply but merely an obligation to explain in detail in case of non-compliance.[66] On this basis, the Court concluded that the guidelines could not be regarded as producing binding legal effects vis-á-vis the competent authorities. This decision is also supported by the judgment in the *Koninklijke* case.[67]

The Court in the *FBF* case also commented on the EBA's different competences, some of which concern the issuing of recommendations and guidelines while others concern the drawing up of technical standards to be adopted by means of regulations or decisions in accordance with article 15(4) of the EBA Regulation.[68] The Court therefore concluded that, by authorising the EBA to issue guidelines and recommendations, the EU legislature intended to confer on that authority the power to exhort and to persuade, which is distinct from the power to adopt acts having binding force.[69] Even though the Court found, due to the lack of any legal binding effect, that an annulment case was ruled out, the Court found itself competent to give a preliminary ruling on the validity of the guidelines.[70] The Court found that the guidelines were valid. Unfortunately, the Court did not consider whether the adoption of the guidelines by the NCA created legally binding effects. The answer to this question could have intrinsic value for the future treatment of soft law instruments issued by EU agencies. Nonetheless, the Court's statement regarding the conferral of competence highlights the powers conferred on the ESAs, stressing the regulatory interventive characteristics of the ESAs' issuance of soft law instruments.

TFEU article 288 lists the Union's legal acts, though the ESAs have to some degree deviated from these as they also use instruments such as guidelines and Q&As to exercise their conferred powers. This deviation could be explained either by assuming that TFEU article 288 only refers to EU institutions, and

[65] Case C-911/19 *FBF* para 42.
[66] Case C-911/19 *FBF* para 44.
[67] Case C-28/15 *Koninklijke KPN NV and Others v Autoriteit Consument en Markt* [2016] EU:C:2016:692 paras 34, 35.
[68] Case C-911/19 *FBF* para 47.
[69] Case C-911/19 *FBF* para 48; and analogy to the judgment in *Belgium v Commission*, C-16/16 P (20 February 2018) para 26.
[70] Case C-911/19 *FBF* paras 54–57.

hence not to agencies like the ESAs, or it could be necessary to look at the conferred powers in the founding regulations. The latter is most likely to contain the answer, as the founding regulations specifically mention in articles 16, 16a, and 16b that the ESAs can issue guidelines, opinions, and Q&As to exercise their powers and fulfil their delegated purposes.

Although the *FBF* case could have been utilised better to secure legal certainty on the understanding of the legal value of soft law instruments, one could argue that the *SV Capital OÜ* case[71] has already settled the score. In this case, the ESAs' Board of Appeal ruled that instruments issued with authority in article 16 of the EBA Regulation are to be used for interpretation measures. This also correlates to the purpose of the instruments: to secure a common, uniform, and consistent use of the substantive provisions of the Single Rulebook,[72] as is stated directly in the wording of article 16.

Concluding on these considerations, the term 'regulation' in the EU financial markets covers more than merely the acts listed in TFEU article 288. As the EU institutions have conferred power on the ESAs in the founding regulations, and often in individual regulations and directives, the instruments issued by these authorities, binding as well as non-binding, are within the scope of the term 'regulation'. Regulation can therefore be considered any form of intervention in a market by a national government body, EU institutions, or authorities delegated such power by either national or EU institutions when the intervention prescribes rules to govern the market, interprets existing rules, fills gaps, or decides on disputes.

[71] Ref EBA C 2013 002 *SV Capital OÜ against European Banking Authority* BoA 2013-008 para 56.

[72] Niels Skovmand Rasmussen, 'Den retlige prøvelse af henstillinger og retningslinjer i EU-kapitalmarkedsret' in Nis Jul Clausen and others (eds), *Festskrift til Hans Viggo Godsk Pedersen* (Djøf Forlag 2017) 471.

3

FAILURES, GOALS, AND STRATEGIES IN THE EU PAYMENT SERVICES MARKET

1 Introduction

The relationship between the market and regulatory intervention can best be described as a circular movement.[1] In a pro-market-based system such as the EU,[2] the rationale for regulation is the presence of one or more market failures.[3] Regulation can be prescribed to address and mitigate these failures.[4] This sort of government intervention in the market, impairing the invisible hand by inserting the visible hand, calls for attention yet again. When government has intervened, it is necessary to evaluate whether the original market failure has been efficiently addressed and dealt with and whether non-market failures have arisen, and to check if new market failures have surfaced. As such, the circle is complete, and the process will continue to cycle as the subject covered by the legal framework evolves. The circle is also illustrated in Figure.3.1 which symbolically does not end but continues to cycle.

This chapter will present the analytical framework developed to conduct the analysis of EU payment services regulation and its ability to accommodate innovation. In accordance with the circular description and as illustrated in Figure 3.1, section 2 will identify the market failures and non-market failures present at the time of implementing the PSD2. This section builds upon the theoretical contributions depicted in chapter 2. The failures will be found through a literature review investigating the problems the EU payments

[1] To some extent supported by John Armour and others, *Principles of Financial Regulation* (OUP 2016) 61.

[2] Marios Costa and Steve Peers, *Steiner & Woods EU Law* (14th edn, OUP 2020) accounts for the developments in the TEU's articulation of this perception on p 56, most recently TEU art 3(3) refers to a highly competitive social market economy.

[3] Andrea Minto, 'Law and Economics: Theory, Methodology and Policy Application' in Carina Risvig Hamer and Sten Schaumburg-Müller (eds), *Juraens Verden Metoder, Retskilder og Discipliner* (DJØF Forlag 2020); George J. Stigler, 'The Theory of Economic Regulation' (1971) 2 The Bell Journal of Economics and Management Science 3; Armour and others, *Principles of Financial Regulation* 70.

[4] For example as suggested by Arthur Cecil Pigou, *The Economics of Welfare* (MacMillan and Co. 1921) to tax or subsidise to alter the market behaviour.

EU Payment Services. Louise Damkjær Christensen, Oxford University Press.
DOI: 10.1093/9780198949084.003.0003

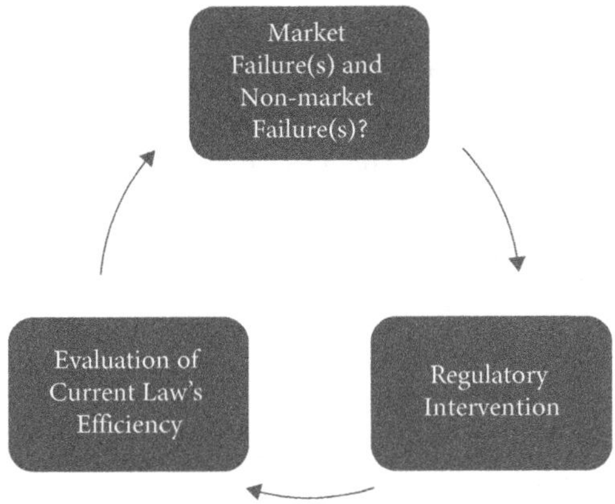

Figure 3.1 The relationship between the market and regulatory intervention as circular movement (own configuration)

market has faced, and using material from the European Commission, the relevant European Supervisory Authorities, and other relevant EU institutions. Furthermore, reports and similar instruments from international organisations will also contribute to the process of identifying existing market failures. It is possible to identify both market and non-market failures, as the scope of the analysis is what is covered by the second Directive (hence its predecessor, the first Directive, was already in existence and could potentially have caused non-market failures to arise).

Section 3 will deal with regulation and legal considerations when intervening in the market, such as the regulatory strategy applied and the underlying goals of regulation. This section is structured with two subsections, one treating the goals and objectives of financial regulation in general, and the other specifically the goals and objectives of the PSD2. The second subsection deals with relevant regulatory strategies which should be considered when intervening in the market with regulation. Goals of regulation can be perceived as a guideline when constructing legislation. They aim to ensure legislative quality, and a unified direction for the specific piece of legislation and in the wider context within which that piece of legislation will have to function. The goals of the PSD2 will be identified by processing the EU goal of the internal market and the meta-goals of financial regulation, followed by a breakdown into the Directive's specific goals. To identify the Directive's specific goals, preparatory works for the adaptation of the PSD2, especially from the European Commission, have been reviewed and secondary sources have been used to buttress the stated goals. Next, the relevant regulatory strategies will be identified and presented. Initially, these strategies will be presented through a literature review to set a framework for the analysis. This will be followed by a specification of the individual strategies applied through the Directive. These have been identified by analysing the PSD2. Supplemental material from the European Commission, the European Supervisory Authorities, and relevant international organisations has also been included to support the argumentation made on the applied strategies.

With section 4 which covers evaluation, the circle will be completed. This section will set out the guidelines for conducting the evaluation. The evaluation's purpose is to discuss whether, or how well, the PSD2 has addressed the initial failures. Given the variety of cases, the content of each chapter's evaluation section will differ from case to case, but elements which naturally span all cases will be introduced in these sections.

The purpose of this chapter is twofold. First, to explain the interplay between market failures, goals of regulation, and regulatory strategies specifically in relation to the PSD2. Second, to identify and select appropriate cases for analysis in the following chapters, creating an analytical framework for these. How the Directive has addressed the identified problems will be analysed and presented in the following chapters, with this chapter only setting out the framework for the analysis. The last and fifth section is structured to introduce the case selection criteria and the cases selected for analysis in the following chapters. For each case the failures, goals, and strategies are briefly presented to prepare the reader for the thorough analysis carried out in the following chapters.

2 Market failures

The purpose of this section is to identify relevant market failures in the EU internal market for payment services. Although the section title suggests a focus merely on market failures, non-market failures will also be addressed. Non-market failures are possible in the EU payment services market because of prior regulation; hence there was not a blank canvas or a free market when the PSD2 was drafted, adopted, and implemented. When drafting regulation, the first step should be to identify and determine the nature and extent of existing market failures,[5] underlining the importance of this step in the analytical

[5] Armour and others, *Principles of Financial Regulation* 52.

framework. Before diving into Directive-specific market failures, some considerations on meta-failures of financial markets will first be presented. The overview of meta-failures of financial markets aims to provide the necessary context to fully understand the failures of the payment services market, and the complexity, when drawing the lines between failures and regulation.

The first subsection will give an overview of meta-failures of financial markets which have been found to be of value for understanding the context within which the payments market is placed. The focus of the second subsection is then narrowed down to present the failures related specifically to the payment services market and the PSD2.

2.1 Meta-failures of financial markets

The financial markets can be described as suffering from some general failures—market as well as non-market failures. These manifest themselves in some generally acknowledged categories: financial crime, systemic or financial stability risks, and asymmetric information that harms both investors and consumers.[6] These categories will be described further in the following paragraphs.

The first category, financial crime, includes one of the most discussed topics within financial markets—money laundering and terrorist financing.[7] Money laundering and financial crime in general, is a negative externality of financial markets.[8] When money is laundered, the collective taxable sum in society is reduced, resulting in less money for society to spend to uphold any version of a welfare state. It is therefore not in society's interest to let money laundering occur. Looking through the economical lens, money laundering is not efficient either. For instance, it could never be Pareto efficient to take something from one group, society, and give it to another, the criminals laundering money. This would leave one group better off at the cost of the other group's welfare. Even the less strict efficiency of Kaldor-Hicks cannot be attained, as the value society loses must be considered greater than the value gained for the criminals. With money laundering, someone is intentionally committing an act to launder money, so why are we calling it an externality? The people acting intentionally are doing so by exploiting a flaw or a gap in a financial product, or sometimes

[6] Armour and others, *Principles of Financial Regulation* 55f.

[7] In the following, referred to simply as 'money laundering'.

[8] Kalle Rose, 'Regulating the Externality of Money Laundering—Halfway there' (2019) No 19-12 CBS Law Research Paper Series 4.

simply using a payment feature to execute a transaction. Hopefully, the providers of the financial product did not in their considerations about launching the product, account, in the budget for profit optimisation, for criminals utilising their product to launder money. As this was not a factor that the provider considered in their value or supply chain, it is categorised as an externality. Money laundering therefore also serves as an excellent example of when regulatory intervention is made to incentivise, if not directly nudge, push, or force, market participants to take preventive measures to avoid money laundering.

Another note-worthy market failure which is generally applicable to financial markets is systemic, or financial, stability risks. When we have stability, this is considered to be a public good[9] which society would want to maintain, but society is dependent on financial institutions to create the stability. Since the Global Financial Crisis, the importance of financial stability has been more distinct, and it has received considerable regulatory attention.[10] The relationship between financial stability risks and consumer protection is particularly interesting. It can be argued that improvements to consumer protection have a positive impact on financial stability and vice versa.[11] Given the nature of financial services and their significance to consumers, trust in the relationship between the two is essential. The problem with a public good such as financial stability is that the public depends on the financial institutions to produce enough of it, but these institutions do not necessarily have the incentive to do so. When too little is produced, for example if trust among consumers in financial services is damaged as happened after the Global Financial Crisis, a market failure is present. Legislators have given high priority to avoiding problems relating to financial and systemic stability risks through intervention, often already at the point of identifying potential risks.[12]

Another generally applicable market failure in financial markets is information asymmetry, which also holds the potential to create moral hazard. As described in chapter 2, information asymmetry is when the parties bargaining do not possess the same information. A sub-category hereof is biased consumer decision-making that entails not only information asymmetry but also variance in the ability, and even desire, to process information correctly. The

[9] Niamh Moloney, Eilís Ferran, and Jennifer Payne (eds), *The Oxford Handbook of Financial Regulation* (OUP 2015) 4f.

[10] Charles A E Goodhart, *The Regulatory Response to the Financial Crisis* (Edward Elgar Publishing 2009) 38.

[11] Also see the link made between consumers and financial stability in European Banking Authority, *EBA Financial Education Report 2019/2020* (2020) 19.

[12] On the correlation between trust in financial institutions and the public's position on government intervention through regulation see Paolo Pinotti, 'Trust, Regulation and Market Failures' (2012) 94 The Review of Economics and Statistics 650.

market failure can arise in both investor and consumer situations. This is inexpedient, as, in order to function, the financial markets need investors willing to invest and consumers willing to buy, which is not the case if neither group can trust the information available on the market and the counterparty. Regulatory intervention is therefore often applied in the attempt to correct this problem, for example in the form of disclosure requirements, such as is the case, for example, in the Market Abuse Regulation and the Prospectus Regulation.[13] The problem of information asymmetry also appears in the process of drafting legislation, where authorities cannot possibly possess full information prior to doing so. It is therefore of the utmost importance that measures such as public consultations are used to collect and process sufficient information about the market and its functioning prior to intervening.[14]

As outlined, the financial market by nature exhibits a variety of market failures, which legislative bodies attempt to correct through regulatory intervention. The following subsection will provide a more detailed overview of the Directive-specific market failures relevant for the PSD2 to address.

2.2 Directive-specific market and non-market failures

In the European Commission's 2013 impact assessment,[15] the Payment Services Directive of 2007 was evaluated. The impact assessment was completed to accompany the proposal on revising the Payment Services Directive. The report gives an account of the issues existing on the market for payment services through an identification of problem drivers, specific problems, and their effects.[16] Notable in the report is the separation of problem drivers into market failures and regulatory and supervisory gaps. This substantiates the analytical framework applied in the following chapters, as it represents the separation of market and non-market failures and using them as a basis for drafting new legislation. The drivers are divided into more tangible problems

[13] Regulation (EU) No 596/2014 of the European Parliament and of the Council of 16 April 2014 on market abuse (market abuse regulation) and repealing Directive 2003/6/EC of the European Parliament and of the Council and Commission Directives 2003/124/EC, 2003/125/EC and 2004/72/EC [2014] OJ L 173/1; Regulation (EU) 2017/1129 of the European Parliament and of the Council of 14 June 2017 on the prospectus to be published when securities are offered to the public or admitted to trading on a regulated market, and repealing Directive 2003/71/EC [2017] OJ L 168/12.

[14] Friedrich A von Hayek, 'The Use of Knowledge in Society' (1945) 35 The American Economic Review 519.

[15] European Commission, *Commission Staff Working Document Impact Assessment* SWD(2013) 288 final (2013).

[16] European Commission, *Commission Staff Working Document Impact Assessment* SWD(2013) 288 final 34.

to be addressed, such as the diverging licensing systems, inconsistent application of the PSD1, and market fragmentation. Furthermore, the effects derived from the problems are described. The impact assessment's findings will be presented in the following sections to build a basis for outlining relevant market and non-market failures in relation to the PSD2's management of these and will be substantiated with further material where relevant.

2.2.1 Market fragmentation and ineffective competition

The market failure of imperfect competition is seen in multiple ways in the EU market for payment services. Prior to the PSD2, the market was driven by restrictive business rules and practices, and new entrants especially lacked market access. As the market was largely controlled by incumbent credit institutions, their market position in comparison to new entrants enabled them to restrict access to payment infrastructures.[17] Such access is crucial for new entrants such as third-party PSPs, as they do not offer customers a payment service account, but only the service of initiating a payment or disseminating account information. By upholding these restrictive business rules and practices, incumbent PSPs could effectively withhold access to crucial components for new entrants and thereby distort the market by avoiding effective competition, while also hampering innovation.[18]

A specific problem identified in the impact assessment related to market failure was market fragmentation.[19] By neglecting standardisation and improvement of interoperability, the market became fragmented both in terms of the size of service providers and across borders. Furthermore, innovation was obstructed from reaching its full potential when dominant market players could control market access. Gaps in standardisation and interoperability reduced competition further, as these are essential in an increasingly digital market. Standardisation is necessary to ensure interoperability, which supports competition when market participants share their proprietary network effects.[20] Gaps in the standardisation and framework for interoperability contributed to ineffective competition, as the market for payment services prior to the implementation of PSD2 was heavily controlled by large, incumbent credit institutions which could effectively set and control practical entry barriers for

[17] European Commission, *Commission Staff Working Document Impact Assessment* SWD(2013) 288 final 16; Iris H Y Chiu, 'A New Era in Fintech Payment Innovations? A Perspective from the Institutions and Regulation of Payment Systems' (2017) 9 Law, Innovation and Technology 190, 205f on the market failures of payment systems.

[18] European Commission, *Commission Staff Working Document Impact Assessment*SWD(2013) 288 final 130.

[19] Alan Brener, 'Payment Service Directive II and Its Implications' in Theo Lynn and others (eds), *Disrupting Finance* (Palgrave Pivot, Cham. 2019) 108.

[20] Marc Bourreau, Jan Krämer, and Miriam Buiten, *Interoperability in Digital Markets* (2022) 19

new entrants.[21] This also meant an excess of legacy systems used in the market, making it more difficult than necessary for innovation to grow in the market.[22]

At the time of the impact assessment's preparation, the market for mobile payments was in a nascent state while internet payments were on the rise.[23] For both solutions the same problem was identified to be stalling further innovation—a lack of standards and interoperability. The impact assessment clearly shows that setting standards and ensuring interoperability are key to creating a payments market which can foster innovative growth.

Combining the growing multilateral interchange fees and the strict business rules applied by card schemes, the ECJ's ruling in the MasterCard case[24] concurred with the direction set forth by the European Commission who initially launched the case.[25] The Court ruled that multilateral interchange fees restrict competition, are forbidden under the competition rules, and are not justified for efficiency reasons. Although the case is significant to improving competition, it only concerns cross-border card-based payments. Changes to domestic-only payments would require interference by national competent authorities, and such interference would be unlikely to result in the same ruleset across the board.[26] Therefore, EU wide regulation could be used as an intervention to create alignment across Member States, increase harmonisation, and improve competition in the payments market. The growing multilateral interchange fees for card-based payments also had a negative impact on competition for new providers in the payment services market. What is most notable considering the topic treated here, is the interchange fees' impact of creating barriers to entry for cheaper and more efficient payment solutions offered by third-party PSPs etc. This inefficient competition state of the market also had a negative impact on the development of innovative payment solutions.[27]

Furthermore, market restrictions caused by incumbent institutions caused a lack of access to information on the availability of funds in a payment account,

[21] European Commission, *Commission Staff Working Document Impact Assessment* SWD(2013) 288 final 15.

[22] Carlo R W De Meijer and Jonathan Bye, 'The increasing adoption of mobile payments in Europe — and remaining challenges to growth' (2011) 5 Journal of Payments Strategy & Systems 273; Niina Mallat and Virpi Kristiina Tuunainen, 'Exploring Merchant Adoption of Mobile Payments: An Empirical Study' (2008) 6 e-Service Journal 24.

[23] European Commission, *Commission Staff Working Document Impact Assessment* SWD(2013) 288 final 17.

[24] Case C-382/12 *MasterCard and Others v Commission* [2014] EU:C:2014:2201.

[25] Case COMP/34.579 *Commission Decision of 19 December 2007 (C(2007)6474) relating to a proceeding under Article 81 of the EC Treaty and Article 53 of the EEA Agreement* [2007] OJ C 264 8-11 C 264/8.

[26] European Commission, *Commission Staff Working Document Impact Assessment*SWD(2013) 288 final 129.

[27] European Commission, *Commission Staff Working Document Impact Assessment* SWD(2013) 288 final 21.

when requested by third parties. Third-party PSPs were dependent on the willingness of the account servicing PSP to provide this information in order to initiate and guarantee a payment requested by a customer. Incumbent institutions, often banks, also held a competitive advantage when it came to payment systems compared to small payment institutions. The latter experienced difficulties participating directly in designated payment systems under the PSD1.[28] This further underlines the issue of ineffective competition and an unlevel playing field between banks and non-banks on the payment services market under the PSD1.

2.2.2 Legislation surpassed by market development

A well-known universal truth is that the market will always develop in a manner to surpass existing legislation. It is therefore essential for the legislator to create flexible regulatory frameworks and to regularly evaluate the need to update current legislation.[29] The rapid development and growth among third-party PSPs, in particular, was unforeseen by the EU legislator when adopting the PSD1 in 2007.[30] One of the problems this caused was the omission of third-party PSPs from the scope of the first Directive. By omitting the category of PSPs, the legislator essentially put systemic stability at risk, as the third-party PSPs were under no obligation to follow the PSD1 requirements, nor were they supervised by any competent authority—national or supranational. Other problems included a lack of legal certainty on issues such as consumer protection, liability, security and safety of services, competition, and protection of data.

With new services such as the payment initiation service and the account information service, the former regulatory framework met a new challenge. These services were not covered by its scope. This caused a legal vacuum to appear. The appearance of the legal vacuum for third-party PSPs can be attributed to the legislator as an internalisation. This non-market failure stemming from the first Directive was caused by the somewhat narrow scope of the Directive but can also be ascribed to the rapid technological developments which were overlooked by the legislator at the time of drafting the former regulatory framework. Almost as a derivative of this non-market failure is the next

[28] European Commission, *Commission Staff Working Document Impact Assessment* SWD(2013) 288 final 24.

[29] Brener, 'Payment Service Directive II and Its Implications' 107 also argues for the high importance of the Directive being evidenced by the impact assessment launched so early after implementation.

[30] European Commission, *Commission Staff Working Document Impact Assessment* SWD(2013) 288 final 26; Mary Donnelly, 'Payments in the digital market: Evaluating the contribution of Payment Services Directive II' (2016) 32 Computer Law & Security Review 828.

issue appearing in the payment services market, the systemic risk caused by the scope being too narrow.

Excluding third-party PSPs from the scope of the PSD1 potentially caused risks to systemic stability, as these providers were not obliged to comply with the rulebook set out by the regulatory framework.[31] This included the rules on capital requirements, safeguarding customer funds, and liability questions, to name a few. Even though these providers were operating without the need for a license, their customers (i.e. consumers) were most likely unaware of this, or its significance. Combined with the competitive advantages this can give third-party PSPs, for example in setting a lower price for their services, leaving them out of the scope of regulation could have detrimental effects on consumer welfare and systemic stability.

Although the market already suffered from market fragmentation and ineffective competition, the non-market failure made by the EU regulator did not provide for a stronger market either. The flawed scope of the Directive caused systemic stability risks to appear and resulted in a less level playing field between PSPs, as some were regulated while others were not. It left new innovative providers in a legal vacuum full of uncertainty, potentially hampering further innovation, and finally, it left consumers unprotected. A revision of the regulatory framework to amend these flaws was therefore justified.

2.2.3 Information asymmetry in a consumer-heavy market

Information covers several different aspects when dealing with the payment services market, where innovation and digitalisation have added new features. Although the failure of asymmetric information was not specifically mentioned in the Commission's impact assessment, it has been included here, as it constitutes an essential element in ensuring appropriate and suitable legislation. When speaking of information asymmetry in the market for payment services, the market failure shows itself in various relationships. Between providers, especially between incumbents and third-party PSPs, there is a knowledge gap where the account servicing PSP has access to information on not only a consumer's availability of funds, but also on the broader picture of the consumer's spending pattern.[32] Availability of funds is essential in order to initiate and execute payment transactions, and financial data about consumers creates an advantage for the data holder in creating and developing tailored products and services for specific target groups.

[31] Rui Gong and Frank Page, 'Shadow Banks and Systemic Risks' (2016) SRC Discussion Paper 33.
[32] Brener, 'Payment Service Directive II and Its Implications' 112.

Another relationship is between the PSP and the payment service user, particularly when the payment service user is a consumer.[33] Even with an extensive disclosure regime, it is not a given that consumers are able to make sound financial decisions. This is often explained by the individual, biased decision-making process, as explained in chapter 2, section 2.1.1. Consumers who have had all relevant information disclosed prior to deciding to use a payment service have been put in the best possible position to make their decision. However, if the consumer does not understand the information provided, or perhaps is pressured by personal financial or social problems, it is not certain that the consumer will be able to make the rational decision which best serves their interests. This can be illustrated using the third-party PSPs who were not covered by the PSD1. The simple awareness that the third-party PSP is not subject to regulation or supervision, as the consumer's account servicing PSP is, will rarely be sufficient for the consumer to understand the impacts on their liability, data protection, prices, etc. when using the third-party PSP, compared to using their account servicing PSP.[34] The objective of improving consumer protection when using payment services will therefore justify regulatory intervention to this end.

The last relationship to be considered here is the one between PSPs and supervisory authorities and regulators. Cooperation and communication between market participants and supervisory authorities are essential elements in a well-functioning market. Supervisory authorities are responsible for enforcing the regulatory framework adopted by the legislator, but this requires continuous information about market participants. Without symmetric information, the enforcement of the regulatory framework may be misguided, and there is a risk supervisory measures may be applied too harshly or too softly. This can cause a negative impact on the provision of services when the enforcement is too harsh, and could, for example, damage consumer protection if applied too gently to PSPs that fail to comply with the regulatory framework. To protect both the effective provision of payment services and consumers of those services, measures for supervisory authorities to secure sufficient information about the PSPs can arguably be justified.

[33] On the importance of this consumer trust or acceptance of digital solutions also see Donnelly, 'Payments in the digital market: Evaluating the contribution of Payment Services Directive II' 828.

[34] European Banking Authority, *EBA Financial Education Report 2019/2020* also concludes that the financial literacy among EU consumers is below the expected level.

3 Regulatory intervention

After identifying and categorising market and non-market failures, it is possible for the legislative organs to start addressing them if intervention is deemed appropriate. Regulatory intervention is appropriate when a legislative measure is expected to mitigate the issue, or to create a situation which is more efficient than without regulatory intervention. The Commission concludes in its impact assessment that regulatory intervention is necessary to create more optimal and efficient market circumstances, particularly considering the legislator's desire to enhance innovation and ensure a competitive edge for the EU payment services market.[35]

When it has been decided by the legislative powers that regulatory intervention is appropriate, some consideration should be given to the contents and strategies of this regulation. It is immensely important to be aware of the goals of the regulation at hand, and the wider context that it will have to contribute to, during the drafting process. The following sections will therefore clarify the context which the PSD2 must function within, and the goals and objectives the Directive must contribute towards. Such clarification provides valuable insights when evaluating current law, as the context of not only the Directive's goals but also of the financial market that it functions within is decisive in determining whether regulatory intervention has been successful. The second subsection 3.2, will introduce the relevant regulatory strategies applied in the PSD2. This serves to provide knowledge of available strategies compared to those applied, which substantiates and explains the regulatory measures analysed in the following chapters. An understanding of regulatory strategies is also useful when evaluating the appropriateness of applied measures.

3.1 Goals of regulatory intervention

In order to set a direction or work towards a certain optimal market situation, it is necessary to have set out the goals and objectives which the regulation aims to achieve. By identifying the goals of the PSD2, it becomes possible in the following chapters to analyse the adopted measures and evaluate their appropriateness and efficiency. However, before moving on to the Directive-specific goals, it is necessary to consider the overarching goals of financial regulation. This is necessary to provide the context which the Directive must fit into and

[35] European Commission, *Commission Staff Working Document Impact Assessment* 27.

contribute to. The context is provided through a top-down approach, starting from the top of the pyramid with the goals of the EU Treaties, then the meta-goals of financial regulation in general, and finally the goals of the PSD2. It should be clear, when looking from the bottom to the top, that each level of goals supports the level above it. Specifically, when identifying the goals of the PSD2, these should represent how the payment services market is expected to contribute to reaching the goals of financial services in general, which again are intended to contribute to the goals set out in the EU Treaties.

The following will first briefly consider the goals set out by the EU Treaties which bear relevance to financial markets. This will be followed by a more substantial discussion of the goals of financial regulation in general, the so-called meta-goals. The goals of the PSD2 will then be identified. The EU Treaties clearly set out their goals, but for the other two levels further exploration must be conducted. For the meta-goals, goals stated in legal acts and uncovered through a literature review will provide an overview of these, whereas the specific goals of the PSD2 will be identified through the Directive, its recitals, reports from the Commission, and reports ordered by the Commission in relation to payment services.

Before moving on to the identification of the above-mentioned goals and objectives, the meaning here of a goal or an objective should be defined. A recurring theme in this book is the notion of regulatory goals and objectives. The term goal or goals is defined as the high-level purpose of government intervention—the purpose that is desired on a societal level. Where the goals are on a higher purpose level, objectives are placed below them which aim to work towards achieving the goals. In many ways, objectives correlate with regulatory strategies, which will be presented in subsection 3.2.

3.1.1 Goals of the EU Treaties

The Treaty of the European Union (TEU) states in article 3(3) that a purpose of the Union is to establish and ensure an internal market. This is still a central purpose of the EU.[36] In the Treaty on the Functioning of the European Union (TFEU) article 26, the internal market is defined as 'an area without internal frontiers in which the free movement of goods, persons, services, and capital is ensured'. In the case of payment services, both the free movement of services and capital hold importance.[37] Without these freedoms, it would be up to Member State regulation

[36] Costa and Peers, *Steiner & Woods EU Law* 327.

[37] European Commission, *Commission Staff Working Document Impact Assessment* SWD(2013) 288 final 35.

to enable the movement of services and capital across borders. Fragmentation in legislation across the Union, which this would result in, would not have a positive impact on the desired harmonisation of legislation within the EU.

The Treaty goals can also be categorised as supranational objectives.[38] They aim towards integration of markets and law within the European Union. With the internal market, the European Council intended to create a more favourable environment for stimulating enterprise, competition, and trade.[39] This intention has since developed concurrently with societal progress. From aiming towards an open market economy, to a harmonious, balanced, and sustainable development of economic activities, to the current objective of a highly competitive social market economy,[40] this testifies to the Union's adamant objective of securing an internal market, yet still being mindful of societal developments. Although TEU article 3 describes the Union's main objectives, the provision does not itself impose legal obligations on Member States. However, even without direct legal impact, the provision still carries interpretative value in matters related to EU law.[41]

The value placed on goals in the Treaties accentuates the importance of regulatory goals. They do not, as rules of law do, prescribe rights and obligations. Instead, they set the direction when drafting legislation and aid in the later interpretation of such legislation. When dealing with the internal market, payment services play an indispensable role. Without payment services no other part of the market could function, as payment for goods, services, labour, and so on is essential to the functioning of the internal market. In the treatment of the regulatory framework for payment services within the EU, the objective of the Treaty—to ensure an internal market that supports a highly competitive social market economy—is important to keep in mind.

3.1.2 Meta-goals of financial regulation

The meta-goals of financial regulation can in economic terms be described as the macro level, while the Directive-specific goals constitute the micro level. An understanding of the functioning of the financial system at the macro level makes it possible to thoroughly investigate the micro level, here the EU market for payment serivces. Providing an understanding of the meta-goals of financial regulation will therefore contribute to the analytical work and evaluations

[38] Mads Andenæs and Iris H-Y Chiu, *The Foundations and Future of Financial Regulation—Governance for Responsibility* (Routledge Taylor & Francis Group 2014) 16.

[39] European Commission, *Completing the Internal Market* (COM(85)310 final) (1985) 4.

[40] Costa and Peers, *Steiner & Woods EU Law* 56.

[41] Costa and Peers, *Steiner & Woods EU Law* 56.

regarding the further examination of regulatory intervention on the payment services market. Furthermore, the meta-goals should also be included in the considerations when dealing with the management of specific market failures, as these cannot be mitigated in a way that is not in alignment with the Directive-specific goals, the meta-goals, and the goals of the European Union.

There are varying points of view on the more specific formulation of goals of financial regulation. John Armour and others[42] argue that there are in general six accepted goals of financial regulation. These constitute the protection of investors and other users of the financial system, consumer protection, financial stability, market efficiency, competition, and preventing financial crime.[43] The formulation of the six goals stems from an economic analysis considering which market failures exist in the financial system and how to amend these. Armour and others also highlight the inevitable issue of the meta-goals conflicting with one another when legislators develop regulatory frameworks. The potential spill-over resulting from regulatory intervention in pursuit of one goal could have implications for the achievement of equivalent goals.[44] This is also another example of how economics and law work well together. As earlier presented in chapter 2, section 2.2.1, spill-over is a known non-market failure which stems from regulatory intervention. If regulatory intervention is used to address a market failure, and the intervention is based on a strategy that aims to achieve the goals of that particular area, for example payments, and yet produces spill-over effects impacting other equivalent goals for the market of payments, or other markets entirely, a non-market failure has occurred and must be addressed. However, the question arises, if regulatory intervention created this issue in the first place, is it truly the most appropriate measure to correct it?

Ross Cranston[45] puts forward similar observations to Armour and others regarding the goals of financial regulation, or as he puts it, the reasons for regulation.[46] Although Cranston's focus is primarily on banks, the objectives he stipulates of their regulatory rationale are worth considering here. The main objectives consist of preserving the stability of financial institutions, enabling orderly recovery and resolution for financial institutions, protection of depositors and consumers of banking services, preservation of market confidence, protection against systemic shocks, and preservation of provision of infrastructure services including payment services. While these are considered the

[42] Armour and others, *Principles of Financial Regulation.*
[43] Armour and others, *Principles of Financial Regulation* ch 3, section 3.4.
[44] Armour and others, *Principles of Financial Regulation* 71.
[45] Ross Cranston and others, *Principles of Banking Law* (3rd edn, OUP 2017).
[46] Cranston and others, *Principles of Banking Law* 27.

explicit objectives, Cranston poses an implicit objective—to foster economic prosperity by protecting systemic stability and safeguarding access to finance for creditworthy borrowers.[47] Perhaps the most important observation made by Cranston is that banking regulation, and this is true for any regulation, cannot and should not seek to create a zero failure environment, but rather an environment where failure can be managed so that it does not endanger the stability of the financial system and create market dislocation.[48] Regulation is not the answer for all market failures, and regulation's increased complexity has contributed to less effectiveness. Where market failures can either self-correct or be corrected by regulation, regulation is less flexible and hence not likely to be the right solution.

Moloney, Ferran, and Payne account for the goals of financial regulation in a slightly different manner.[49] The trio sets out three main objectives of financial regulation. The first is the support of financial stability, the second is market efficiency, transparency, and integrity, and the last is the protection of consumers. Underpinning these three objectives is the concern to ensure that the financial system supports economic growth and does not put taxpayers' funds at risk.[50] The authors have managed to make the list of goals much shorter than the other contributions, but the essence remains very similar.

Across the different contributions, a list of meta-goals seems to be generally accepted. These constitute consumer and investor protection, competition, economic growth and efficiency, financial and systemic stability, and the prevention of financial crime. Going forward, any mention of the meta-goals of financial regulation is a reference to these five goals. The reason for leaving out important elements such as market transparency and integrity is that these, in the context of this book and its topic, constitute objectives which work towards the five listed goals. As such, they are to be understood as measures which can be used to achieve the meta-goals.

3.1.3 Directive-specific goals

Zooming in on the PSD2, three primary goals stand out when reviewing the Directive, its recitals, and the consultations and pre-legislative works such as the impact assessment. These goals are competition, consumer protection, and

[47] Cranston and others, *Principles of Banking Law* 28.
[48] Cranston and others, *Principles of Banking Law* 28.
[49] Moloney, Ferran, and Payne (eds), *The Oxford Handbook of Financial Regulation*.
[50] Moloney, Ferran, and Payne (eds), *The Oxford Handbook of Financial Regulation* 6.

innovation.[51] This grouping is also supported by the European Commission's statements when proposing the Directive and is mentioned directly on the Directive's FAQ webpage.[52] Subsections 3.1.3.1–3.1.3.3 will describe each goal in detail and consider the interplay between the different goals.

3.1.3.1 Competition

One of the main goals of the PSD2, and of financial regulation in general, is to improve and support fair competition in the internal market for payment services.[53] Competition is important, as it provides incentives for market participants to innovate. By innovating, market participants develop new products or improve current products, and this is assumed to be beneficial for the consumer in the end. Furthermore, competition creates an incentive for providers to offer their products and services at a fair price and not overcharge consumers. Competition also ensures fair barriers for entry to and exit from markets, which creates incentive to enter the market with innovative products. In perfect competition, it will also be easier for consumers to change their provider of services. The ability account servicing PSPs had under the PSD1 to block new entrants undermined competition. This justified regulatory intervention.

In the press release[54] accompanying implementation of the Directive, the European Commission highlighted that it intends to open the EU payment services market to companies offering payment services by giving them access to information about payment accounts. With this measure, the Directive aims to create more and fairer competition in the payments market, while also promoting innovation in the payment services market.

The need to implement technological developments in the regulatory framework for the EU to remain competitive was also highlighted in the ROFIEG[55] report as necessary in order to increase the value of technology companies in

[51] European Commission, *Green Paper: Towards an integrated European market for card, internet and mobile payments* (COM(2011) 941 final) (2012) where the Commission highlighted these three goals for a revision of the PSD1.

[52] European Commission, 'FAQ: Making Electronic Payments and Online Banking Safer and Easier for Consumers' (2019) <https://ec.europa.eu/commission/presscorner/detail/en/qanda_19_5555> accessed 16 June 2022.

[53] Directorate-General for Financial Stability Financial Services and Capital Markets Union, *Revised rules for payment services in the EU—Summary of Directive (EU) 2015/2366 on EU-wide payment services* (2016); European Commission, *Green Paper: Towards an integrated European market for card, internet and mobile payments* (COM(2011) 941 final) 2.

[54] European Commission, *Payment services: Consumers to benefit from cheaper, safer and more innovate electronic payments* (European Commission 2018).

[55] Expert Group on Regulatory Obstacles to Financial Innovation (ROFIEG), *30 Recommendations on Regulation, Innovation and Finance* (2019) 11.

the EU and promote values such as fair competition. The expert group also emphasised the need for a considerably more harmonised framework to increase competitiveness in a technology-driven financial sector.[56] In this respect, a harmonised framework across Member States could be perceived as a measure to achieve greater competition in a single EU payments market.

In existing literature covering the area of payment services and the PSD2 there exists a general consensus that the PSD2 aims to encourage competition and innovation in the payment services market. It is also agreed that this is attempted by expanding the scope of the first Directive, introducing regulation of third-party PSPs.[57]

At the end of the day, it all comes down to incentives. To foster fair competition there must be sufficient incentive for market participants to continuously provide and develop payment services. By securing access to payment accounts, the Directive creates incentive for new entrants to enter the market, as the access which they depend on is guaranteed. Bringing new entrants into the market also creates greater incentive for incumbents to perform better and improve their current services, as they otherwise risk losing customers if they do not evolve their product portfolio. For both incumbents and new entrants, there is an incentive to offer their services at a fair price, as the price of services can be a deciding factor for consumers,[58] who make up a large group of payment service users.

To fully understand why enhanced competition in the market became a challenge, it is necessary to analyse a little bit of the history of the development of modern banking. Historically, consumers have held their money at a traditional credit institution where they had one or more deposit accounts. To transfer money from their account, either to a recipient or to their own deposit account in another credit institution, it was necessary to ask the credit institution servicing the payer's account to make the transfer. The credit institution would then communicate with the payee's account servicing credit institution to execute the transaction. This was a rather slow process for consumers requiring the involvement of multiple intermediates. Modern technology, the

[56] Expert Group on Regulatory Obstacles to Financial Innovation (ROFIEG), *30 Recommendations on Regulation, Innovation and Finance* 12.

[57] See Ben Regnard-Weinrabe and Jane Finlayson-Brown in Jelena Madir (ed), *FinTech Law and Regulation* (Elgar Financial Law and Practice, 2nd edn, Edward Elgar Publishing 2021) 31; Donnelly, 'Payments in the digital market: Evaluating the contribution of Payment Services Directive II'; Benjamin Geva, 'Title 1 "Subject Matter, Scope and Definitions" (arts 1–4)' in Gabriella Gimigliano and Marta Bozina Beros (eds), *The Payment Services Directive 2—A Commentary* (Edward Elgar Publishing 2021) 6.

[58] For more on the benefits of consumers when adressing market failures see Jean Tirole, 'Market Failures and Public Policy' (2015) 105 The American Economic Review 1665, 1667.

outcome of technological innovation, has made it much faster and simpler for consumers to initiate such transactions with fewer intermediaries. Using an app on a mobile device, it is now possible to initiate the payment transaction through a payment initiation service which will then access the deposit account and initiate the transfer to the chosen payee's deposit account at the same or another credit institution. This is possible due to the Application Programming Interface (API).

In addition to the payment initiation service, another newcomer to the market is the account information service, which allows customers to review their deposit accounts across credit institutions in one app that shows them all their accounts in one place. For both types of services, access to the consumer's deposit account(s) at their credit institution(s) is essential for the service provider to be able to provide their services. These two services are also known as third-party payment services, which were not regulated under the former PSD1. Prior to the implementation of the PSD2, there were no rights for these providers to have access to their users' deposit account through API's. They were dependent on the good will of credit institutions through bilateral agreements. This allowed incumbent institutions to keep new entrants out by not allowing access to the deposit accounts despite the owner of the account requesting such access.[59] This undermined competition and lowered consumer welfare by giving consumers fewer choices.

The PSD2 aims to create a comprehensive regulatory framework for the internal payment services market.[60] The Directive establishes a right for customers to grant third-party PSPs access to payment accounts maintained at credit institutions.[61] This significantly lowers the entry barrier to the market and underlines the Directive's goal of improving competition.

3.1.3.2 Consumer protection

Whether we call it consumer protection, consumer interest, or consumer welfare, a more precise definition of the term is warranted. In the context of payment services regulation, consumer protection is to be understood as protecting the interests of consumers. This covers price, service, quality, and

[59] Regnard-Weinrabe and Finlayson-Brown in Madir (ed), *FinTech Law and Regulation* 32.

[60] Directorate-General for Financial Stability Financial Services and Capital Markets Union, *Revised rules for payment services in the EU—Summary of Directive (EU) 2015/2366 on EU-wide payment services*.

[61] Directive (EU) 2015/2366 of the European Parliament and of the Council of 25 November 2015 on payment services in the internal market, amending Directives 2002/65/EC, 2009/110/EC and 2013/36/EU and Regulation (EU) No 1093/2010, and repealing Directive 2007/64/EC [2015] OJ L 337/35 arts 66 and 67.

choice.[62] The different consumer terms can be used interchangeably. This definition of consumer welfare also stands apart from the purely technical and economic sense applied by the Chicago School.[63] Instead, it represents a balance between economics and law, where both areas play an interdependent role in the use and understanding of the term.[64]

The incentives created for service providers by the goal of competition, as mentioned in section 3.1.3.1, undoubtedly impact consumer protection positively.[65] As such, the efforts toward achieving the goal of competition are also considerably advancing the all-important goal of consumer protection.[66] This prompts one to consider why consumer protection has become of such high importance in financial regulation. The Global Financial Crisis was not only followed by years of financial crisis but also lowered consumer trust in financial institutions.[67] Such lowered trust naturally leads to less willingness to entrust credit institutions with personal savings, which are to some extent a necessity for traditional banking operations. Simply put, when financial institutions protect consumer interests, they increase consumer trust in them. But this might not be sufficient incentive for all financial institutions to observe consumer interests without further encouragement. It is therefore necessary for financial regulators to provide incentives to encourage financial institutions to work towards efficient consumer protection, in order to ensure and protect financial stability.[68]

In the case of the digital development of financial technology it is not only for the sake of financial stability that consumer protection is an important goal. Technology also leads to the creation of new forms of personal, financial data that were not as easily accessible prior to digitalisation. Consumers are now

[62] Eugène Buttigieg, *Competition Law: Safeguarding the Consumer Interest*, vol 40 (International Competition Law Series, Kluwer Law International 2009) 1.

[63] Robert H Bork, *The Antitrust Paradox—A Policy at War with Itself* (Basic Books Inc. 1978) 50

[64] This definition would also seem to be in accordance with the views stated in Armour and others, *Principles of Financial Regulations.*

[65] Tirole, 'Market Failures and Public Policy' (n 58) 1667.

[66] Moloney, Ferran, and Payne (eds), *The Oxford Handbook of Financial Regulation* 6 for one manages to highlight the importance of consumer protection. The handbook also designates three whole chapters to consumer related issues.

[67] Bahriye Basaran and Mahmood Bagheri, 'The Relevance of "Trust and Confidence" in Financial Markets to the Information Production Role of Banks' (2020) 11 European Journal of Risk Regulation 650 also calls the GFC a crisis of confidence (in financial markets) at 663; Pinotti, 'Trust, Regulation and Market Failures' 65; Torben Hansen, 'The role of trust in financial customer-seller relationships before and after the financial crisis' (2014) 13 Journal of Consumer Behaviour 442 which found trust to have less decisive factor after GFC than before.

[68] Basaran and Bagheri, 'The Relevance of "Trust and Confidence" in Financial Markets to the Information Production Role of Banks'; Frank Partnoy, 'Financial Systems, Crises, and Regulation' in Niamh Moloney, Eilís Ferran, and Jennifer Payne (eds), *The Oxford Handbook of Financial Regulation* (OUP 2015) 80.

more prone to giving access to, and producing more, data that service providers can utilise. Protecting consumers from involuntarily or unknowingly sharing personal financial data is therefore an objective of the Directive. Furthermore, by using financial services digitally, consumers create data on their financial actions which can be utilised by financial service providers to sell more products to the same consumers. Making these processes ethical and reasonable for both consumers and financial service providers is of importance.

A Danish study of consumer behaviour in relation to payments,[69] shows an uptake in consumers' use of digital payment solutions with approximately 80% having used such solutions within the last year. The respondents use digital payment solutions because they are easily accessible and fast,[70] especially when paying online the consumers tended to prefer a digital payment solution.[71] Among the respondents who do not use digital payment solutions, their reasons for this choice were that they were accustomed to paying with a physical payment instrument, and around 10% do not trust digital solutions and up to 20% do not think that they are protected from payment fraud if they use a digital payment service.[72] The numbers partly show that some consumers are unfamiliar with the ruleset covering their digital payments, while others focus on the accessibility of the solution without considering the increasing complexity of digital payment services. In a report on consumer vulnerability in the digital age, the OECD also warns that the increasing complexity of online transactions and new technologies expose consumers to greater risk of financial harm.[73] These observations highlight the importance of the PSD2 specifically having consumer protection as a regulatory goal, as innovative developments must be aligned with this goal to ensure safe payment services for all consumers.

Another dimension that it is also necessary to shed some light on is financial crime. Criminal actors could potentially exploit the consumer position for financial fraud and money laundering. Safety measures, such as strong customer authentication (SCA), are therefore a necessary tool to secure safe payments. SCA makes access to payment services a little less smooth for the consumer, having to authenticate for each use, but considering the extra security it

[69] Konkurrence-og Forbrugerstyrelsen (Danish competition and consumer authority), *Betalingsrapport 2024* (2024).

[70] Konkurrence-og Forbrugerstyrelsen (Danish competition and consumer authority), *Betalingsrapport 2024* 41.

[71] Konkurrence-og Forbrugerstyrelsen (Danish competition and consumer authority), *Betalingsrapport 2024* 39.

[72] Konkurrence-og Forbrugerstyrelsen (Danish competition and consumer authority), *Betalingsrapport 2024* 42 fig 5.5.

[73] OECD, *Consumer vulnerability in the digital age* (2023) 16.

provides this is a small price to pay. In any case, instruments like strong customer authentication are a necessity to protect against financial crime.

Financial crime in the economic framework can perhaps best be perceived as a negative externality, as the activity of using a service available on the market is not ineffective as such, but the outcome—money laundered or consumers defrauded—impacts society negatively on multiple levels. This is true whether it be lowered trust in financial services due to fraud or lowered tax income due to money laundering, resulting in less total welfare. The SCA enforced by the Directive[74] can therefore be perceived as a regulatory intervention to correct the market failure that would otherwise continue to create a negative externality for society, with the aim of improving consumer protection as well. By enforcing the SCA on PSPs, the regulator makes the PSPs adopt a higher degree of precaution, ensuring the production of a public good.

Furthermore, as the third-party payment services were previously unregulated, the PSD2 also had to create legal certainty about consumer rights in relation to this part of the payment services market. Aspects such as liability and refund rights have therefore also been specified. Compared to the previous rules for payment services, consumer rights are now enhanced.[75] This is yet another aspect where the market's invisible hand is insufficient. Left on its own, the market would not deliver these consumer rights, as consumers do not group sufficiently to put the necessary pressure on providers to include the rights voluntarily in their provision of services. Furthermore, the concept of consumer protection includes the notion of consumers not being able to collect and process information sufficiently to be an equal counterparty to a financial institution when bargaining. The rights are therefore ultimately paid for by the providers of services, and the incentive to voluntarily offer the rights would most likely be a severe price increase to cover potential costs arising from liability protection, or the fixed cost of covering other costs such as surcharges. The rationale for regulatory intervention is therefore present and aims to secure the societally desired level of consumer protection.

The European Commission states a desire to make it easier, cheaper, and safer to make payments.[76] These objectives are also encouraged by reports on

[74] The Directive's art 98 mandates the EBA to develop draft regulatory technical standards on strong customer authentication, which were adopted with minor changes by the European Commission and came into full force in September 2019.

[75] Directorate-General for Financial Stability Financial Services and Capital Markets Union, *Revised rules for payment services in the EU—Summary of Directive (EU) 2015/2366 on EU-wide payment services* 4.

[76] European Commission, *Payment services: Consumers to benefit from cheaper, safer and more innovate electronic payments.*

FinTech such as the ROFIEG report, which argue that FinTech can serve as a tool to help financial inclusion by enabling new or cheaper services and potentially increase consumers' control of their finances.[77] Ensuring transparency for consumers is therefore essential when regulating towards the goal of enhanced consumer protection.

These considerations also relate directly to perhaps the most famous market failure concerning consumer protection—the issue of asymmetric information, which also relates to the consumer's individual, biased decision-making. This justifies a generous amount of regulatory intervention, though it is important for regulators to be cautious how they intervene. The PSD2 has, with the aim of enhancing consumer protection, indirectly enforced transparency into the regulatory framework. Transparency requirements cover prices, products, consumer rights, and liability, and set out to create legal certainty in the provider/consumer relationship.

The need to consider and use different regulatory strategies can be illustrated when securing consumer protection through consumer rights. As consumers are considered a weak and non-unified group, efficient enforcement of the rules laid down in the Directive is important. The PSD2 has ensured this by implementing strict rules on the rights of consumers, and through an easily accessible resolution system,[78] compared to the alternative of national court systems. Furthermore, the Directive empowers the supervisory architecture at both Member State and EU level. As such, the Directive uses a combination of strategies to enhance and secure consumer protection in the desired EU payment services market.

The number and strictness of rules aiming for stronger consumer protection are easily justified. The free market would, and does, fail to provide sufficient incentive for service providers to deliver these consumer rights voluntarily. All of these rights are directly or indirectly paid for by the providers. The issue of surcharges perhaps best illustrates the problem. Prior to regulating surcharges, it was negotiable who the bearer of this cost would be. Providers of payment services placed the surcharge on the consumer for requesting the transaction. This could be added to the requested amount, or deducted from the amount transferred, leaving both the payer and the payee with uncertainty about the amount paid or received. By regulating this at the EU level, the cost has been placed on the service provider, creating legal certainty for consumers about

[77] Expert Group on Regulatory Obstacles to Financial Innovation (ROFIEG), *30 Recommendations on Regulation, Innovation and Finance* 90.

[78] Directive (EU) 2015/2366 (PSD2) arts 101–103.

what amount will be debited from their account, and what amount a payee can expect to receive.

3.1.3.3 Innovation

As mentioned under the competition section, a rationale for regulatory intervention promoting innovation and competition is the market failure of imperfect competition, whereby incumbents effectively keep start-ups with innovative products or services from entering the market by not allowing them access to the all-important customer payment accounts. The market has failed to develop and accommodate these new, innovative solutions. If the market cannot secure the necessary competition to incentivise incumbents to innovate their portfolios, it will have a direct, negative impact on consumers. Consumers are protected through fair competition, as this ensures fair prices and the best possible selection of options. Regulatory intervention can therefore potentially provide the necessary room for innovation to thrive and is a reasonable solution. Regulation in favour of innovative development is a way to address market failure, and marks innovation as a goal of the PSD2.[79]

Innovation stands out when compared with the goals of competition and consumer protection, as innovation is also a particular policy goal set by the European Commission. In the press release for the implementation of the PSD2 of 12 January 2018, it is stated that the Directive will promote the development of innovative solutions for online and mobile payments.[80] Even the title of the press release highlights the European Commission's focus on innovation as a goal for the PSD2. Furthermore, the European Commission's focus on innovation is also underlined in its strategy for retail payments adopted in September 2020.[81]

In 2017, the European Commission conducted a consultation process on FinTech with the aim to create a more competitive and innovative European financial sector.[82] Respondents, ranging from incumbents to start-ups and supervisory authorities, generally agreed that innovation is a driver of financial

[79] European Commission, *Green Paper: Towards an integrated European market for card, internet and mobile payments* 3 also highlights the potentials of improving innovation in the market through an updated directive.

[80] European Commission, *Payment services: Consumers to benefit from cheaper, safer and more innovate electronic payments.*

[81] European Commission, *Communication from the Commission to the European Parliament, the Council, the European Economic and Social Committee and the Committee of the Regions on a Retail Payments Strategy for the EU* (COM(2020) 592 final) (2020).

[82] European Commission, 'Public Consultation on FinTech: a more competitive and innovative European financial sector' 2017) <https://finance.ec.europa.eu/consumer-finance-and-payments/payment-services/payment-services_en> accessed 11 October 2021.

services development. Respondents expressed the view that innovation was an enabler for better access to finance, cost-savings, increased efficiency, and competition.[83] As such, innovation is a multi-faceted goal of both the PSD2 and financial regulation in general in recent years.[84]

Innovation brings both positive and negative effects. On the positive side, it contributes to competition, perhaps in much the same way it contributes to consumer protection, by creating incentives for service providers to improve their products, prices, processes, and so on. Although these are undoubtedly positive externalities, innovation also poses new risks, such as cyber risks or risks of technological breakdowns, which could have a negative impact on consumers. A recent example is the Wirecard scandal, which severely affected consumers relying on innovative (open) banking options, as they were left for days without access to their bank accounts.[85]

By harmonising the European Union legal framework in member states to create a level playing field, the PSD2 also ensures a future with room for innovation in the provision of payment services. Innovation creates an incentive for market players to develop their service and product portfolios. And incentives are essential for maintaining an efficient market.[86] But regulatory intervention is also necessary in a continuously innovative field to avoid legal uncertainty in regard to new products or services that do not fit the scope of current regulation. By aiming towards some degree of technology neutrality, the PSD2 sets out to create a future-proof framework by implementing rules that are not entirely prejudiced against new applied technology.

The phrase 'some degree' of technology neutrality is used, as even though there is no prejudice regarding the technology applied, PSD2 article 4(3) does define payment services by reference to Annex 1, which lists specific services that are considered 'payment services' with a focus on their function. This effectively excludes any new functions that could also constitute a payment service resulting from future innovative efforts, leaving room for legal uncertainty in the future. Incentives to promote innovation are connected to competition. Fair competition promotes innovation to increase efficiency and cost savings

[83] European Commission, *Summary of contributions to the 'Public Consultation on FinTech: a more competitive and innovative European financial sector'* (2017) 4.

[84] Brener, 'Payment Service Directive II and Its Implications' 111.

[85] Ryan Browne, 'Wirecard scandal hits UK consumers as online banking apps freeze accounts' (*CNBC*, 2020) <https://www.cnbc.com/2020/06/29/wirecard-scandal-hits-users-of-uk-fintech-apps-curve-anna-and-pockit.html> accessed 8 October 2021.

[86] The relation between innovation and economic growth was also explored extensively by Joseph A Schumpeter, *The Theory of Economic Development: An Inquiry into Profits, Capital, Credit, Interest, and the Business Cycle* (Harvard University Press 1934).

for market participants in order to obtain greater market share. Ensuring legal certainty in the regulatory framework can therefore also promote innovation.

3.1.4 The interplay of goals

Recapitulating on section 3.1.3, the interdependent effect between goals and the applied measures is rather clear. The interdependency of the goals of competition, consumer protection, and innovation can be illustrated by the fact that the incentives each goal creates support the remaining goals. Competition promotes innovation in the development of payment services, and innovation promotes competition by incentivising market participants to evolve their product portfolio, their operational efficiency, cost savings, and so on. These factors also affect consumer protection positively, for example by increasing the number of options available for consumers and lowering the price of services. Consumer welfare is then improved by increasing their choices and lowering prices. Whether this has a positive effect on quality and service is another discussion.

Investigating the goals of the PSD2 and the measures applied to reach these goals, the interplay between goals and objectives become clear. Though the terms and their categorisation can be used differently in different scholarly works, this book will distinguish between the above defined goals and other objectives, such as harmonising legal frameworks across the EU and creating and securing a level playing field. Such objectives are considered to be applied as measures towards achieving the greater goals of competition, consumer protection, and innovation. Essentially, objectives are tools to contribute to the Directive-specific goals, and in the end also the meta-goals of financial regulation.

Legal certainty can be promoted through harmonised regulatory frameworks, both on the national Member State level, as well as in cross-border cases. Legal certainty promotes competition and innovation.[87] Furthermore, ensuring a level playing field on the payment services market improves competition by setting fair entry barriers regarding information, licensing, and access to accounts. As such, these measures can also be perceived as appropriate or proportional for tackling the market failure of imperfect competition that led to entry barriers for non-banks.

Looking at the incentives to promote consumer protection, the picture of the interplay of the goals changes. As discussed above, a free market does not supply sufficient incentive for market participants to improve consumer rights,

[87] Directive (EU) 2015/2366 (PSD2) recital 6.

as these costs are ultimately paid by the market participant providing the service. The promotion of the goal of consumer protection is therefore a good case when considering different regulatory strategies that competent authorities can apply to ensure greater consumer protection on the EU payment services market.

As illustrated so far, it is possible to a wide extent to create harmony between the Directive's goals, but creating this balance can also be difficult. All three goals can be at odds with each other, and conflicting interests can also arise between Directive goals and meta-goals. How these goals are balanced in the legislative process can be analysed when examining legislation. This aspect will therefore also be analysed and discussed in the following chapters.

3.2 Regulatory strategies

When pursuing the perfect regulatory framework—one that can manage and address identified market failures and non-market failures—it is appropriate to consider the different regulatory strategies that are suitable for pursuing the regulatory goals. The first thing to consider is whether to use standards or rules. This distinction, and its economic consequences, has been described well by Louis Kaplow,[88] who argues that rules are more costly to make but cheaper for the subject to use, whereas standards are cheaper to make but can be more difficult for the subject to understand and comply with. Though, Kaplow posits that the central factor influencing the desirability of rules and standards is the frequency with which a law will govern conduct.[89] Rules are necessary when the law intents to impact the behaviour, or conduct, of the subjects, while standards can prove more fertile as an ex ante measure. Given the nature of the topic treated here, it comes as no surprise that the majority of provisions in the regulatory framework, that the PSD2 constitutes, takes the shape of rules. To understand this further, it is necessary to examine the regulatory strategies further.

When looking at the regulatory framework from the perspective presented in this book, the strategies of regulation are important in order to understand the analytical elements. Sections 3.2.1–3.2.3 will therefore introduce different regulatory strategies that are relevant for financial regulation, and hence also apply to the market for payment services. The section uses the separation of

[88] Louis Kaplow, 'Rules Versus Standards: An Economic Analysis' (1992) 42 Duke Law Journal 557.
[89] Kaplow, 'Rules Versus Standards: An Economic Analysis' 621.

conduct-related rules and prudential-related rules as its basis, and supplements this with a section on supervision.

3.2.1 Conduct rules

The target of conduct rules is to mould the subject's behaviour, or conduct. They can state what the subject can, cannot, should, or must do in described situations. The use of conduct rules can be separated into client-facing and market-facing conduct. This is to be perceived from the viewpoint of the market participant subject to the regulation, but in some cases conduct rules are also applied, for example, to consumers.[90] As such, client-facing rules regulate the market participant's conduct towards their customers, consumers as well as commercial customers. Market-facing regulation focuses on the conduct of market participants towards each other or the market, for example to avoid market control or abuse.[91]

Conduct rules can also be divided into ex-ante and ex-post measures. On the ex-ante side, we have regulation related to entry, conduct, information, prudential matters, and governance. Ex-post strategies consist of regulation related to insurance and resolution.[92] The regulatory framework moves from the ex-ante rules to the ex-post rules, for example when an unauthorised transaction is completed, or when an authority decides not to grant authorisation or decides to withdraw an authorisation. These situations place the parties in a conflict situation with diverging interests. It is then the legislator's task to set out rights and obligations. Before these situations arise, ex-ante measures seek to, among other things, prevent the necessity of ex-post measures.[93]

Ex-ante rules can be divided into different sub-categories or tools. The specific classification of these tools varies depending on which author you ask. In a chapter on 'Conduct of Business Regulation', Andrew Tuch[94] argues that conduct of business rules govern the conduct of financial intermediaries toward their clients, in contrast to market stability regulation and safety and soundness regulation.[95] In his adopted approach of a division between client-facing and firm-facing rules, Tuch delimits product-related rules from conduct of business rules, but does not distinguish entry-rules from conduct-rules. The

[90] An example of this are the obligations placed upon payment service users in PSD2 art 69.

[91] Moloney, Ferran, and Payne (eds), *The Oxford Handbook of Financial Regulation* 6.

[92] Armour and others, *Principles of Financial Regulation* 73.

[93] This can be illustrated with the relationship between preventive measure against money laundering in AMLD4 which also aims to minimise the necessity of the sanctions on money laundering in criminal law.

[94] Andrew F Tuch, 'Conduct of Business Regulation' in Niamh Moloney, Eilís Ferran, and Jennifer Payne (eds), *The Oxford Handbook of Financial Regulation* (OUP 2015).

[95] Tuch, 'Conduct of Business Regulation' 538.

latter distinction is the approach taken by John Armour and others in their 2016 'Principles of Financial Regulation'.[96] Armour and others divide the regulatory strategies into ex-ante and ex-post regulation, where entry rules and conduct rules are in the first category but make up two different sub-categories, and where product rules are covered by the conduct of business section.[97] As the exact naming of this category of rules does not materially impact the analysis conducted in chapters 4–6, the distinction between conduct and prudential rules has been adopted instead. It is considered that this separation provides a sufficient classification and division of rules without overly complicating matters.[98]

As mentioned in the beginning of this subsection, conduct rules can also have the user of the financial product as the subject. But users of products can be difficult to regulate efficiently, especially considering the problems of information asymmetry and individual, biased decision making among consumers. Making the company that provides the product the subject of regulation instead can, from a regulatory and supervisory perspective, be much more manageable. This is also clearly illustrated when considering the available tools focusing on the company as the subject of regulatory obligations. These tools range widely from licensing to capital requirements, to disclosure rules, ownership restrictions, resolution procedures, etc.

When considering which strategy to apply to a given issue, it is important to also consider what market failure the strategy is supposed to address and the goal of regulation. The market failure of information asymmetry will rarely be addressed by implementing rules on board structure or ownership restrictions, whereas rules on disclosure or consumer education would appear more suitable for that specific problem. However, the strategy will not only have to be appropriate for addressing the market failure that constitutes the rationale for regulation, but also for aiding realisation of the goals of regulation. As such, there are three elements which need to be considered when deciding which measure to apply to an issue; failure, goal, and strategy.

3.2.2 Prudential rules

Where conduct rules govern the market participants' conduct, prudential rules are directed towards financial stability and have two sub-categories.

[96] Armour and others, *Principles of Financial Regulation* ch 3.

[97] Armour and others, *Principles of Financial Regulation* 73.

[98] The division is drawn from the simple classification provided by Moloney, Ferran, and Payne (eds), *The Oxford Handbook of Financial Regulation* 6 which is found to be most suitable for the analytical work carried out here.

Micro-prudential rules seek to address the stability of individual financial system participants. Essentially such rules are directed to the inside of the financial institution. Macro-prudential regulation focuses on the system as a whole, aiming to soften the periodic blows of the economic cycle.[99]

Micro-prudential regulation focuses on the health and soundness of the individual financial institution. This focus starts when the institution applies for authorisation, where demands such as capital requirements and fit-and-proper rules regarding members of the institution's board and management form essential tools. Micro-prudential rules can generally be understood as imposing obligations on the individual financial institution to ensure its safety and soundness. This ultimately serves to protect users of the financial system such as investors and consumers.[100] But by addressing the individual institution's management of capital, assets, board members, risk-management, etc., the micro-prudential level risks interfering with the systemic stability which calls for cooperation with macro-prudential regulation.

The boundaries, where macro-prudential regulation begins and micro-prudential ends, cannot always be easily delineated. The most important difference between the two is perhaps that micro-prudential regulation is concerned with the individual financial institution, i.e. specifically how healthy the institution is, whereas macro-prudential regulation is concerned with the relationship between any financial institution and the safety and soundness of the system as a whole.[101] The target for macro-prudential regulation is the causes of systemic risk, as the purpose of these rules is to ensure financial stability. The tools available to pursue this target can be divided into cyclical and structural rules, where cyclical rules relate to the overall economic cycle and include countercyclical elements, while structural rules relate to the structure of the financial market.[102] The focus of macro-prudential regulation can also be divided into more specific links between market actors, which require different tools. These links can be classified as the inter-institution channel, the payment systems channel, the information channel, and the psychological channel.[103] All four need to be addressed through macro-prudential tools to ensure systemic stability.

[99] Moloney, Ferran, and Payne (eds), *The Oxford Handbook of Financial Regulation* 6.

[100] Armour and others, *Principles of Financial Regulation* 76.

[101] Rosa Lastra, 'Systemic Risk and Macro-Prudential Supervision' in Niamh Moloney, Eilís Ferran, and Jennifer Payne (eds), *The Oxford Handbook of Financial Regulation* (OUP 2015) 316.

[102] Lastra, 'Systemic Risk and Macro-Prudential Supervision' 318.

[103] Rosa M Lastra, 'Defining forward looking, judgement-based supervision' (2013) 14 Journal of Banking Regulation 221.Moloney, Ferran, and Payne (eds), *The Oxford Handbook of Financial Regulation* 6.

The tools can have a varying impact on micro-prudential rules, for example through requirements for capital buffers to be higher in good times to prepare for bad times. Some of the main tools for macro-prudential regulation are countercyclical capital buffers, sectorial capital requirements, loan-to-value requirements, loan-to-income requirements, restrictions on funding sources, structural systemic risk buffers, large exposure restrictions, and deposit protection.[104] A recurring theme for these tools is the focus on the financial institution's behaviour or acts, and their potential impact on the stability of the market as a whole.

Specifically, for the payment services market, the regulator can adopt stricter or less stringent regulation in relation to, for example, capital requirements when applying for authorisation, depending on the stability of the market and the current needs for more or less providers and innovation. In essence, the regulator can, as we saw with the conduct rules, assess the market to observe relevant failures, consider the regulatory goals, and adjust the prudential requirements if this is deemed necessary to address one or more failures.

3.2.3 Supervision

The last category which deserves special attention here is supervision. Although not traditionally considered a regulatory strategy, it does hold significant importance in regulating financial markets. For example, in the area of financial markets, the EU has created the ESAs to ensure cooperation and harmonisation across Member States, aiming to create a single rule book for the internal market.[105]

Supervision is not regulatory intervention per se, though it is a natural course after such intervention. For regulation to be efficient, enforceability is necessary. To enforce regulation, the market participants must be supervised to monitor compliance. Under the current supervisory and regulatory architecture, supervisory institutions are to varying degrees vested with the power to formulate different (legal) acts. The best example can be seen in the ESAs, which are vested with delegated powers in Directives and Regulations to formulate draft technical and implementing standards, guidelines, decisions, and more. As such, these authorities—intended to be supervisory—have been delegated the power to draft and issue regulatory measures. These soft law

[104] A full overview of objectives, tools, and their connection to market failures is provided in Lastra, 'Systemic Risk and Macro-Prudential Supervision' 320–322.

[105] For more on the Single Rulebook see European Banking Authority, 'The Single Rulebook' (*European Banking Authority*, <https://www.eba.europa.eu/regulation-and-policy/single-rulebook> accessed 16 December 2022.

instruments are considered to have significant legal value in financial law areas where hard law is in need of specification and there is limited case law.[106]

To ensure compliance and efficiency in regulation, government delegates power to one or more supervisory authorities with the task of monitoring and enforcing current law. When analysing legislation, it is therefore not only important to note the different regulatory tools used by the legislator, but also which supervisory powers the legal framework warrants. It is through rules set up in regulation that supervisory measures are defined. At the same time, the obligations for supervisors to monitor market participants are also set out in regulation.[107]

The purpose of including supervision in the regulatory strategies when examining the EU payment services market is to highlight the importance of supervision when regulating financial markets. In chapters 4–6, supervisory authorities will be of importance when analysing the PSD2 and its ability to address market and non-market failures and accommodate innovative developments. This can be seen either in provisions granting supervisory authorities' competence to draft technical standards or issue guidelines, or in expectations about their monitoring or sanctioning of the market.

4 Evaluation

One might ask the questions 'Why do we need incentives?' and 'Why do we wish to alter people's behaviour?' From the perspective of law and economics, incentives are a way of ensuring or maintaining market efficiency, where the market maximises utility or welfare. In case of market failures, such as externalities or information asymmetry, incentives can be an effective instrument to influence the behaviour of market participants to restore market efficiency. But why is this even necessary? As Ronald Coase states in his Notes on the Problem of Social Cost,[108] producers, or here service providers, are normally not interested in social cost but only in maximising their own incomes. Although Coase was well-known to be a proponent of government intervention, social cost does constitute an externality which is important to society, and therefore this author argues that government intervention in the form of incentives can be

[106] Niamh Moloney, *The Age of ESMA: Governing EU Financial Markets* (Hart Publishing 2018) 145f.
[107] For more on macro-prudential supervision see Lastra, 'Systemic Risk and Macro-Prudential Supervision'.
[108] Ronald H Coase, *The Firm, the Market and the Law* (University of Chicago Press 1990) 158.

necessary to persuade producers or service providers to take account of social cost.

The role of incentives when drafting legislation and other legal measures is essential. When applying an economic term such as incentives to this context, an ex-ante approach is used. Here, focus is placed on the ability of different incentives to influence people's behaviour.[109] The use of the term incentives in this context is based on microeconomic analysis, with the concept of man as a rational maximiser of self-interest. This implies that people, being rational, respond to incentives in a default way where maximisation of welfare is the key motivator.[110] An exception from the benchmark of man as a rational maximiser is the consumer's biased, individual decision-making. This concept will be used throughout when considering legislative measures which are targeted particularly at or for consumers.

While economics, especially market failure theory, provides a reason for government to intervene in markets, economics is also necessary to include in considerations on public policy. When government tries to affect how people, or financial institutions, behave and make decisions, this must be done in a well-informed manner. It is necessary for government to understand how people and the market function in order to be able to create plausible change. The subjects must be motivated to conform to regulation, and the catalogue created by economic theory of how the market works and fails is essential to create viable public policy and regulation.[111] As such, economic theory justifies government intervention, but it is also a necessary component for the legislator when addressing market failures.

All these elements are considered in the evaluation, which completes the circle of Figure 3.1. This can also be referred to as legal public policy work. It is important, when doing legal public policy work, to keep it clearly separated from the legal analysis that is the foundation for proposing recommendations.[112]

Alf Ross argues[113] that there exist two kinds of legal public policy. One that is irrational and based on a sense of justice, which we should abhor, and one that is rational and based on so-called factual reasons and considerations. The

[109] Kenneth G Dau-Schmidt and Thomas S Ulen, *Law and Economics Anthology* (Anderson Publishing Co. 1998) 23.

[110] Dau-Schmidt and Ulen, *Law and Economics Anthology* 2.

[111] Mark A R Kleiman and Steven M Teles, 'Market and Non-Market Failures' in Michael Moran, Martin Rein, and Robert E Goodin (eds), *The Oxford Handbook of Public Policy* (OUP 2006) 646.

[112] Sten Schaumburg-Müller and Bjarke Viskum, 'Retspolitik og metode' in Carina Risvig Hamer and Sten Schaumburg-Müller (eds), *Juraens Verden Metoder, Retskilder og Discipliner* (DJØF Forlag 2020).

[113] Alf Ross, *Om ret og retfærdighed* (Nyt Nordisk Forlag 1953); for an English version see Alf Ross, *On Law and Justice* (OUP 2019).

latter's purpose is not to make law less flawed, but to use legal expert knowledge as a tool to make law more efficient. Ross says that the work of legal public policy can be configured into three phases. In the first phase, it is necessary to identify societal goals and settings. In the second phase, the legal scholar must identify which legal tools or measures, for example through legislation, would be appropriate to apply to achieve the aforementioned goals. In the last phase, which Ross argues is not scientific, the recommendations are formulated.

The reasoning from Ross on this not being scientific is based on his understanding of the decision-making on which recommendations to put forward as not being rational. Though one must argue that in the case of using both a legal and economical perspective, this statement is not true. Within the field of law and economics, such recommendations would be based on economic analysis of the law to select the most efficient set of recommendations. Hence, all three phases would in the case of this book be considered as scientific legal scholarship.

Chapters 4, 5, and 6 deal with specific issues in relation to the PSD2 and the financial innovation development in payment services. This serves as an ideal basis for formulating public policy recommendations. By identifying the regulatory goals and measures in the analytical section, the recommendations can be thoroughly supported by this work, combined with the economic insights from applying market and non-market failure theory to the subject matter. The application of non-market failure theory especially contributes to identifying aspects where previous intervention has failed and needs amendment. Furthermore, the rapid development of financial innovation increases the probability of further market failures appearing, which must be considered in the process of formulating policy recommendations. With clear identification of current issues in the market of payment services and deduction of regulatory goals and available measures the recommendations posed throughout are transparent in their composure and argumentation, making them ideal for application.

The evaluation sections will also discuss notions of fairness in the regulatory framework. 'Fairness' as a concept is applied as a weighing of the welfare of opposing parties and the costs placed on them through regulation.[114] In the evaluation sections, considerations given to the notion of fairness build on the goals of the PSD2 and the goals of financial regulation in general. As

[114] Henrik Lando, 'A Pragmatic View of Fairness and Social Welfare in the Analysis of Law' (2020) 20 CBS Law Research Paper Series highlights the importance of substantiating what is meant when applying these terms.

such, societal desires and welfare can play a key role in the formation of public policy agendas but can also be affected by economic drivers such as the need for growth and the efficiency of markets.

The combination of failures, goals, and analysis of regulatory intervention makes for both practically relevant and theoretical contributions to the area of EU payment services regulation, making it possible to discuss the area's ability to accommodate innovation and future regulatory developments. The evaluation sections also makes it possible to recapitulate the regulatory interventions appropriability in light of initial problems, whether these be market or non-market failures, and to illustrate if any new failures has occurred. This will also be benchmarked to the stated goals of the specific provisions examined, to clarify whether these have indeed been reached, and if not, how they could be achieved in the future.

4

THE LICENSING REGIME

1 Introduction

The market for payment services is of immense importance to society. It holds the potential to disrupt systemic stability and threaten the ability of society to function if we cannot trust that payments initiated are executed, settled, and received by the payee. If ordinary citizens cannot pay for their groceries using a payment card, how are they supposed to eat that day? Expanding from ordinary citizens to corporations and government, all participants in society need to use payment services in the ordinary functions of everyday life and the functioning of a business. Given what is at stake, it is reasonable to regulate the ability of PSPs to enter the market. This control of access is achieved in practice through the licensing regime, or rules of authorisation, in the PSD2. Similar regimes apply, for example, to credit institutions, which must be authorised in accordance with national rules implementing Directive 2013/36/EU. A licensing regime can also be seen as an entry barrier to the market, erected to uphold a desired standard which the providers must comply with. Legal entry barriers can as such be used as a regulatory tool to ensure a level playing field, while also combatting fraudulent service providers. While legal entry barriers hold great potential to create a balanced and safe market, the risks stemming from any regulatory intervention are still present.

When legislators intervene in the market to set legal entry barriers through a licensing regime, they risk setting the barriers too high or too low. They might also make the scope too narrow, excluding some providers, or too wide, covering more than is required to ensure an efficient market. This chapter will examine the licensing regime of the PSD2, to enable an evaluation of its fitness and how it accommodates innovations in the market for payment services. First, in section 2, the market and non-market failures relevant to consider in this case will be presented. The focus is on the scope of legal entry barriers, the problem with asymmetric information and moral hazard, and systemic risks. Section 3 will illustrate how the PSD2 has addressed the failures covered in the foregoing section by presenting the licensing regime. This section will also

EU Payment Services. Louise Damkjær Christensen, Oxford University Press. © Louise Damkjær Christensen 2025.
DOI: 10.1093/9780198949084.003.0004

link the goals of the Directive to the regulatory strategy applied to manage the initial failures. Finally, section 4 will evaluate the regime's fitness to address the failures and discuss whether new failures have surfaced since implementing the current regulatory framework.

2 Failures deriving from innovation

The development in financial innovation has surged since the PSD1 was drafted and adopted, leaving the payments market with new solutions. While innovation is generally considered desirable,[1] some of these innovations, the third-party PSPs, fell outside of the Directive's scope. When legislation is not able to capture technological developments, this is traditionally recognised as the non-market failure of internalisation.[2] No piece of legislation can be expected to be fully future proof, but society should expect regulators to take action when it is discovered that current regulation is insufficient. When this happens, it is not only the initial non-market failure that has to be mitigated. The non-market failure can cause one or more market failures to develop. In this case, where the PSD1 did not cover third-party providers, it gave rise to market failures of asymmetric information, resulting in moral hazard, and systemic risks, as will be explained further below.

In a free market, there is a risk of moral hazard and adverse selection existing for participants. Akerlof's 'Market for Lemons'[3] and its inherent risk of consumers (or just buyers) being exposed to fraudulent car salesmen trying to offer them a lemon for the price of a tank illustrates this. In the market for payment services, it is of great importance to avoid fraudulent service providers and moral hazard, as financial integrity and trust play a vital role in making financial services appealing to consumers.[4] There is also a risk that payment service users might use 'lemon' payment services if the market was entirely free. This could be manifested in service providers with insufficient safeguarding measures potentially jeopardising the payment service user's funds, or through unreasonable surcharges for the use of services. Both instances would impact

[1] As is also highlighted by the Commission in European Commission, *Payment services: Consumers to benefit from cheaper, safer and more innovate electronic payments* (European Commission 2018).

[2] Internalisation is thoroughly described in chapter 2.

[3] George A Akerlof, 'The Market for "Lemons": Quality Uncertainty and the Market Mechanism' (1970) 84 The Quarterly Journal of Economics 488.

[4] European Banking Authority, *EBA Financial Education Report 2019/2020* (2020) 19.

consumer trust and financial integrity negatively, which is undesirable for society.

A free market driven by the decisions of private actors, and only subject to the most necessary regulation, does not inherently entail a licensing regime. The purpose of authorisation is to ensure that all providers on the market comply with regulatory requirements. In an area such as the financial system, trust and integrity are key elements to ensuring a stable system which society can use, trust, and contribute to. Implementing a licensing regime would therefore be in accordance with the objective of creating an efficient market. Before examining the licensing regime of the PSD2, a further discussion of the potential risks and issues in the market for payment services is necessary. The following subsections will describe the non-market failure created through the narrow scope of the PSD1, and the market failures emerging from this. Subsection 2.1 will deal with the non-market failure of the legislator's inadequate regulatory framework, considering innovation, as this is the initial problem. This leads us to the two other failures, moral hazard and systemic risk. The former will be explained in subsection 2.2, highlighting the potential issues arising from moral hazard on the market for payment services. The last subsection, 2.3, will delve into the relationship between payment services and the correlated systemic risk, explaining why this is a potential market failure and its impact on society.

2.1 When legal entry barriers become a non-market failure

At the time of drafting the PSD1, the expected development in future payment service solutions was severely underestimated. For one, the Directive's scope did not include third-party PSPs which operate and provide payment services without maintaining payment accounts for their payment service users. This flaw in the legislative framework is a classic non-market failure in the category of internalities. It is uncertain whether the EU legislator, at the time of drafting and adopting the PSD1 in 2007, was aware of the potential technological development. But whatever the cause, the result was a framework that was unfit for purpose shortly after its implementation in late 2009.[5] The failure was expressed in two ways. First, the technological advance in financial services hastily outpaced the Directive, with new payment services

[5] European Commission, 'questions 1 and 2' (*Payment Services Directive: Frequently Asked Questions*, 2018) <https://ec.europa.eu/commission/presscorner/detail/en/MEMO_15_5793> accessed 7 March 2022.

being excluded from its scope.[6] The second factor relates to the acquisition and processing of information. As a centralised legislator, the acquisition of information can be flawed as the legislator's main purpose is to regulate and govern society, whereas the market's main purpose is to deliver goods and services. Information might therefore be lost between the parties when drafting legislation.[7] Furthermore, the legislator has to take care of societal goals, which will naturally conflict with the interests of the market and its providers. In summary this leaves us with the failure of a too narrow scope.

The presence of a failure is not itself sufficient reason to perform regulatory intervention on the market. The justification of a second regulatory intervention must be more extensive than the mere existence of a problem. In this situation, the limited scope of the PSD1, which left an entire segment of payment services unregulated and hence not in compliance with the PSD1 requirements, also left them outside of supervision by any competent authority. To understand how problematic this is, it is necessary to reiterate that in order for third-party providers to perform their services they must be given access to the payment service user's payment account, maintained by an account servicing PSP. This access to the consumer's online banking credentials raises a series of issues in relation to consumer protection, consumer security, liability, competition, and data protection.[8] Leaving third-party PSPs excluded from the scope of regulation countered the Directive's efforts towards improving consumer protection and competition on the market for payment services. As the non-market failure did not conform to the Directive's purposes it was necessary to revise the Directive to ensure consumer protection and fair competition.

2.2 The problem with information asymmetry and moral hazard

In any market, there exists a risk of some participants acting opportunistically, and in some cases these actions harm other market participants such as consumers. When one actor, say a provider of a payment service, acts to maximise their own profit, they do not—on a free market—consider spill-over effects. These spill-overs can be both positive and negative, but in the case of

[6] This is also supported by the Commission's own statement in question 2 of European Commission, *Payment Services Directive: Frequently Asked Questions*.

[7] This problem is also excellently described in Friedrich A von Hayek, 'The Use of Knowledge in Society' (1945) 35 The American Economic Review 519.

[8] European Commission, *Commission Staff Working Document Impact Assessment* SWD(2013) 288 final (2013) 24.

financial fraud they will be negative for the group whom the legislator aspires to protect—the consumers. When thinking about financial fraud, money laundering naturally comes to mind, but this problem is not treated specifically in the PSD2 as it belongs within the scope of the Anti-Money Laundering Directives and the forthcoming Regulation. Money laundering will therefore not be included in further discussions here. Instead, focus will be on financial fraud where payment service users are defrauded of banking credentials and money.

To defraud a payment service user, it will be necessary to possess information which the payment service user does not possess, and for the fraudster to be aware of this advantage. This situation creates the opportunity to act opportunistically and exploit the information advantage. There is thus a risk of moral hazard. Moral hazard is most directly linked to the problem of asymmetric information. When two parties possess different or unequal information their motives to negotiate, or act, will be affected. Of course, moral hazard does not only cover actual fraud, but also situations where the party acts in an ethically questionable manner without acting illegally. For consumers though, the protection of their data is of high priority, and any exploitation of it is potentially a problem for them. Asymmetric information can, for example, be caused by differences in access to information or information processing choices. This can pose a problem in general, but when the consumer perspective is added, the problem is magnified. As previously explained,[9] consumers are generally expected to perform individual, biased decision-making.[10] This is due to individual bias, or preference, and differences in ability to process available information. Biased, individual decision-making and moral hazard place consumers in a vulnerable position where they are at a higher risk of being defrauded when using payment services.

The problem touches directly on the core values of consumer welfare—price, service, quality, and choice. While a regulatory vacuum might bring more choices, and even lower prices due to the distorted competition, the quality of available services will undoubtedly be lower. This is particularly true because legal requirements, which set a minimum standard for providers to comply with, also add costs for the provider. To maximise profit, it is necessary to keep costs low and find the optimal price. This might not include complying with costly standards which are not mandatory when the average service user does not possess information about this or is unable to understand the

[9] See chapter 2.
[10] John Armour and others, *Principles of Financial Regulation* (OUP 2016) 60.

importance of such standards. Without a regulatory framework which covers all service providers, consumer welfare will be diminished. As consumer protection is both a meta-goal and a Directive-specific goal, the presence of this market failure has justified regulatory intervention to re-frame the scope of the Directive.

2.3 Payment services and systemic risk

Systemic stability, much like financial stability, is considered a public good[11] and is a meta-goal of financial regulation. Public goods are available to all, and one person's use does not affect another's. This is particularly true for systemic and financial stability. Society does not consciously use systemic stability. This happens implicitly whenever financial services are utilised. But for society to be able to enjoy this public good it must be maintained by financial institutions. As a public good does not directly affect the costs and income for a financial institution, it will most often be necessary for the regulator to provide incentives to ensure stability. Though in some cases, as here, the systemic risk does not lie within the activities of currently regulated institutions. Instead, the activities carried out beyond the scope of current legislation—the unregulated activities and entities—are the cause of systemic risk.

In contrast to neoclassical tradition, where regulatory intervention is only justified to rectify market failures which cause inefficient allocation of resources, the issue treated here is not yet a market failure. The market for payment services holds eminent value for society. For the market to fail or be inefficient would cause disruptions to systemic stability. This threat is so serious that legislators are not willing to risk it occurring.[12] They have therefore chosen to safeguard against potential market failure using preventive measures. Leaving a sub-category of PSPs, like the third-party providers, excluded from the scope of the regulatory framework, and placing more stringent requirements upon authorised entities, will have negative effects on systemic stability.[13] While serious damage might not yet have occurred by the time the

[11] Niamh Moloney, Eilís Ferran, and Jennifer Payne (eds), *The Oxford Handbook of Financial Regulation* (OUP 2015) 4f; Rosa Lastra, 'Systemic Risk and Macro-Prudential Supervision' in Niamh Moloney, Eilís Ferran, and Jennifer Payne (eds), *The Oxford Handbook of Financial Regulation* (OUP 2015) 313.

[12] As described in Rosa M Lastra, 'Defining Forward Looking, Judgement-based Supervision' (2013) 14 Journal of Banking Regulation 221, the Global Financial Crisis also accelerated the focus on macro-prudential supervision to promote systemic stability.

[13] Rui Gong and Frank Page, 'Shadow Banks and Systemic Risks' (2016) SRC Discussion Paper 33.

PSD2 was adopted, it could be argued, even from a neoclassical perspective, that intervention was reasonable to ensure systemic stability and an efficient payment services market.

3 The licensing regime

A licensing regime serves two purposes. First, it serves to avoid fraudulent behaviour in the market by setting entry requirements that limit the possibility of fraudulent providers appearing on the market. The second purpose is to establish an agreed standard that all participants must observe. This contributes to maintaining a level playing field and ensuring fair competition in the market. An agreed standard which providers are required to comply with also contributes towards the meta-goal of maintaining systemic stability. A licensing regime, when framed and shaped appropriately, can therefore contribute to fulfilling the PSD2's goals of competition and consumer protection, while also helping to maintain systemic stability. In order to be able to evaluate the Directive's licensing regime and its appropriability to serve these goals, the following subsections will analyse the regime.

The structure of the PSD2 has been used to guide the structure of this section. As with the Directive, the first subject treated is the 'full license', whereby a payment institution is authorised in accordance with the rules in the Directive's title 2, chapter 1, section 1. This includes observations related to the application process, the requirements to the financial institution's funds, and the safeguarding of customer funds. Following the full licence are the exemptions placed in articles 32 and 33 which illustrate how the Directive attempts to balance the goals of competition and consumer protection with the goal of innovation by having the option of a 'small' license. Finally, the findings of the section will be summarised, and remarks will be made on the regime's ability to accommodate financial innovation.

3.1 The full license

Although the market for payment services prior to the PSD2 suffered from incumbents' market control oppressing new entrants, a balance of who can enter the market also needs to be upheld with legal entry barriers. In this respect, PSD2 article 5 establishes general rules for applications for authorisation as a payment institution, and article 7 sets requirements for the initial capital of these authorised payment institutions, which are supplemented with article 8 regulating their 'own funds' and article 9 on how to calculate these. These rules have a clear purpose—to ensure consumer protection by setting an equal and fair level of requirements on market participants prior to them becoming authorised to provide their services. Furthermore, these rules aspire to maintain a level playing field for entrance to the market and thereby contribute to fair competition.

By setting legal barriers for entry, the legislator must find an appropriate balance between not setting the bar too high, especially for new entrants, and not setting it too low, and risking moral hazard and the many negative effects this would have. In this legislative effort, it is important to also remember the goals which the Directive aspires to achieve. The legislator must apply the right regulatory tool to the problem identified. Whether this is the case for the full license of the PSD2 will be investigated below. The structure follows the natural order of the Directive but is supplemented with adjacent provisions where appropriate.[14]

3.1.1 Applying for authorisation

The first step for an aspiring PSP is to apply for authorisation as a payment institution, as this is a requirement in order to provide payment services.[15] The rules for applying for such authorisation follow from article 5. Applications for authorisation must be submitted to the national competent authority (NCA) which has been delegated authority to grant authorisation in article 11. It should be noted that the Directive has chosen to follow the tradition of decentralised supervision and enforcement within EU financial markets law by making the NCA the competent authority in preference to the EBA. The information required to accompany an application is listed in article 5(1), litra a-q, and spans several important topics, to enable the NCA to scrutinise the application and the applicant's ability to provide payment services without creating systemic or financial instability.

The application's guiding principles can be divided into four groups—financial soundness, security, risk management, and (corporate) governance. To ensure the financial soundness of applicants, they are first required

[14] It is noted that not all provisions of the Directive are treated here as the scope of treatment has been limited to what is necessary to give an understanding of the framework and enable an evaluation in section 4 of this chapter.

[15] See the prohibition against providing payment services without authorisation in Directive (EU) 2015/2366 of the European Parliament and of the Council of 25 November 2015 on payment services in the internal market, amending Directives 2002/65/EC, 2009/110/EC and 2013/36/EU and Regulation (EU) No 1093/2010, and repealing Directive 2007/64/EC [2015] OJ L 337/35 art 37.

to provide evidence of holding the initial capital as provided for in article 7, cf. article 5(1)(c). They must also provide a business plan, which demonstrates their ability to apply appropriate and proportionate systems, resources, and procedures to operate soundly, and a budget calculation for the first three financial years, cf. article 5(1)(b). The latter can be difficult for a new business to estimate but can be compared to the requirement when a company is going public in an initial public offering (IPO) and must provide three years of financial reports. As is also the case with IPOs, if the company is too young to have concluded three financial years, reasoned financial projections must be submitted instead which can also be sufficient to comply with the requirement of article 5(1)(b).

To provide evidence of soundness, the applicant must describe their business continuity arrangements, clearly identifying critical operations, effective contingency plans, and a procedure to regularly test and review the adequacy and efficiency of these plans, cf. article 5(1)(h). The requirements listed to ensure the applicant's financial soundness are well in line with the meta-goal of financial regulation—to ensure financial and systemic stability. This is sought to be achieved by ensuring that the applicant has considered and set internal rules to ensure financial soundness. This also contributes to enhancing consumer protection by setting a standard for all PSPs to comply with which seeks to ensure financial soundness in payment institutions.

Compared to the financial soundness requirements, security covers more diverse elements. These range from article 5(1)(d) requiring a description of the measures taken to safeguard payment service users' funds in accordance with the Directive's article 10, to anti-money laundering and counter terrorist financing measures in article 5(1)(k), which demands internal control mechanisms be established to comply with the obligations laid down in Directive (EU) 2015/849 of the European Parliament and of the Council and Regulation (EU) 2015/847 of the European Parliament and of the Council. Security also covers providing a description of the procedures in place to monitor, handle, and follow up on security incidents and security related customer complaints, cf. article 5(1)(f). This latter aspect is also specifically treated in the Directive's articles 95 and 96, which place considerable requirements on the PSP to ensure safe payments.[16]

Finally, consideration is also given to the payment service user's sensitive payment data, as a description must be provided of the process to file, monitor, track, and restrict access to such data, cf. article 5(1)(g). With the last

[16] This aspect is also treated later in chapter 6.

provision, the expectation that market participants comply with the General Data Protection Regulation (GDPR) becomes evident, although the GDPR was not yet implemented at the time the PSD2 was enacted.[17] In summary, the security-related requirements all contribute directly to improving consumer protection, albeit not in a manner that most consumers will notice. Whether the consumer is aware of these protective measures bears no value. What is important is the Directive's efforts toward improving consumer welfare by imposing a certain level of quality among providers.

For the NCA to evaluate the applicant's risk management, article 5(1)(j) requires the applicant to provide a detailed risk assessment in relation to its payment services and a description of security control and mitigation measures taken to protect payment service users adequately against the risks identified. The security policy document, combined with the security documentation, is an essential part of balancing access to the market with the protection of consumers.

The last group, which consists of requirements with a high degree of (corporate) governance characteristics, is the most extensive one. Spanning eight provisions, the legislator has focussed on ensuring applicants have taken appropriate measures to put in place well-functioning organisations. The requirements range from a description of the structural organisation and intended use of agents, branches, and outsourcing including control thereof, to a mere description of the principles and definitions applied for collecting statistical data on performance, transactions, and fraud. Somewhere in between are requirements related to the identity of shareholders, their holdings, and evidence of their suitability, considering the need to ensure sound and prudent management of the payment institution. This can be compared to the fit and proper requirement in credit institutions, but for qualifying holdings in payment institutions.[18] Note, however, that the requirements for holdings in payment institutions are not nearly as demanding as those for directors and persons responsible for the management of the payment institution. Shareholders and management must be identified in the application, with evidence of their good repute and that they possess appropriate knowledge and experience to perform payment services. What this entails is left to the home Member State to determine, but the EBA can provide guidelines, opinions, or Q&As on this aspect. Overall, in applications for authorisation, the legislator has put great

[17] GDPR art 94 amends the PSPs responsibility to comply with the GDPR instead of the predecessor. Directive 95/46/EC.

[18] Within the meaning of point 36 of art 4(1) of Regulation (EU) no 575/2013 stating the limit as 10% or more to possess a qualifying holding, although less is possible if this constitutes the power to exercise a significant influence over the management of the undertaking.

weight on some of the same criteria as we see with credit institutions,[19] that is, a focus on ensuring responsible and sound management of financial institutions with the aim of supporting financial stability.

While the regulator stipulates that authorities must collect a wide array of information with an application for authorisation, as an extra safeguard article 5(1)(o) also requires the identity of statutory auditors and audit firms to be stated. For the purposes of article 5(1)(d), (e), (f), and (l), a description of the audit and organisational arrangements must also be provided. This is considered necessary to ensure that all reasonable steps are taken to protect the interests of the payment institution's users and ensure continuity and reliability in the payment system's performance, cf. article 5(1). Through external monitoring, the regulator can feel a greater sense of control over the institution, although we must keep in mind even this measure is not bullet-proof.[20]

On top of the general requirements reviewed above, applicants applying for authorisation to provide payment initiation services or registration to provide account information services will also have to hold either professional indemnity insurance or some other comparable guarantee they can meet any liability claims, cf. article 5(2) and (3). Putting this condition on third-party PSPs, who at no point hold client funds, might seem a bit odd at first. The reason for this extra requirement can be found in article 9. The PIS and AIS are not covered by the own funds provision in article 9, which functions as a safeguarding measure for client funds and could in the end protect clients in cases of failing payment institutions. Comparing the two measures, an insurance condition is proportionate for third-party PSPs compared to the more burdensome own funds scheme. The requirement is therefore actually a measure to lower the entry barrier for third-party providers to create room for more competition and innovation in the market for payment services.

The remaining paragraphs of article 5 are interesting from a legislative technical perspective. Article 5(4) delegates competence to the EBA to issue guidelines in accordance with article 16 of the EBA Regulation[21] on the criteria for

[19] Directive 2013/36/EU of the European Parliament and of the Council of 26 June 2013 on access to the activity of credit institutions and the prudential supervision of credit institutions and investment firms, amending Directive 2002/87/EC and repealing Directives 2006/48/EC and 2006/49/EC [2013] OJ L 176/338; European Banking Authority, *Guidelines on internal governance under Directive 2013/36/EU* (2017); European Banking Authority and European Securities and Markets Authority, *Joint ESMA and EBA Guidelines on the assessment of the suitability of members of the management body and key function holders* (2021).

[20] As we have seen recently with the Wirecard scandal and previously with cases such as ENRON and Danske Bank in Estonia.

[21] Regulation (EU) No 1093/2010 of the European Parliament and of the Council of 24 November 2010 establishing a European Supervisory Authority (European Banking Authority), amending Decision No 716/2009/EC and repealing Commission Decision 2009/78/EC [2010] OJ L 331/12.

stipulating the minimum monetary amount of the professional indemnity insurance or comparable guarantee referred to in paragraphs 2 and 3. These guidelines are to be used by NCAs when deciding on granting authorisation to PIS and AIS applicants. The paragraph sets out what the guidelines must take into account. The paragraph focuses on the risk profile of the specific undertaking, including whether it provides other payment services or is engaged in other business, and it sets out how to measure the size of the applicant's activity. As the purpose of the professional indemnity insurance is to protect the payment service user, as well as the stability of the financial system, which is naturally connected to service users, it is natural to focus on the business' risk profile. This is also in line with the Directive's goal of consumer protection, as it is expected that many payment system transactions will be within the retail payments market.[22] The technical aspect of this paragraph is also interesting. Since these guidelines are to be issued in accordance with article 16 of the EBA Regulation, and are addressed to NCAs, the NCAs are obligated to make every effort to comply with them. This raises the question of whether provisions such as this one transform what is known as a soft law instrument into 'hard' law? The same question is relevant when looking at article 5(5), where the EBA is to issue guidelines in accordance with article 16 of the EBA Regulation concerning the information to be provided to NCAs when applying for authorisation. The provision goes a step further with article 5(6) which delegates the competence to the EBA to draft regulatory technical standards based on the experience acquired in paragraph 5, which the Commission has delegated power to adopt without consulting the European Parliament and the Council as the Treaty otherwise prescribes for EU legislation. As such it could be said that the transfer from being a soft law instrument to becoming hard law is only under the Commission's scrutiny.

3.1.1.1 Soft law and the ECJ

An attempt has been made to test before the ECJ whether such a change of character for soft law instruments is indeed plausible. In the *FBF* case[23] the ECJ decided on the legally binding effect of guidelines issued by the EBA. The court posed, as a prerequisite to this question, that in order to determine whether an act produces binding legal effects, it is necessary, in accordance with the settled

[22] European Commission, *Communication from the Commission to the European Parliament, the Council, the European Economic and Social Committee and the Committee of the Regions on a Retail Payments Strategy for the EU* (COM(2020) 592 final) (2020).

[23] Case C-911/19 *Fédération bancaire francaise (FBF) v Autorité de contrôle prudentiel et de résolution (ACPR)* [2021] EU:C:2021:599.

case law of the Court, to examine the substance of the act and assess its effects on the basis of objective criteria, such as the content of the act, taking into account, as appropriate, the context in which it was adopted and the powers of the EU institution, body, office, or agency which adopted it.[24]

The Court went on to highlight that guidelines issued by the EBA are subject to the same rules of law as recommendations issued by the EBA, which are not binding upon those to whom they are addressed, and therefore, in principle, have no binding force.[25] This is also supported by the second paragraph of the contested guidelines, which states that these guidelines are merely the EBA's view of appropriate supervisory practices within the European System of Financial Supervision or of how Union law should be applied in a particular area.[26]

The ECJ then commented on the NCA's obligation under article 16(3) of the EBA Regulation to comply or explain, and noted that this does not trigger an obligation to comply, but merely to explain in detail if the NCA decides not to comply with the guidelines.[27] On this basis, the Court stated that the guidelines issued by the EBA cannot be regarded as producing binding legal effects vis-á-vis the competent authorities, which is also supported by analogous judgment in the *Koninklijke* case.[28]

Finally, the Court commented on the EBA's various competences. Some relate to issuing recommendations and guidelines while others relate to drawing up technical standards to be adopted by means of regulations or decisions in accordance with article 15(4) of the EBA Regulation.[29] The Court therefore found it apparent that, by authorising the EBA to issue guidelines and recommendations, the EU legislature intended to confer on that authority a power to exhort and to persuade, which is distinct from the power to adopt acts which have binding force.[30] Even though the Court found that due to the absence of legal binding effect an annulment case is ruled out, the Court found itself competent to give a preliminary ruling on the validity of the guidelines.[31] The Court found that the guidelines were valid. Unfortunately, the Court did not consider whether the adoption of the guidelines by the NCA caused legally

[24] Case C-911/19 *FBF* para 38.
[25] Case C-911/19 *FBF* para 42.
[26] Case C-911/19 *FBF* para 39.
[27] Case C-911/19 *FBF* para 44.
[28] Case C-911/19 *FBF* para 45. *Koninklijke KPN and Others* [2016], C-28/15 paras 34 and 35.
[29] Case C-911/19 *FBF* para 47.
[30] Case C-911/19 *FBF* para 48; and by analogy the judgment of 20 February 2018, in C-16/16 P *Belgium v Commission*, para 26.
[31] Case C-911/19 *FBF* paras 54–57.

binding effects. The answer to this question could have intrinsic value for future treatment of soft law instruments issued by EU agencies.

While the Court decided not to comment on the question of binding effects when the NCA adopts the guidelines, Advocate General (AG) Bobek did touch upon this question in his Opinion. He stated that when the NCA makes the decision whether to opt in or to opt out of guidelines, their initially non-binding nature becomes very much binding, as the 'nominal addressee' (the NCA) becomes an effective enforcer. This leaves truly little, if any, choice with the financial institutions, the real addressees of the guidelines, on whether to comply with them.[32] The AG goes on to critique the Court for not looking beyond the EU level in previous case law. This would, according to the AG, lead to the finding that the EU soft law instrument, when adopted by the NCA at Member State level, effectively becomes hard law.[33] Here, the AG also referred to the *Belgium v Commission* case,[34] stating that the Court chooses to focus on the act and its author, detached from the real life of the act and its addressees.

One can only applaud the AG's efforts in calling for reality in the Court's judgments, as they would perhaps seem to weigh formalities over substance, something the Court is not otherwise known for.[35] However, it must also be noted that the guidelines contested in the case have been issued in accordance with the delegating act. As the Court also reiterates, the EU legislator has chosen to confer on the EBA the power to exhort and to persuade, which the issued guidelines result from. To question the validity of the guidelines could therefore also be interpreted as questioning this conferral of power by the EU legislator. Since no Member State NCA is forced to adopt the guidelines at the national level, but does so voluntarily, the ECJ is right in not considering whether these soft law instruments possess binding force.[36]

3.1.1.2 The Procedure in Practice—A case from the Danish FSA

In a case before the Danish Competition and Consumer Authority in a matter related to PSD2 article 36, the Danish Financial Services Authority (Danish

[32] Case C-911/19 *Fédération bancaire francaise (FBF) v Autorité de contrôle prudentiel et de résolution (ACPR)* [2021] Opinion of AG Bobek EU:C:2021:294 para 48.

[33] Opinion of AG Bobek in Case C-911/19 *FBF* paras 52–55.

[34] Case C-16/16 P *Kingdom of Belgium v European Commission* [2018] EU:C:2018:79.

[35] Case C-370/12 *Thomas Pringle v Government of Ireland* [2012] EU:C:2012:756 paras 53 and 55; Case C-62/14 *Peter Gauweiler and others v Deutscher Bundestag* [2015] EU:C:2015:400 para 46.

[36] The position of the Court was also reinforced with Case C-822/21 *Latvia v Sweden (Systèmes de garantie des dépôts)* [2024] EU:C:2024:373 ignoring the credentials of the *FBF* case while the EBA in *Spain v Belgium* [2023] Decision of the European Banking Authority EBA/DC/499 relied on the Court's admission in the *FBF* case to reinforce the value of the comply or explain principle embedded in its founding regulation.

FSA) was consulted, among other matters, on the authorisation process for payment institutions.[37] The payment institution being denied access to payment accounts at a credit institution claimed that by authorisation, the competent authority had approved of their business model, something the credit institution in question did not. In the consultancy process, the Danish FSA replied to the claim by rebutting the assertion that approval was automatic due to authorisation having been granted. The Danish FSA continued by noting that the authorisation process was simply to attest and ensure that all legal requirements were adhered to by the applicant before authorisation was to be granted. As such, the authorisation process does not automatically include an approval of the applicant's business model.

Recapitulating PSD2 article 11(4), this statement causes concern considering the goals of the Directive. The provision states: *The competent authorities shall grant an authorisation only if, taking into account the need to ensure the sound and prudent management of a payment institution, the payment institution has robust governance arrangements for its payment services business, which include a clear organisational structure with well-defined, transparent and consistent lines of responsibility, effective procedures to identify, manage, monitor and report the risks to which it is or might be exposed, and adequate internal control mechanisms, including sound administrative and accounting procedures; those arrangements, procedures, and mechanisms shall be comprehensive and proportionate to the nature, scale, and complexity of the payment services provided by the payment institution.* The provision clearly sets out an obligation for the competent authority to evaluate whether the applicant can ensure sound and prudent management of a payment institution. This entails more attention to the authorisation process than the statement in the aforementioned case would suggest. This is problematic, as the authorisation process is directly linked to the quality parameter of consumer welfare. To ensure at least an agreed standard among PSPs—an agreed lowest quality—it is important that NCAs uphold the responsibilities laid on them in article 11 in practice.

3.1.1.3 Summarising

Overall, article 5 draws up comprehensive rules as to how an applicant wishing to provide payment services should apply for authorisation at Member State

[37] See CDP-18/19832 *Afgørelse vedrørende Betalingslovens § 63, stk. 1 om adgang til betalingskonti, der føres i kreditinstitutter—Ringkjøbing Landbobank A/S* [2020] Konkurrence-og Forbrugerstyrelsen (Danish Competition and Consumer Authority).

level. The article solely focuses on the market participant wanting to provide payment services and, as such, functions as an access restriction. With the PIS and AIS specific regulations in paragraphs 2 and 3, and the information requirements when applying for authorisation, the legislator sets the entry barrier at a reasonable level to balance the goal of competition (with an improved level of innovation) and the goal of consumer protection.

3.1.2 The payment institution's financial soundness

To obtain authorisation as a payment institution, the applicant must satisfy the capital requirements set out in PSD2 article 7 at the time of application. The capital requirements are differentiated depending on the payment services which the payment institution provides. If a payment institution only provides money remittances, the requirement is not to be less than EUR 20,000.[38] If the payment institution only provides the payment initiation service, the capital limit is to be no less than EUR 50,000.[39] For payment institutions that provide not only money remittances or payment initiation services, but also at least one of the services listed in the PSD2's Annex 1, number 1–5, the minimum required initial capital is EUR 125,000.[40] The regulator has chosen here to deviate from the formal capital requirements set for limited companies in national company law.[41] This differentiation in thresholds reflects the increased risks associated with the provided services and their importance to financial stability. The increasing capital requirement between the different types of payment services also mirrors increasing risks, particularly for the users of the payment services, and also reflects the kind of contact with user funds each type of payment service necessitates. For example, the initial capital requirement for payment institutions that only provide the payment initiation service is lower than for payment institutions that execute payment transactions, as the PIS is not, at any point, allowed to hold the customers' funds.[42] The PIS only initiates a transaction, and hence there is little risk of the loss of customer funds in case of the PSP's insolvency.

An interesting observation on article 7 is that it does not cover initial capital requirements for account information service providers.[43] As defined in

[38] Directive (EU) 2015/2366 (PSD2) art 7(1)(a).
[39] Directive (EU) 2015/2366 (PSD2) art 7(1)(b).
[40] Directive (EU) 2015/2366 (PSD2) art 7(1)(c).
[41] See for example the Danish Companies Act (Selskabsloven) § 4 or the German Companies Act (Aktiengesetz) s 7.
[42] Directive (EU) 2015/2366 (PSD2) art 66(3)(a).
[43] It should also be noted that AISPs are generally referred to apply for authorisation through the Directive's art 33, as will be analysed further below in section 3.3.

chapter 1, the AIS is an online service providing consolidated information on payment accounts held by the payment service user with one or more account servicing PSPs. The AIS only accesses and uses information to provide its services, and therefore never holds or processes the user's funds in any way. It would therefore have no direct monetary impact on the user if the AIS became insolvent. This explains why no special threshold for initial capital has been set for the AIS, leaving this matter entirely to the Member States' national company law.[44] Leaving this to the discretion of the Member States could contribute to innovation on the national level, as the PSD2 capital requirements will often be higher than those for companies under national law. The PSD2 sets higher capital requirements to ensure better liquidity and financial stability in select sectors which impact society more significantly than others.[45]

By creating different classes of capital requirements, the legislator manages to address the goal of increasing innovation in payment services. Having a lower initial capital requirement to obtain authorisation as a third-party provider enables more service providers to comply with the requirements for a full license, as they will have to raise less funds prior to authorisation. This regulatory choice therefore effectively allows more innovative providers to enter the market by using a differentiated, subjective initial capital provision. Linking the composition of initial capital to provisions in the Capital Requirements Regulation,[46] seeks to achieve continuity and harmonisation across financial institutions. Like the capital requirements for other financial institutions, those for payment institutions are justified by the institutions' importance to society.[47] It is therefore important to create a balance between making room for innovation and ensuring the stability of payment institutions. Creating such a balance does not wholly rely on the initial funds—provisions on the payment institution's own funds and safeguarding initiatives are also necessary to consider, both of which will be examined below.[48]

[44] I refer to national company law as the PSD2 does require payment institutions and payment service providers to be a legal person, see art 11(1).

[45] Ciro G Corvese, 'Title 2 "Payment Service Providers", chapter 1 "Payment Institutions", section 1 "General Rules" (art. 5–18), section 2 "Other Requirements" (art. 19–21)' in Gabriella Gimigliano and Marta Bozina Beroš (eds), *The Payment Services Directive—A Commentary* (Edward Elgar Publishing 2021) 45f.

[46] Regulation (EU) No 575/2013 of the European Parliament and of the Council of 26 June 2013 on prudential requirements for credit institutions and investment firms and amending Regulation (EU) No 648/2012 [2013] OJ L 176/1.

[47] Corvese, 'Title 2 "Payment Service Providers", chapter 1 "Payment Institutions", section 1 "General Rules" (art. 5–18), section 2 "Other Requirements" (art. 19–21)' 45.

[48] Douglas Diamond and Philip Dybvig, 'Bank Runs, Deposit Insurance, and Liquidity' (1983) 91 Journal of Political Economy 401 makes a well-known argument for considering different factors to avoid bank runs, although this book concerns itself with payment institutions, similar considerings are useful.

While the provision on initial funds merely covers the Directive's requirement of a payment institution at the time of application for authorisation, article 8 covers the demands set for the payment institution's own funds at any given time. The provision builds upon the limits set out in article 7, which states that the payment institution's own funds must not fall below these limits, or the amount of own funds as calculated in accordance with the Directive's article 9. The highest of the two amounts is the one the payment institution must comply with. Where the composition of initial capital follows the rules set out in the Capital Requirements Regulation,[49] the calculation in PSD2 article 9 of own funds takes a different approach.

PSD2 article 9 presents three different methods for calculating a payment institution's own funds. They all share the common feature that the institution's primary activity—providing payment services—is in focus. The first method, method A, states that the payment institution's own funds shall amount to at least 10% of its fixed overheads in the preceding year. This method is easy to apply but entails a risk of the payment institution holding too much or too little in funds if the payment institution is decreasing or increasing its activities.

The second method, method B, is a little more complicated. According to method B, the payment institution's own funds must amount to at least a specific percentage of payment volume (this percentage decreases as payment volume increases), multiplied by a scaling factor of 0.5 or 1, depending on whether the institution provides only money remittances, or the remaining services listed in points 1–5 of Annex 1, respectively. While method A does not account for actual activity, method B is based on the payment institution's actual payment service activity.

The last method, method C, is based on the sum of the payment institution's interest income, interest expenses, commissions and fees received, and other operating income, but expenses such as outsourcing services can also be included in the calculation. The sum represents an indicator which is then multiplied by a factor, which decreases as the indicator increases. This is multiplied by the same scaling factor as used in method B (0.5 for money remittances and 1 for the remaining services in points 1–5 of Annex 1). Method C thus presents yet another option, which can be appropriate for payment institutions whose primary activity is not the execution of payments, but who perhaps hold deposits or provide credit instead.

[49] PSD2 art 7 specifically refers to art 26(1)(a) to (e) of Regulation (EU) No 575/2013 (CRR) for the composition of items to fulfil the initial capital requirement.

Article 9(3) leaves discretion to NCAs to increase or decrease the amount calculated by up to 20% based on an evaluation of the risk-management processes, risk loss database, and internal control mechanisms of the payment institution. This discretion for Member States leaves the NCA with a valuable tool to level the playing field where calculations would otherwise force some payment institutions to hold too much in own funds, compared to what is efficient, and in other cases to require them to hold more if risks are deemed to be higher than average or if internal control mechanisms make this necessary. This can also be a relevant tool to apply for securing systemic stability, as, for example, decreasing markets could call for more stringent requirements to bolster the payment institutions against future stress.[50]

The thresholds set in article 9 are material, rather than formal like the capital requirements in national company law and the diverging requirements in article 7. Setting a material capital requirement makes it possible to take the individual payment institution's circumstances into consideration. This can cause the requirement to be higher or lower depending on how well the payment institution is doing, and how the institution's business model is performing. The purpose of applying material capital requirements to financial institutions is to increase the institution's ability to absorb losses, making it more robust or sound. This serves to protect the financial system, and hence to protect users of the system as well. The rules on own funds therefore contribute towards the meta-goal of financial stability and have the derived effect of contributing towards improving consumer protection.

As a further precaution, in the case of groups of financial institutions, where one or more are payment institutions, article 8(2) instructs Member States to take the necessary measures to prevent multiple use of elements eligible for own funds. This applies if the payment institution belongs to the same group as another payment institution, credit institution, investment firm, asset management company or insurance undertaking, or if the payment institution has a hybrid character, carrying out activities other than providing payment services. It is common sense that an element to ensure financial stability and the soundness of the institution cannot be double counted towards reaching the threshold in more than one financial institution if it is to achieve its purpose.

Where the second paragraph of article 8 narrows the rules on calculating own funds, the third and last paragraph offers a deviation from the rules in article 9. This exemption is applicable only if the conditions laid down in article 7

[50] Rafael Repullo and Javier Suarez, 'The Procyclical Effects of Bank Capital Regulation' (2013) 26 The Review of Financial Studies 452.

of the Capital Requirements Regulation[51] are met, and if the payment institution is included in the consolidated supervision of the parent credit institution pursuant to Directive 2013/36/EU. If these conditions are met, the payment institution is considered to be financially sound and to hold enough own funds in the event of financial turmoil, providing justification for the exemption.

The provisions on the payment institution's funds serve an important purpose in setting efficient legal entry barriers. The rules contribute to maintaining financial stability and aim to ensure each payment institution is financially sound. Ensuring financial stability is a meta-goal of financial regulation and is of immense importance for society. With the increase in financial innovation, and with a regulatory desire to improve conditions for innovative providers of payment services, the rules on initial capital and own funds also serve to create a balance between the regulatory goals of financial stability and innovation. By exempting PISPs and AISPs from the stricter requirements set out in article 9, it can be argued that the Directive attempts to create such a balance. Since PSPs that only provide these two services never touch client funds, there is no significant risk of loss of funds for payment service users. This creates a balance between the meta-goal of financial stability, the Directive's goal of innovation, and the goal of consumer protection, including the protection of payment service users in general.

3.1.3 Safeguarding funds

Regulators are concerned about the risk of payment institutions' insolvency, fraudulent service providers, and the protection of payment service user's funds. One measure to address these concerns is the safeguarding requirement in article 10. The provision sets requirements on safeguarding client funds for payment institutions that provide the payment services referred to in points 1–6 of Annex 1. These requirements are applicable when funds have been received from the payment service user or through another PSP for the execution of payment transactions.

The first paragraph of article 10 lists two options to safeguard the received funds for payment institutions to choose between. The first option states that the funds shall not be commingled at any time with the funds of any natural or legal person other than payment service users. This means one account is sufficient for handling all the payment institutions' client funds. However, if the funds are not to be transacted no later than the following business day, the payment institution must either deposit them in a separate account in a credit

[51] Regulation (EU) No 575/2013 (CRR).

institution or invest them in secure, liquid low-risk assets, where they must be insulated in accordance with national law to protect the payment service user's funds against the claims of the payment institution's other creditors.

The second option requires the payment institution to cover all funds by an insurance policy or other comparable guarantee from an insurance company or credit institution. The insurance provider must not belong to the same group as the payment institution itself. Since the account balance will naturally vary, the insured amount is to be set as the amount that would have been segregated in the absence of an insurance policy or other comparable guarantee, which would have been payable in the event that the payment institution becomes unable to meet its financial obligations. Whether applying the first or second option, the primary objective is to secure the payment user's funds, particularly in the event of the payment institution's insolvency.

The importance of this article can be illustrated with the *Yourpay* case.[52] Yourpay was a Danish payment institution, licensed according to the rules laid out by the PSD2 and implemented in national Danish legislation[53] by the Danish FSA. It provided payment services listed in Annex 1, points 1–5, and was hence obligated to safeguard client funds according to article 10. The funds on the transaction account were mixed with funds on the company's operating account. As a result, some clients are still missing their funds.[54] The trustee in bankruptcy is investigating whether the requirements set out by article 10 were indeed fulfilled.[55] It is crucial for the payment service users that these requirements were fulfilled, as their funds will not have priority in the insolvency proceedings otherwise, and they will be left to seek remuneration through an indemnity suit against management of the company under national law. The value of article 10's content, and the supervision of its implementation and enforcement in action are clearly significant for payment service users.

3.1.4 Summarising the full license

Looking at the full picture of the authorisation rules for the full license, the Directive applies a range of different regulation strategies in order to pursue

[52] Malte Oxvig and Sofie Højlund, 'Direktør kaster nyt lys over betalingskonkurs: Kunders penge var formentlig ikke godt nok beskyttet' (*JP/Politikens Hus A/S*, 2022)<https://finanswatch.dk/Finansnyt/Fintech/article13576760.ece> accessed 6 January 2022.

[53] LBKG 2021-12-07 nr 2710 Betalingsloven (Danish Payments Act) [2016].

[54] Oxvig and Højlund, 'Direktør kaster nyt lys over betalingskonkurs: Kunders penge var formentlig ikke godt nok beskyttet'.

[55] Malte Oxvig and Sofie Højlund, 'Kurator undersøger om regler for betalingsinstitutter er overholdt i konkursramt selskab' (*JP/Politikens Hus A/S*, 2022)<https://finanswatch.dk/article13575248.ece?utm_campaign = FinansWatch%20Morgen&utm_content = 2022-01-14&utm_medium = email&utm_source = finanswatch> accessed 14 January 2022.

different goals. The primary goal of a licensing regime is to create fair, legal entry barriers. The barrier must be low enough to ensure competition and room for new innovative service providers, yet high enough to discourage potential fraudulent service providers. The legal entry barriers also serve to contribute to systemic stability by creating a licensing regime covering all PSPs. The rules for obtaining authorisation are of a prudential character, designing the infrastructure of payment institutions in a manner which is expected to ensure sound and responsible institutions. This is achieved through the provisions on initial capital, own funds, and the calculation of own funds, which all serve to ensure the financial soundness and sufficient buffering of payment institutions.

When an NCA grants authorisation to a payment institution, this constitutes a stamp of approval for the payment service user as the licensing regime provides a mark of trust for users. As payment service users rarely possess full information, it is important they can trust the authorisation process, and the associated standard of quality, in order to make payment related decisions. This highlights the importance of the role of supervisory authorities, who after granting authorisation have to supervise entities and enforce current regulation.

Having a harmonised framework for licensing in the EU eases the cooperation between NCAs in different Member States, who must trust their counterparties when a payment institution authorised in one Member State seeks to use the passport to provide services in another Member State. This right is granted to all authorised payment institutions according to article 11(9) and seeks to improve competition across the European Union. The passport can be considered the final detail in the licensing regime, which seeks to effectively harmonise the licensing regime across all Member States, to fulfil the Directive's goals of competition and improved conditions for innovative providers. For some PSPs, applying for the full license at an early stage of their business life cycle might be too high a barrier to overcome. For these providers, the PSD2 offers an alternative, which will be examined further in the following section 3.2.

3.2 The 'small' license

To allow smaller PSPs to deliver their services without conforming to the requirements set out for the full license, article 32 offers an exemption.[56] The

[56] In any case it is not possible to be exempted from arts 14, 15, 22, 24, 25, and 26 as these provisions aim to secure registers of providers, the designation of competent authorities, professional secrecy, the right to apply to courts and provisions on the exchange of information among relevant authorities.

exemption is only applicable to PSPs that provide the services listed in points 1–6 of Annex 1. To be exempted, two cumulative conditions must be fulfilled. The first condition concerns the provider's monthly average value of payment transactions executed during the preceding 12 months, which must not exceed EUR 3 million, although Member States have the option to set a lower limit.[57] The other condition concerns the natural persons responsible for the management or operation of the business, who must not have been convicted of offences relating to money laundering, terrorist financing, or other financial crimes. If the PSP fulfils these conditions (or if a provider has not yet been in operation for 12 months, and their business plan shows they will not exceed the limit on transactions), the Member State or their NCA can exempt the provider from all or parts of the procedure and conditions set out in sections 1, 2, and 3 of Title 2 of the PSD2. Although such PSPs are exempted from parts of the authorisation procedure of the PSD2, they are not exempted from the anti-money laundering requirements of Directive (EU) 2015/849 or of national anti-money laundering legislation.[58]

The exemption in article 32(1) has some strings attached. In exchange for the considerably lower legal entry barrier, the PSP will be required to have its head office in the Member State in which it carries out its business,[59] and even though they are to be treated as payment institutions, the passporting rules of article 11(9) and articles 28–30 do not apply to them, limiting their business to the Member State in which they are registered.[60] Furthermore, Member States can choose to limit the allowed activities listed in article 18 for these exempted providers.[61]

To help new entrants to the market, article 32 addresses one of the first issues they will face—the demanding process of acquiring authorisation. The provision lowers the legal entry barrier to ensure earlier and easier access to the payment services market for new, low value providers. The goals of fair competition and increased innovation are clearly balanced throughout the subsequent paragraphs of the provision. By gaining less strict authorisation requirements in the home Member State, cross-border provision is waived. This

[57] This discretion for Member States to differentiate the limit might seem disharmonious but one also needs to remember the very varying population sizes and economies across the EU and hence the expected number of payment service users and transactions.

[58] Directive (EU) 2015/2366 (PSD2) art. 32(6).

[59] Directive (EU) 2015/2366 (PSD2) art. 32(2).

[60] Directive (EU) 2015/2366 (PSD2) art. 32(3).

[61] Directive (EU) 2015/2366 (PSD2) art. 32(4).

serves as a balancing measure for competitors who have to comply with the full prudential authorisation package, and to protect consumers. The provision thus manages to address both the non-market failure of high legal entry barriers and the market failure of market control which makes it difficult for new and smaller actors to enter the market. In essence, the provision sets out fair entry barriers to the market, at the cost of the option to provide payment services outside the home Member State.

A central goal of the exemption in article 32 is to improve conditions for innovative PSPs. The exemption helps them enter the market at an earlier stage than would otherwise have been possible, but this also raises the question of whether such provisions render new initiatives such as regulatory sandboxes unnecessary? Regulatory sandboxes rose rapidly in popularity across the EU after the UK Financial Conduct Authority launched the first version in 2016.[62] A regulatory sandbox allows businesses to test new innovations in the market with real consumers, but with a restricted authorisation, individual guidance, and waivers or modifications to current rules that otherwise apply. This gives new, innovative players an opportunity to develop their product and raise funding before applying for full authorisation. But with the exemption in article 32, it can be argued that PSPs already have this opportunity without having to apply for admission to a regulatory sandbox. While these two innovation-driven initiatives appear to oppose each other, it could also be argued that the exemption rule in article 32 leaves more room for other non-payment related FinTech initiatives in sandboxes.

3.3 The account information service license

For PSPs that only provide the account information service, there is a different regime specifically designed for AISPs which also allows them to provide services on a cross-border basis.[63] The Directive's article 33 exempts AISPs from some of the requirements in the application to obtain authorisation. The provision's first paragraph reads:

> Natural or legal persons providing only the payment service as referred to in point (8) of Annex I shall be exempt from the application of the procedure and

[62] Financial Conduct Authority, 'Regulatory Sandbox' (2022) <https://www.fca.org.uk/firms/innovation/regulatory-sandbox> accessed 27 October 2022.

[63] This is also supported by Directive (EU) 2015/2366 (PSD2) recital 48.

> conditions set out in Sections 1 and 2, with the exception of points (a), (b), (e) to (h), (j), (l), (n), (p) and (q) of Article 5(1), Article 5(3) and Articles 14 and 15. Section 3 shall apply, with the exception of Article 23(3).

The provision clearly states which requirements must be fulfilled for an AISP to obtain authorisation in a Member State. The requirements in article 5(3) are naturally carried over as they specifically target AISPs. The remaining provisions which an application must document relate to the programme of operations, the business plan, governance arrangements and internal control mechanisms, security arrangements, processes for access to sensitive payment data, business continuity arrangements, a security policy document, the structural organisation of the business, identification of directors and management, the legal status and articles of association for the company, and the address of its head office. This information can be considered to cover the most necessary information and requirements to ensure a minimum standard across all PSPs. Even though the AISPs can obtain an authorisation to provide their services at a lower cost than those service providers that have to comply with the full license requirements, this does not impact competition on the market unfairly in terms of range of services provided. AISPs only access and process payment data upon request from the payment service user, this means that they never access, hold, or in any way touch client funds. It is therefore impossible for them to initiate an unauthorised payment or put client funds at risk in case of insolvency etc.

The exemption in article 33 is important to the Directive's aim of improving innovation in payment services, as the AIS is an example of FinTech solutions in action. Since the exemption only covers AISPs that only provide the AIS, it does not impede the goal of competition significantly. The exemption does make it easier for new entrants that only provide this service to enter the market, but their competitors will either be at the same stage or be established market participants providing other financial services. The latter group, in particular, is not expected to be affected significantly by new, exempted entrants due to their established position and market share. The goals of innovation and competition are therefore balanced in this case. The protection of consumers[64] is also expected to be sufficient, as the requirements that still apply maintain a standard which guarantees consumer welfare on the quality

[64] Directive (EU) 2015/2366 (PSD2) recital 28 also notes that covering AIS under the PSD2 provides adequate protection of consumers and legal certainty about the status of AISPs.

parameter, while the choice parameter is improved by allowing more players to enter the market.

Another important thing to notice is the article's second paragraph, it reads:

> The persons referred to in paragraph 1 of this Article shall be treated as payment institutions, save that Titles III and IV shall not apply to them, with the exception of Articles 41, 45 and 52 where applicable, and of Articles 67, 69 and 95 to 98.

The provision states which rules of the Directive apply to the exempted AISPs, while also making it unmistakable that AISPs are payment institutions, despite not interacting at any point with payment transactions. Articles 45 and 52 primarily deal with the information and conditions payment service users must be provided with prior to using the service, while article 41 places the burden of proof for the information requirements upon the PSP. Article 67 constitutes the rules on access to and use of payment account information for AISPs, making it essential for these providers—even under the very limited license—to be covered by this provision. The obligations placed upon payment service users in article 69 in relation to payment instruments and personalised security credentials are also significant for AISPs, to ensure that their users are legally obliged to treat their security credentials with sufficient care. The remaining provisions, articles 95 to 98, relate to operational and security risks and authentication. Even though the AIS does not entail a transfer of funds, it does give the provider access to the user's financial data. This calls for the same standards for risk management, incident reporting, and authentication requirements as the PSPs under the full license.

Exempting AISPs from large parts of the Directive creates a balance between making room for innovative providers, taking sufficient care of payment service users, and maintaining a level playing field. The AIS does not pose the traditional payment service threat of unauthorised or wrongful transactions. It would therefore not be proportionate to enforce the parts of the PSD2 which aim to ensure financially sound PSPs and protect payment service users.[65] Instead, the AIS accesses payment account information, processes it according to its described service functionality, and delivers personal, financial

[65] As for what goes for own funds requirements also see Directive (EU) 2015/2366 (PSD2) recital 35.

information to payment service users. Where these users are consumers, this also contributes toward improving financial literacy and inclusion among consumers. But one question which does not seem to be tackled in the exemption package is the AISP's definition of its service, and the access and use of data this can entail.

3.4 Summary of the licensing regime

The PSD1 established the single license regime for payment services, but unfortunately the scope of this regime was too narrow to cover new, innovative PSPs. The PSD2 makes up for this by expanding the scope to cover third-party PSPs, such as the AISP and PISP. This expansion addresses the problem of systemic risks created due to some PSPs being outside any regulatory framework, and creates legal certainty for service providers and service users alike.

Given that the PSD1 also contained an almost identical exemption to the one in PSD2 art. 32, the only truly novel addition is the special account information service license in article 33. The special exemption for AISPs is an example of the regulatory framework accommodating innovation, as it constitutes a specific evaluation of the service which is then instructive for the content of registration requirements. The provision takes into account the characteristics of the AIS and creates a proportional framework for the providers, to allow for more competition in the market.

The licensing regime is a measure in the legal toolbox which has a primarily prudential character. It strives to design a regulatory framework which supports the meta-goals of financial regulation, while also considering the Directive-specific goals. The requirements on initial capital and own funds are good examples of prudential rules, with the purpose of ensuring financial soundness among payment institutions. This contributes to the meta-goal of financial stability, as well as the goal of consumer protection. Covering all PSPs under the same regulatory framework also enhances fair competition and ensures a level playing field when all have to comply with the same ruleset. Although the licensing regime cannot cover all issues, it does attend to all the goals of the Directive, without severely demoting the value of any of the goals. How the applied measures manage the initial failures described in section 2, and whether new challenges have arisen, will be evaluated further in the following section 4.

4 Evaluating the licensing regime

The initial failures in this chapter revolved around the non-market failure of internalisation due to speedy technological development making the former legislative framework outdated. This yielded further market failures in the forms of moral hazard and systemic risk. To address these failures, the legislator reconfigured the licensing regime in the PSD2. Whether this reconfiguration has addressed the failures appropriately will be discussed in this section. To make the section more comprehensible, the discussions have been sorted into themes. These cover the licensing regime's accommodation of innovation, and its impact on competition and the ability to ensure a 'more' level playing field. The themes have been selected by considering the initial failures, the intentions laid out by the legislator, and the measures applied through the PSD2.

4.1 Accommodating innovation

A goal for the PSD2 was to accommodate innovative development in financial technology. This accommodation involved the re-configuration of the licensing regime, which was expanded to include third-party PSPs. In shaping the new licensing regime for payment institutions, the legislator set forth a definitive list of payment services to be covered by the rules set out in the Directive.[66] This method rightfully fulfilled the purpose of including third-party PSPs, but the execution of it failed to take into account previous experiences. The flaw in the PSD1 was the non-market failure of internalisation, where government did not allow for technological developments. The same problem has arisen with the PSD2. By setting a restrictive list of included services, the Directive excludes new innovations, such as the developments within cryptocurrency payments.[67][68]

[66] Directive (EU) 2015/2366 (PSD2) Annex 1.

[67] For more on the development in crypto payments see PYMNTS, 'PYMNTS Intelligence: The Promise of Faster Transactions Using Blockchain Technology' (*PYMNTS.com*, 2022) <https://www.pymnts.com/blockchain/2022/pymnts-intelligence-the-promise-of-faster-transactions-using-blockchain-technology/> accessed 18 August 2022; Charles X, 'Cryptocurrency Payment Gateway Development—Best Crypto Development Solutions' (*Finextra*, 2021) <https://www.finextra.com/blogposting/20872/cryptocurrency-payment-gateway-development--best-crypto-development-solutions> accessed 18 August 2022.

[68] The critique has also been raised by Mary Donnelly, 'Payments in the digital market: Evaluating the contribution of Payment Services Directive II' (2016) 32 Computer Law & Security Review 837; Louise Damkjær Christensen, 'Crypto payments – a danger to consumer protection?' (2022) 16 Law and Financial Markets Review 197.

While the restrictive list excludes new services such as cryptocurrency payments, the expansion of the services on the list has accompanied the introduction of AIS and PIS into the regulated sphere of payment services. The PIS and AIS were invented prior to the regulatory framework including them, and as described above in section 2.3, this left the potential for systemic risks that are undesirable for society. By including the services in the regulatory framework of the PSD2, the legislator manages to embrace the innovative development, while also strengthening competition in payment service solutions and improving consumer welfare.

Despite becoming regulated by the PSD2, this has not affected the number of new innovative PSPs. Across the EU there was a surge in the number of newly incorporated payment institutions.[69] After the adoption of PSD2 there was a 70% increase, though lowered by 36% the year after when the PSD2 was implemented in national legislation of the Member States. This shows that market actors welcomed the expansion of the regulatory framework to include third-party PSPs, and the incentives created with the PSD2 can be said to have worked. The market actors can therefore also be considered to have benefited from the changes in regulation introduced by the PSD2.

Including the AISP and PISP in the legislative framework, making them regulated and supervised, also improves consumer welfare in several ways. For one, the inclusion creates more regulatory clarity for providers wishing to enter the market. This clarity can be essential for the business' decision to develop and provide their payment services. Making the services regulated could also deter some providers, but considering their often malevolent motives, this does not affect the increase in choice for consumers. By setting a legal standard for all providers to comply with, one would expect the quality and service of these payment services to improve as well. The price aspect is less positive. The rising transaction costs for PSPs from having to comply with the ruleset might cause a rise in price for the services.[70] Given the circumstances, it is clear that the inclusion of new innovative services in the regulatory framework has impacted consumer welfare positively.

Accommodating new innovations in financial services also impacts competition in the market for payment services. By allowing more new providers to enter the market, the legislator can incentivise incumbent institutions to

[69] Michał Polasik and others, 'The impact of Payment Services Directive 2 on the PayTech sector development in Europe' (2020) 178 Journal of Economic Behavior & Organization 385, 394.

[70] Although, as proposed by Louis Kaplow, 'Rules Versus Standards: An Economic Analysis' (1992) 42 Duke Law Journal 557 the costs might have been higher had the regulator chosen standards instead of rules.

improve their own product portfolios and invest more in innovation.[71] Having a competitive and incentivised payments market would also reduce moral hazard, although this measure cannot stand alone to mitigate moral hazard. Disclosure requirements would also have to be in place, which is also the case with the PSD2.[72] Furthermore, the improvements in competition from accommodating innovation also impact consumer welfare positively by pushing prices down.

To summarise, the Directive manages to sufficiently accommodate innovation in the form of third-party PSPs following the re-configuration of the Directive's scope and the licensing regime. This has had a positive impact on the two other goals—competition and consumer protection. Unfortunately, the legislative style, using restrictive lists, has proven to exclude further innovative developments within payment services. Leaving new innovations such as cryptocurrency payments out of the scope of the PSD2 could be harmful to consumer welfare and systemic stability, just as it was previously with third-party PSPs.[73]

4.2 Competition and legal entry barriers

Using a licensing regime as a legal entry barrier serves multiple purposes. Those related to competition include ensuring a level playing field and protecting systemic stability. Fencing in all PSPs under the same regulatory framework and setting the same minimum standard serves the purpose of creating fair competition. Although the authorisation rules in the PSD2 entail exemptions in articles 32 and 33, these are rational and proportionate considering the PSPs eligible for exemptions and the accompanying restrictions. Agreeing on the minimum requirements for PSPs is an important foundational element of a well-integrated EU Payment Services Market.

[71] Which effect was already supported by Joseph A Schumpeter, *The Theory of Economic Development: An Inquiry into Profits, Capital, Credit, Interest, and the Business Cycle* (Harvard University Press 1934).

[72] Directive (EU) 2015/2366 (PSD2) also cover important rules on disclosure, for example, the information requirements for framework contracts in art 52 and art 45 for single payment transactions.

[73] European Fintech Association, *Position Paper on the Revised Payment Services Directive 2* (European Fintech Association 2022) also calls for greater coherence with other overlapping regulation such as the Markets in Crypto Assets Regulation; Iris H Y Chiu, 'A New Era in Fintech Payment Innovations? A Perspective from the Institutions and Regulation of Payment Systems' (2017) 9 Law, Innovation and Technology 190, 227 also points to the need for PSD2 to cover payments in virtual currencies.

Having a market where some providers exist outside of the regulatory framework is harmful to the goal of fair competition. The providers covered by regulation and hence obliged to comply with the ruleset must pay the costs of compliance, which the providers outside of the regulatory framework do not have to pay. Providers excluded from the scope thus hold an advantage by being able to set the price for their services lower, as their costs are not affected by compliance requirements. This distorts competition and makes for a more unlevel playing field.

It could be argued that the smart payment service user would be able to distinguish between the two providers, and assume that service and quality, including security, would be higher with the more expensive, regulated provider. Unfortunately, a considerable group of these payment service users are consumers with limited financial literacy.[74] Consumers are generally believed to be biased, individual decision-makers.[75] This means that we already have an information asymmetry problem on our hands, which is exacerbated by the complexity of the products and services provided on the market for payment services. The technical workings and information that have to be processed to provide these services are complex and difficult for consumers to understand prior to selecting a provider. It must therefore be assumed that the consumer is not able to distinguish the qualities of a regulated provider from an unregulated one. Expanding the scope of the licensing regime to include third-party PSPs therefore also contributes to improving consumer welfare and reducing the risk and impact of biased, individual consumer decision-making.

The regulatory strategy of using a licensing regime to regulate a market also contributes positively to systemic stability by minimising the risks arising from unregulated activities, which can be harmful on a systemic level. The systemic risks create an interesting conflict with the Commission's desire to advance innovation in financial services, as these innovations have proved to be possible threats to systemic stability. As noted above in section 2.3, the PSD1's scope, which excluded third-party PSPs, was a factor that increased systemic risks. By including the service providers in the scope of the PSD2, attention has been given to creating balance between innovative developments and the meta-goal of systemic stability.

It is worth questioning whether financial and systemic stability improve consumer welfare, or if consumer protection rules improve financial and

[74] European Banking Authority, *EBA Financial Education Report 2019/2020* and OECD, *OECD/INFE 2020 International Survey of Adult Financial Literacy* (2020) have both examined financial literacy among consumers and found the average level to be low.

[75] Armour and others, *Principles of Financial Regulation* 60.

systemic stability. Considering that consumers account for a large share of end users in any market, the latter must, at least, be true. Setting legal entry barriers can help the regulator and supervisor to ensure a certain standard among providers on the payment services market. This has a positive impact on the quality of services, and hence improves consumer welfare. The downside of setting minimum standards and authorisation rules is the impact this has on prices. These rules tend to add costs for the provider who has to comply with them, and these costs are transferred to the end-price of the service purchased by the end-user, who is often a consumer. When we have to weigh quality, including greater security, against higher prices, the former must be of greatest importance. Managing the potential threat to systemic stability ideally improves consumer protection as well. As such, there exists an interdependent relationship between the two goals, where changes in one can be reflected in the other.

Summing up, expanding the scope of the licensing regime in the PSD2 has had a positive impact on competition by levelling the playing field for incumbent institutions regulated under the previous regime, and new third-party PSPs that were previously unregulated. This has also addressed the potential systemic risks arising from a market that consists of both regulated and unregulated entities and activities. Furthermore, creating a clear ruleset increases the likelihood of innovation and new providers, while also improving consumer welfare in terms of quality, service, and choice (although this is expected to have a slightly negative impact in the form of higher prices).

Overall, the licensing regime contributes to improved competition and also addresses systemic risks by covering all PSPs under one regime. The regime also accommodates innovation through two different exemptions depending on the type of PSP. While these might be the primary goals of the measures, they also impact consumer welfare positively by improving the quality, choice, and service available to consumers. The only aspect of the regime which might cause new failures in the future is the exclusion of cryptocurrency payments, which continue to exist outside the regulatory framework. It can only be highly recommended that the legislator either includes these service providers in a revised Directive or ensures proper regulation of the activity in other ways, although the latter option too entails a risk towards systemic stability.[76]

[76] Christensen, 'Crypto payments – a danger to consumer protection?'.

5

COMPETITION IN THE EU PAYMENT SERVICES MARKET

1 Introduction

One of the greatest problems to be addressed by the PSD2 was the market failure of market control and entry barriers on the EU market for payment services making competition inefficient. The market was dominated by incumbent institutions which were able to prevent new entrants entering the market. This chapter examines how the PSD2 has addressed the market failure of imperfect competition through regulatory intervention on the market for payment services. This is done through an analysis of three legislative measures applied by the Directive. In accordance with the circular process presented in chapter 3,[1] section 2 will discuss the market and non-market failures that the PSD2 was expected to address. The focus for this chapter is the market failure of imperfect competition, which manifested itself in incumbent providers being able to control the market and create unfair entry barriers. One group of providers distorted competition on the market, causing negative effects on new entrants and payment service users. Note, however, that with its prior regulatory intervention, the PSD1, the legislator did not address the former issues adequately, leading to non-market failures for the PSD2 to mitigate. These will also be presented in section 2.

After explaining the relevant market failures which the legislative measures address, following the circle clockwise, focus is turned to the three relevant measures to analyse in section 3. The first is article 35, which is the rule regulating access to payment systems. It would in many cases not be possible for a PSP to provide its services if they did not have such access. The second measure examined is the right of payment institutions to hold a payment account at a credit institution, as set out in article 36. Access to a payment account in a credit institution is crucial for any business, but especially for a business providing payment services (but not yet offering payment account services). Without

[1] Ch 3, figure 3.1.

EU Payment Services. Louise Damkjær Christensen, Oxford University Press. © Louise Damkjær Christensen 2025.
DOI: 10.1093/9780198949084.003.0005

access to a payment account in a credit institution, it would not be possible for a business to receive payment for services or to manage financial operations. Having examined the most basic necessities for providing payment services, the transfer of power in articles 66 and 67 that allows third-party PSPs to access a customer's payment account(s) upon consent is examined. These provisions are interesting for two primary reasons. The first is the transfer of power to payment account owners from market participants, who could previously decide to whom they granted access to payment accounts. This allowed them to deny access upon the customer's request, even though the customer owned the payment account. The second reason relates to the rise in innovation of financial services, where third-party PSPs such as Account Information Services (AIS) and Payment Initiation Services (PIS) were not formerly covered by the scope of the PSD2. By including these services in the Directive's scope and implementing articles 66 and 67, the legislator intends to lower the entry barriers considerably for new, innovative service providers.

These measures have been selected as they represent crucial rights for both PSPs and users. They are also measures dedicated to addressing the issues of imperfect competition, high entry barriers, and the narrow scope of the PSD1. They are therefore excellent examples illustrating how the EU institutions function, combining economic and legal considerations in the legislative process. The contents of the provisions will be analysed further in this chapter, as well as the correlation of failures, regulatory goals, and strategies when drafting and adopting legislation in the EU. The three regulatory measures all entail elements of all three Directive goals, as well as sharing a regulatory strategy.

Whether this can be considered appropriate management of the failures presented in section 2, or ends up creating new issues, will be discussed in section 4. The last section completes our circle from chapter three by summarising the findings of the preceding sections and discussing the collective appropriateness of the applied measures and their ability to accommodate future developments in financial innovation.

2 Imperfect competition

As illustrated by the impact assessment[2] in chapter 3, there were issues of inefficient competition and unbalanced entry barriers set by incumbent

[2] European Commission, *Commission Staff Working Document Impact Assessment* SWD(2013) 288 final (2013).

institutions in the EU market for payment services prior to the implementation of the PSD2. This section will outline the market and non-market failures in detail, to provide an understanding of the failures which needed to be addressed by legislation. Explaining the problems on the payment services market is necessary in order to understand the regulatory measures applied, analyse their impact, and evaluate their appropriability. Simply examining an adopted article would not tell us why it was drafted nor explain any of its peculiarities. The context it has been drafted in is necessary in order to understand its purpose, interpret how it ought to be applied in practice, and evaluate whether it is fit for purpose. With the Commission applying economic and market considerations when it identifies problem areas and drafting legislation, an analysis of such legislation requires reflection on these economic considerations, and it is necessary to include these reflections in the analytical work of the legal scholar.

In subsection 2.1, the market failure of imperfect competition will be explored, specifically the issue of market control. As described above, there were severe problems with market access due to incumbents possessing market control to a degree whereby competition was distorted by being able to set practical entry barriers for new entrants. The second subsection, 2.2, will present the non-market failure of not sufficiently accommodating innovation in the previous legislative framework. Although regulation cannot possibly be made to fit all future developments, it is possible to accommodate some development and to draft flexible, technology-neutral legislation. As will be presented in detail in subsection 2.2, the PSD1 contained one such failure where, despite proper warning, the legislator decided against adding foreseeable innovative developments into the scope of the Directive. How leaving third-party PSPs out of the scope of the PSD1 resulted in a non-market failure will be explained in subsection 2.2.

2.1 Market control

The market failure of market control has incurred when one or a few providers control the market. This affects the efficiency of competition in a market, as competition ensures fair pricing, incentivises providers to innovate, and can positively impact the number of alternatives or choices available to consumers. When one or a few participants control the market, these effects fail to materialise. Market control can also be effected through the power to keep new entrants from entering the market. This has negative consequences for customers on the market, including consumers, as they will miss out on innovation in services and the positive effects of stronger competition on the market.

The market for payment services prior to the PSD2 was dominated by incumbent institutions, with few payment institutions authorised or registered, as most providers were authorised as credit institutions.[3] On this market, incumbent institutions could control the entrance of new providers into the market. Incumbents had a particular advantage when new providers did not offer payment account services, as these providers were dependent on entering into bilateral agreements with credit institutions, which were also direct competitors regarding the services new entrants wished to provide. This had negative consequences both for competition in the market and for innovation in financial services.[4]

These situations can also be described as entry barriers. On the market for payment services, the entry barriers we are concerned with at present are those of a practical nature.[5] Entry barriers can originate from market control, although other sources also exist, which will be described further in the following with specific relevance to the PSD2. Prior to the PSD2, new PSPs, and especially third-party PSPs, had trouble entering the market. New entrants needed access to payment account services for their business, and third-party PSPs were dependent on bilateral agreements with incumbent institutions to offer their services. Things were further complicated by the fact that legislators, when drafting PSD1, had decided against including third-party PSPs in its scope. This left a category of PSPs without a regulatory framework, including the associated rights and obligations. The problem of unfair entry barriers to the market therefore consists of both market failures and non-market failures. The focus will here first be on the former, whereas the latter will be explained in subsection 2.2.

Entry barriers should not only be perceived in a negative sense as they can also contribute appropriate and fair requirements for entering a market. There can exist both legal entry barriers, most often enacted through legislation, and practical entry barriers created in the market by its participants, either intentionally or not. Considering the goals and purpose of regulation, a certain balance should be pursued to set fair entry barriers that protect or aim towards achieving the prescribed goals. The legal entry barriers are more manageable,

[3] European Commission, *Commission Staff Working Document Impact Assessment* SWD(2013) 288 final 21.

[4] Pieter T J Wolters and Bart P F Jacobs, 'The security of access to accounts under the PSD2' (2019) 35 Computer Law & Security Review 29, 30.

[5] The legal entry barriers were examined in chapter 4.

as they can be adjusted through regulation as the market develops. With legislation, it is possible to lower or raise the entry barriers depending on what is necessary to achieve an efficient market, as was examined in chapter 4.

This chapter focuses on the practical entry barriers set by market participants, which are different and not easily adjusted by regulators. Incumbent institutions with large market share can under certain circumstances control entry into the market, or they can exploit economies of scale to set prices too low for new entrants to be able to compete.[6] The attributes of incumbents' products can also be of such quality or quantity that new entrants struggle to attract customers. Other issues such as subscriptions or servicing contracts with excessive termination terms can also lock customers into one service provider. The impact of these situations can be extremely negative for customers, especially consumers. Possible effects include price redundancy, lack of innovation, too few providers for customers to choose between, product quality being compromised, etc. Such a development in the market, which interferes with the market's efficiency, justifies regulatory intervention to restore fair competition and access to the market for new PSPs.

2.2 The Directive's scope and innovation

When the first Payment Services Directive was drafted and adopted in 2007, third-party PSPs were slowly advancing on the market. Despite being aware of this fact, the EU legislator chose not to incorporate these new actors under the scope of the Directive.[7] A possible explanation for this could be that the legislator did not anticipate the rapid development in non-banks providing payment services. This belongs to the non-market failure category of internalities, as the legislative intervention did not account properly for technological advances and did not process and utilise existing information prior to adopting the legislative framework.[8] The goal of the first Directive, to harmonise the Market for Payment Services, failed to account for something the second Directive is making up for, accommodating financial innovation.

[6] We have also seen cases from the ECJ where the Court addresses and defines these issues for example Case 85/76 *Hoffmann-La Roche & Co. AG v Commission of the European Communities* [1979] ECR I-461 EU:C:1979:36; Case 27/76 *United Brands Company and United Brands Continentaal BV v Commission of the European Communities* [1978] ECR I-207 EU:C:1978:22.

[7] Mary Donnelly, 'Payments in the digital market: Evaluating the contribution of Payment Services Directive II' (2016) 32 Computer Law & Security Review 828.

[8] On this problem also see the work of Friedrich A von Hayek, 'The Use of Knowledge in Society' (1945) 35 The American Economic Review 519; Arthur Cecil Pigou, *The Economics of Welfare* (MacMillan and Co. 1921).

By not including third-party PSPs under the scope of the PSD1, the legislator left a legal void for these providers. This caused great legal uncertainty, especially concerning the position of consumers, rights and obligations, and applicable rulesets, as regulation of these providers was left entirely to national legislation in each Member State, which led to further problems for cross-border activities.[9] Leaving third-party providers out of the scope not only worked against the goal of creating a harmonised internal market, but also impeded innovation and efficient competition on the market for payment services. Irrespective of whether Member States created a legislative framework for third-party PSPs, the effects of hampered competition automatically had a negative impact on consumer welfare, giving them less options to choose between at less favourable prices. Furthermore, as third-party PSPs were not covered by regulation, they were also not compelled to implement and comply with the same high standards that applied to payment institutions, resulting in questionable quality of services for consumers.

Leaving a gap in the legislative framework at EU level could also result in derived externalities, for example if this caused third-party PSPs not to be covered by anti-money laundering and counter-terrorism financing legislation. This is not a desired outcome for any regulator. As presented in chapter 3, avoiding, or at least minimising, financial crime, such as money laundering and terrorism financing, is a goal for financial regulation in general. It would therefore seem fair to conclude that by not including third-party PSPs under the scope of the PSD1, the regulator failed to apply an appropriate measure to secure an efficient market with its regulatory intervention. Whether the EU regulator has managed to address this issue appropriately with the PSD2 will be examined in the following section 3. After this, the legislative intervention aiming to improve competition by providing access to new market entrants will be evaluated in section 4.

3 Improving competition via access

To address and manage the problems arising from the market failure of imperfect competition, the EU legislator applied several measures with the PSD2. Common to all three examined here is that they are conduct rules. Articles 35 and 36 are both market-facing conduct rules, whereas articles66 and 67,

[9] Alan Brener, 'Payment Service Directive II and Its Implications' in Theo Lynn and others (eds), *Disrupting Finance* (Palgrave Pivot, Cham. 2019) 107.

although entailing a profound change to market-facing behaviour, are essentially client-facing conduct rules. The measures also share the goal of competition as a key driver, but their balance with the other goals of consumer protection and innovation varies. The details of the provisions will be analysed in the following subsections. Subsection 3.1 treats the provision securing access to payment systems, the Directive's article 35. This is one of the two most fundamental provisions to ensure market access and lower entry barriers for new, non-bank providers. This will be followed by an analysis of article 36, which ensures payment institutions have access to holding a payment account at a credit institution. Why such a provision is even necessary will also be explained in subsection 3.2. The third and last subsection investigates the most novel provisions treated in this chapter, articles 66 and 67, which provide access to payment accounts held with account servicing PSPs upon customer consent. What this entails, why it is necessary, and how it impacts the Directive-specific goals will be analysed in subsection 3.3.

3.1 Access to payment systems

The first measure to be examined in the Directive's handling of the problems related to the failure of imperfect competition is the access to payment systems in article 35. The provision requires Member States to ensure that rules on access to payment systems are objective, non-discriminatory, and proportionate, so that they do not inhibit access more than is necessary to safeguard against specific risks. The intent is for authorised or registered PSPs that are legal persons to be able to participate in payment systems. But to understand the importance of article 35, and the access granted through it, it is necessary to first outline the functions of a payment system.

The PSD2 defines a payment system as a funds transfer system with formal and standardised arrangements and common rules for the processing, clearing and/or settlement of payment transactions.[10] The European Central Bank's Regulation (EU) No 795/2014 on oversight requirements for systemically important payment systems defines a payment system as a formal arrangement between participants with common rules and standardised arrangements for

[10] Directive (EU) 2015/2366 of the European Parliament and of the Council of 25 November 2015 on payment services in the internal market, amending Directives 2002/65/EC, 2009/110/EC and 2013/36/EU and Regulation (EU) No 1093/2010, and repealing Directive 2007/64/EC [2015] OJ L 337/35 art 4(7).

the execution of transfer orders between the participants.[11] Another way to formulate what a payment system is can be found in the UK Banking Act 2009 section 182(1), which defines an inter-bank payment system as an arrangement designed to facilitate or control the transfer of money between banks who participate in the arrangement. While the first two definitions are more comprehensible, the essential purpose of a payment system is more neatly conveyed in the last definition. The definition in the Banking Act 2009 also highlights the importance of PSD2 article 35 granting access to PSPs, as this is necessary in order to move funds from a payer in one bank to a payee in another bank.[12]

As already mentioned above, article 35 requires Member States to ensure that rules on access of authorised or registered PSPs to payment systems are objective, non-discriminatory, and proportionate. The rules cannot inhibit access more than is necessary to safeguard against specific risks, such as settlement risk, operational risk, and business risk, and to protect the financial and operational stability of the payment system. Adding the objectives of financial and operational stability of the payment system to the provision emphasises the legislator's view of the importance of the payment system to the functioning of the financial system. But it also adds discretion to the payment systems in their decisions on which PSPs to grant access.

Furthermore, the provision's first paragraph stipulates that payment systems are not to impose restrictive rules on effective participation in other payment systems, or rules which discriminate between authorised PSPs or between registered PSPs in relation to the rights, obligations, and entitlements of participants, and lastly to not impose restrictions on the basis of institutional status. The latter is especially relevant for PSPs registered with only a limited license being exempted through article 32. Member States are obligated under article 35 to ensure that no PSPs, payment service users, or other participants in payment systems are met with such restrictions. Although this provision is not a new invention, its importance remains high.[13]

Moving the provision from PSD1 article 28 to PSD2 article 35 only entailed minor linguistic changes to the first paragraph, but the widened scope of the

[11] Regulation of the European Central Bank (EU) No 795/2014 of 3 July 2014 on oversight requirements for systemically important payment systems [2014] OJ L 217/16 art 2(1).

[12] It goes beyond the scope of this book to explain further the details of the concepts of clearing, settlement, and netting, for more on this I recommend reading chapter 12, section 3.A of Ross Cranston and others, *Principles of Banking Law* (3rd edn, OUP 2017).

[13] Its importance is also stressed by Nikita Divissenko, 'Title 2 Payment Service Providers, Chapter 2 Common Provisions (arts 35-37)' in Gabriella Gimigliano and Marta Bozina Beroš (eds), *The Payment Services Directive 2 A Commentary* (Elgar Commentaries in Financial Law, 2021) 86.

Directive causes the provision's importance to increase, as third-party PSPs have been included. Looking from the legislative point of view, the widened scope is expected to effectively secure competition in the market for payment services among all types of PSPs. While the provision is of high importance in order to create and ensure competition, it was of lower priority during the revision of the first Directive.[14] This was the case even though it is perceived as a measure to safeguard an open and innovative payment services market. It sets out to secure access for payment institutions to existing payment systems, enabling all PSPs to provide payment services effectively and on a non-discriminatory basis. In any case, considering the current scope and effect enabled by the provision in correlation with other improvements to the Directive, the lack of focus under the revision does not seem to have had negative consequences for the goal of increased competition and better conditions for innovation.

Where article 35's first paragraph obligated Member States to ensure access to payment systems, the second paragraph contains an exemption which has undergone substantial changes from its former PSD1 article 28(2), limiting the scope of exemptions and moving interpretative parts to the recitals. The exemption becomes particularly relevant when sorting payment systems further. One category is the card schemes, with both four-party and three-party schemes. With the four-party scheme, the issuer of the payment card used by the payer is different to the acquirer of the payment through which a merchant rents their point-of-sale, as illustrated in Figure 5.1. In the three-party scheme, illustrated in Figure 5.2, the issuer and acquirer are the same legal entity, often referred to as a closed network. It is in the latter, three party scheme where the exemption becomes relevant.

The second paragraph states that payment systems designated under Directive 98/26/EC and payment systems composed exclusively of PSPs belonging to a group, such as a three-party card scheme, are exempted from the access requirement. Of greatest interest here is perhaps the latter exemption granted in litra b), as this essentially allows more advantageous conditions to three-party schemes than four-party schemes.

The recitals define the payment system group as systems set up and operated by a single PSP.[15] This definition allows not only the three-party schemes

[14] European Commission, *Commission Staff Working Document Impact Assessment* SWD(2013) 288 final 42; Divissenko, 'Title 2 Payment Service Providers, Chapter 2 Common Provisions (arts 35-37)' 87.

[15] Directive (EU) 2015/2366 (PSD2) recital 52.

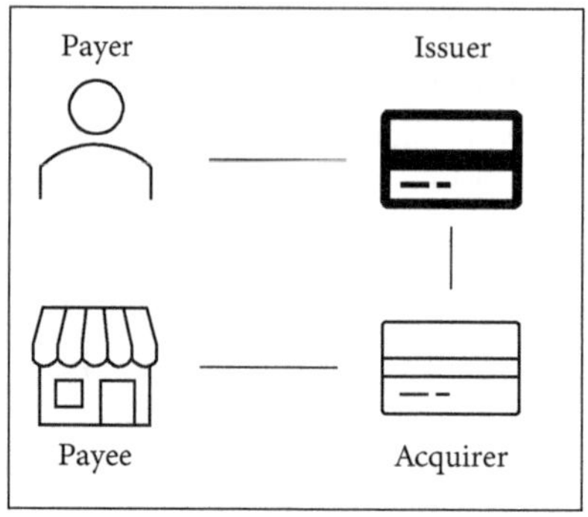

Figure 5.1 The 4-party card scheme (own configuration)

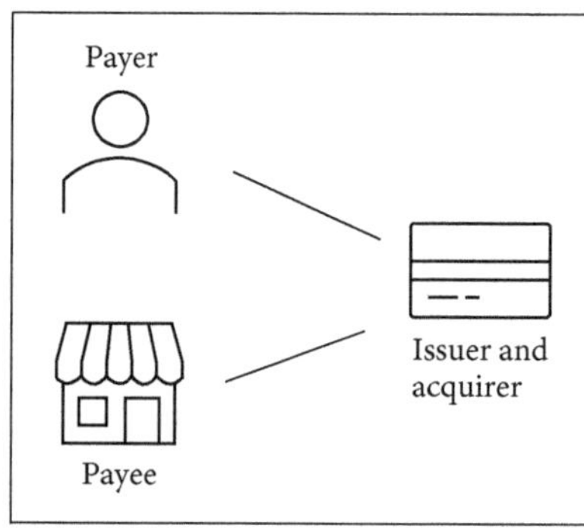

Figure 5.2 The 3-party card scheme (own configuration)

to be exempted, but also services offered by telecommunication providers, internal systems of banking groups, etc. The purpose of the exemption can also be found in the recitals, stating that such closed payment systems can stimulate competition with established mainstream payment systems.[16] However, the recitals also state that such systems should always be subject to competition rules, which may require access to be granted in order to maintain effective competition in the payments market. The placement of such a direct interpretation of the Directive's provision on access to payment systems poses a methodological problem. This issue is also addressed in the *American Express* case before the ECJ.[17] The Court stressed that while a recital in secondary EU legislation may cast light on the interpretation to be given to a legal rule, it cannot in

[16] Directive (EU) 2015/2366 (PSD2).

[17] Case C-643/16 *American Express Company v The Lords Commissioners of Her Majesty's Treasury* [2018] EU:C:2018:67.

itself constitute such a rule.[18] Given that the wording of recital 52 is only to be considered an interpretation, which cannot be directly applicable to any situation, but only on a case-by-case basis, the direct formulation of the recital and its interpretative value does not pose a problem.

To further investigate article 35, subsection 3.1.1 will first examine the provision from a theoretical perspective, while subsection 3.1.2 will substantiate this analysis with examples of the provision's use in practice.

3.1.1 Article 35 in theory

To address the existing market failure of imperfect competition, where incumbents could effectively control the market, article 35 applies a conduct of business rule targeted directly at payment systems, to give access to all PSPs. By keeping the provision in a nearly unchanged form, combined with the expanded scope of the Directive, the legislator expresses a clear intention to continue improving competition on the market for payment services. The impact assessment defines adjustments to the access to payment systems for all PSPs as a fine-tuning measure intended to give PSPs access comparable to that of smaller banks.[19] While improving competition on the market is an important goal of the provision, its relationship to the goal of innovation also becomes abundantly clear when looking at the impact assessment and the motives for the provision.

As preparation for drafting the PSD2, the Commission, through its impact assessment, identified problems of the payment services market under the PSD1. The report divided these into problem drivers consisting of two subsections, market failures and regulatory and supervisory gaps. These drivers led to the problems, which caused a range of effects.[20] Among the problems caused by market failures are market fragmentation of innovative payment solutions, and ineffective competition in certain areas of card and internet payments. By widening the scope of the Directive to include third-party PSPs, the problem was essentially expected to be solved. What can also be deduced from such a division of problems is the legislator's goal of improving market conditions to support innovation.

[18] Case C-643/16 *American Express* paras 49–51; Case 215/88 *Casa Fleischhandels-GmbH v Bundesanstalt für landwirtschaftliche Marktordnung* [1989] ECR I-2789 EU:C:1989:331 para 31.

[19] European Commission, *Commission Staff Working Document Impact Assessment* 43.

[20] European Commission, *Commission Staff Working Document Impact Assessment* SWD(2013) 288 final see problem-tree at 34.

In this case, the problem appears to have been partly a market failure of entry barriers due to incumbents' market control, and partly a non-market failure of setting the scope of the PSD1 too narrowly. The result of these two failures was an unlevel playing field, placing incumbents in a stronger position than new entrants in the market. By forcing payment systems to give access on equal and objective terms to all PSPs, the legislator sought to level the playing field and lower the entry barrier for new, innovative entrants. This measure, in combination with Regulation (EU) 2015/751 on interchange-fees which bans surcharges, was also expected to improve conditions for consumers.

The market was previously suffering from market dominance by expensive card schemes, but forced access and a cap on fees were expected to contribute to lower prices and more transparency. Furthermore, a market without a right of access to payment systems also limited the available payment instruments for both consumers and merchants. Article 35, in combination with the Regulation on interchange-fees, therefore also contributed to the Directive's goal of consumer protection. The provision improves consumer welfare by ensuring fair pricing of services and enabling more choices and seeks to improve the quality and service of the available payment services through competition.

It is clear that the provision's primary goal is to improve competition, and secondarily to improve innovation and consumer protection. It is also obvious that the intent is to achieve this through conduct of business rules, as the provision mandates the behaviour of some market actors—the payment systems. What is less clear to the reader of the provision is when a payment system is covered by paragraph one, and obliged to provide access, and when it can be exempted under the second paragraph.

The four-party payment card scheme is undoubtedly covered by the first paragraph, as the issuer and acquirer are two different providers. But when these two roles belong to the same group, it can be unclear which collaborations with companies outside of the group are permitted. This causes a degree of legal uncertainty for both payment systems and payment institutions wanting to gain access. One of the changes from PSD1 article 28(2) to PSD2 article 35(2) is the relocation of the definition of the closed network group covered by litra b). This definition, and hence its interpretative contribution, has been moved to recital 52 in the PSD2. Legislating in the recitals can hardly be applauded by a legal scholar, but the important question is whether this has caused problems in practice.

3.1.2 Art. 35 in practice

The extent of the exemption can best be analysed through case law. The *American Express* Case can be used to illuminate the relationship between the exemption in article 35(2)(1) and the second sub-paragraph of article 35(2), which reinstates the obligation to give access in accordance with paragraph one. This is to happen in the situation where an exempted payment system allows an authorised or registered PSP, who is not a participant in the system, to pass transfer orders through the system. In this case, the exemption is practically repealed.

The *American Express* case tested when article 35(2)(2) is activated.[21] The case essentially asked whether American Express Company was obligated in accordance with article 35(1) to give access to their payment system to PSPs. American Express Company argued that this was not the case, as the company considered itself to be a three-party payment card scheme, covered by article 35(2)(1)(b) as belonging to a group. As the American Express Company does in fact act as both issuer and acquirer, it does constitute a three-party payment card scheme, but the question before the Court was whether—by entering into co-branding and service provision arrangements with third parties within the EU—American Express was no longer covered by the exception in article 35(2)(1) due to the limitation set out in article 35(2)(2).[22] Here the Court considered the Directive's recital 52 in its reasoning. The Court reasoned that, in order to stimulate the competition that closed payment systems can give to established mainstream payment systems, it would not be appropriate to grant third parties access to those proprietary payment systems.[23]

The Court further stated that with article 35, the EU legislature intended to ensure that all PSPs can make use of such services under the same conditions, in order to maintain effective competition in payment markets.[24] As such, the EU legislature intended to only treat PSPs differently when differences between them justify it.[25] Therefore, the Court found that the determining factor ought to be whether the co-branding partner is a PSP. If this was not the case, and the partner did not in any way provide payment services, the three-party payment card scheme was still to be covered by the exception. Conversely, if the co-branding partner were a PSP, or if the three-party payment card scheme used an agent to provide payment services, they would lose the benefit of the

[21] Case C-643/16 *American Express*.
[22] Case C-643/16 *American Express* paras 10 and 23.
[23] Case C-643/16 *American Express* para 59.
[24] Case C-643/16 *American Express* para 60.
[25] Case C-643/16 *American Express* para 61.

exception and become subject to the obligation to grant access in accordance with article 35(1).[26]

By incorporating a co-branding partner or an agent that provides payment services into the closed network group, treating the schemes differently can no longer be justified. The Court and the EU legislator emphasised the goal of competition as the principal reason for different treatment of the schemes. With the changes to the original three-party scheme in the *American Express* case, the differences between the schemes no longer justified different treatment. Essentially, it would no longer serve the goal of fair competition to continue to treat the American Express scheme differently, compared to four-party schemes.[27]

The Court was also asked to decide on article 35's validity where a three-party scheme could become subject to the access obligation. The validity was questioned as being unfounded in the Directive, not in compliance with the principle of proportionality, or simply a manifest error of assessment.[28] The Court rather briefly rejected the latter charge by deduction. The Court argued that such a system, where third-party schemes can be subject to the access obligation, would contribute to the achievement of the objectives of the Directive.[29] On the principle of proportionality, the Court stated that nothing in the case suggested the provision to be inappropriate for attaining the legitimate objectives pursued by the Directive, and continued to emphasise that in this case it was appropriate. The Court reasoned that it would be difficult to achieve the Directive's objectives, particularly the objective of article 35, if the arrangement of this case was not subject to the access obligation.[30] As for the charge that the article lacked sufficient reason, the Court referred to recitals 49, 50, and 52 of the Directive as showing with sufficient clarity the underlying reasoning for applying the access obligation to three-party payment card schemes. The Court substantiated this claim by stating that:

> those recitals show that the aim of Article 35 is to ensure that, as a general rule, all payment service providers can have access to the services of technical infrastructures of payment systems in order to ensure, throughout the European Union, equal treatment of the various categories of payment

[26] Case C-643/16 *American Express* para 69.
[27] Case C-643/16 *American Express* para 76.
[28] Case C-643/16 *American Express* paras 73, 81, and 84.
[29] Case C-643/16 *American Express* para 83.
[30] Case C-643/16 *American Express* paras 86 and 87.

> service providers and, thereby, to maintain effective competition in payment markets.[31]

In conclusion, the Court confirmed the validity of article 35 underpinning the importance of a Directive's objective, and even a single Article's objective, when interpreting and applying EU legislation.

The case shows how the provision works in practice and documents a positive change to the payment services market. The rule applied to address the initial problem functions in both the theoretical sense and in practice. The reasoning by the Court also highlights the importance which should be placed on the context of a rule, and the objectives, or goals, attached to a Directive and the provision in question.

3.2 Access to payment accounts

The second measure, a right of access to payment account services, addresses the market failure of imperfect competition, particularly the entry barriers set by credit institutions. Without the right to access a credit institution's payment account services, credit institutions could decide not to grant access with the purpose of keeping competition out of the market. It is vital for a third-party PSP to have access to a payment account service. It is an essential part of any business to be able to receive payments from customers and to be able to pay invoices etc. For many PSPs, at least one extra payment account is vital to ensure compliance with the safeguarding requirement in article 10. Therefore the following will examine article 36 further, as this is the provision granting payment institutions access to payment account services.

Article 36 was a new addition to the PSD2 and placed an obligation on Member States to ensure access to credit institutions' payment account services for payment institutions. The services must be accessible on an objective, non-discriminatory, and proportionate basis. Furthermore, the access must be sufficient to enable payment institutions to provide payment services in an unhindered and efficient manner. Although article 36 grants payment institutions a right of access, it can also be deduced from the context of the provision that this right is limited in scope. As such, it is expected that the right to access

[31] Case C-643/16 *American Express* para 75.

payment account services applies to activities covered by the PSD2 and cannot be assumed to cover other unrelated activities.[32]

The provision is a conduct of business rule as it places an obligation on selected market participants to behave in the desired manner. Its firmness, practically forcing credit institutions to provide payment account services to competitors, clearly signals the legislator's intention of securing access to the payment services market for more new providers. By making it possible for more providers to enter the market, competition is naturally expected to improve and become, if not efficient, at least more efficient than it was prior to the implementation of the rule.[33] This will contribute to the Directive's goal of improving competition in the payment services market. To counterbalance the extensive right of access, the legislator has given credit institutions the possibility of denying payment institutions access to payment account services, but this must be on objective, non-discriminatory, and proportionate grounds.

The right of access in article 36 is further balanced by the safeguarding requirements in article 10. The two provisions are intricately linked, as the payment account acquired through article 36 serves as a transaction account for the business providing payment services. Article 10 sets out the requirements to safeguard client funds for payment institutions that provide the payment services referred to in points 1–6 of Annex 1.[34] These requirements apply when funds have been received from the payment service user or through another PSP for the execution of payment transactions.

The first paragraph of article 10 lists in litra a) and b) two options for payment institutions to safeguard the received funds. Under litra a), the funds must not be commingled at any time with the funds of any natural or legal person other than payment service users. This makes one account sufficient for handling all the payment institution's client funds, given that the PSP only deals with transactions in one currency. However, if the funds are not to be transacted no later than the following business day, the payment institution must either deposit them in a separate account in a credit institution or invest them in secure, liquid low-risk assets, where they must be insulated in accordance

[32] Gabriella Gimigliano, 'Title 2 "Payment Service Providers", Chapter 2 "Common Provisions" (art 35-37) sect. F and G' in Gabriella Gimigliano and Marta Bozina Beroš (eds), *The Payment Services Directive 2—A Commentary* (Elgar Commentaries in Financial Law, Edward Elgar Publishing 2021) 98.

[33] For more on the impact of competition on financial services markets see Stijn Claessens, 'Competition in the Financial Sector: Overview of Competition Policies' (2009) 09 IMF Working Papers particularly at 4–9.

[34] It should be noted that points 7 and 8 of Annex 1 are not covered by the provision as the nature of these services does not entail, at any point, the holding of client funds.

with national law to protect the payment service user's funds against the claims of the payment institution's other creditors.

Litra b) calls for the payment institution to cover all funds by an insurance policy or other comparable guarantee from an insurance company or credit institution. The insurance provider must not belong to the same group as the payment institution itself. Given that the account balance will naturally be variable, the insured amount is to be set as the amount that would have been segregated in the absence of an insurance policy or other comparable guarantee, and which would have been payable in the event that the payment institution becomes unable to meet its financial obligations. Whether a financial institution applies the option given in litra a) or litra b), the primary objective is to secure the payment user's funds in the event that the payment institution becomes insolvent.

The importance of this provision can be illustrated with the Yourpay case,[35] concerning a Danish payment institution, licensed in accordance with the rules laid out by the PSD2, which are implemented in national Danish legislation,[36] by the Danish Financial Services Authority (Danish FSA). Yourpay provided payment services to e-commerce covered by point 3 of Annex 1 and was hence obligated to safeguard client funds according to article 10. The funds on the transaction account were mixed with funds on the company's operating account, and as a result, some clients have still not received funds they are owed.[37] The trustee in bankruptcy investigated whether the requirements set out by article 10 were indeed fulfilled.[38] It is crucial for the payment service users that these requirements were fulfilled, as their funds will not have priority in the insolvency proceedings otherwise and they will be left to seek remuneration through an indemnity suit against management of the company under national law. The case also caused the Danish FSA to launch an investigation into payment institutions' attainment of the safeguarding requirements which led to a report with recommendations on how to improve the safety of client funds.[39] The value of article 10's content and the supervision of its

[35] Malte Oxvig and Sofie Højlund, 'Direktør kaster nyt lys over betalingskonkurs: Kunders penge var formentlig ikke godt nok beskyttet' (*JP/Politikens Hus A/S*, 2022) <https://finanswatch.dk/Finansnyt/Fintech/article13576760.ece> accessed 6 January 2022.

[36] LBKG 2021-12-07 nr 2710 Betalingsloven (Danish Payments Act) [2016].

[37] Oxvig and Højlund, 'Direktør kaster nyt lys over betalingskonkurs: Kunders penge var formentlig ikke godt nok beskyttet'.

[38] Malte Oxvig and Sofie Højlund, 'Kurator undersøger om regler for betalingsinstitutter er overholdt i konkursramt selskab' (*JP/Politikens Hus A/S*, 2022) <https://finanswatch.dk/article13575248.ece?utm_campaign = FinansWatch%20Morgen&utm_content = 2022-01-14&utm_medium = email&utm_source = finanswatch> accessed 14 January 2022.

[39] Finanstilsynet (Danish Financial Supervisory Authority), *Temaundersøgelse om betalings-og e-pengeinstitutters sikring af brugermidler* (2023).

implementation and enforcement in action are clearly significant for payment service users.

It is also clear that there is an important connection between PSD2 article 10 and article 36, as the protection of customer funds, including consumers funds, is directly related to the payment institution complying with the safeguarding requirements of article 10. Though this should not undermine the importance of adding article 36 to the revised Payment Services Directive. In Danish administrative case law, there have so far been three cases of this obligation being breached, where credit institutions have declined payment institutions access to payment account services.[40] These will be examined in the following subsection 3.2.1 to analyse the practical impact of article 36.

3.2.1 Credit institutions vs. payment institutions

As article 36 is a novelty of the PSD2, case law is so far limited, and no cases have yet reached the ECJ.[41] In Danish administrative case law there have so far been three cases of the obligation set out in article 36 being breached, where three different credit institutions have declined access for payment institutions to payment account services.[42]

In the first case, decided by the Danish Competition and Consumer Authority,[43] a Danish credit institution (Ringkjøbing Landbobank) had denied access to its payment account services to a payment institution which had requested access in accordance with PSD2 article 36, which was implemented into Danish law with the Payment Services Act[44] § 63(1). The credit institution listed as its reasons for this rejection to the competent authority that 1) the payment institution did not have a transparent business model, 2) the bank *assumed* the payment institution did not comply with current law, and 3) it would be damaging for the credit institution's reputation to be associated with

[40] CDP-19/06783 *Afgørelse vedrørende Betalingslovens § 63, stk. 1 om adgang til betalingskonti, der føres i kreditinstitutter—Arbejdernes Landsbank A/S* [2019] Konkurrence-og Forbrugerstyrelsen (Danish Competition and Consumer Authority); CDP-18/19832 *Afgørelse vedrørende Betalingslovens § 63, stk. 1 om adgang til betalingskonti, der føres i kreditinstitutter—Ringkjøbing Landbobank A/S* [2020] Konkurrence-og Forbrugerstyrelsen (Danish Competition and Consumer Authority); CDP-19/10259-64 *Afgørelse vedrørende betalingslovens § 63, stk. 1 om Sydbanks vilkår* Konkurrence og Fobrugerstyrelsen (Danish Competition and Consumer Authority).

[41] A search in Curia on the Directive 2366/2015 art 36 found 0 (null) results.

[42] Afgørelse vedrørende Betalingslovens § 63, stk. 1 om adgang til betalingskonti, der føres i kreditinstitutter—Ringkjøbing Landbobank A/S; Afgørelse vedrørende Betalingslovens § 63, stk. 1 om adgang til betalingskonti, der føres i kreditinstitutter—Arbejdernes Landsbank A/S; Afgørelse vedrørende betalingslovens § 63, stk. 1 om Sydbanks vilkår.

[43] Afgørelse vedrørende Betalingslovens § 63, stk. 1 om adgang til betalingskonti, der føres i kreditinstitutter—Ringkjøbing Landbobank A/S.

[44] LBKG 2021-12-07 nr 2710 Betalingsloven (Danish Payments Act).

the payment institution and could lead to unnecessary risk exposure.[45] The credit institution repeatedly highlighted to the Authority that it did not wish to be associated with the kind of business which the payment institution and its clients represented. Although the Authority found that reasons 2 and 3 were proportionate, the reasons for the rejection were not objective and were administered in a discriminatory manner. In conclusion, by its rejection and the reasoning behind this, the credit institution had therefore violated the obligation in article 36 to give access to its payment account services on an objective, non-discriminatory, and proportionate basis.

In the second Danish administrative case, also decided by the Danish Competition and Consumer Authority,[46] the credit institution was also found to have breached its obligation according to the Payment Services Acts § 63(1) to provide payment account services to a payment institution. What makes this decision all the more interesting is the Authority's emphasis on the terms of access to payment account services, and especially how these were hindering the effective provision of services by the payment institution.[47] The Authority found that two of the four terms in question were either discriminating against the payment institution or were not compliant with the principle of proportionality. This assessment was to a large extent based on the effect of the payment account terms, which made it impossible for the payment institution to provide part of its services to specific types of clients. On these grounds, the Authority found that the credit institution's terms of access to payment account services were hindering the effective provision of the payment institutions' services. This constitutes a breach of the obligation laid upon the credit institution with the Payment Services Acts § 63(1), implementing article 36 of the PSD2.

The last case also calls out the credit institution's terms and conditions and finds that they breach the obligation to be objective, non-discriminatory, and proportionate. This case, however, is a much more clear breach of the objectivity requirement. The bank, Sydbank A/S, had declined the payment institution's request for payment account services based, first, on the basis that the payment institution provides money remittance services. Secondly, the bank found that money remittance services was a high risk money laundering

[45] Afgørelse vedrørende Betalingslovens § 63, stk. 1 om adgang til betalingskonti, der føres i kreditinstitutter—Ringkjøbing Landbobank A/S 19.

[46] Afgørelse vedrørende Betalingslovens § 63, stk. 1 om adgang til betalingskonti, der føres i kreditinstitutter—Arbejdernes Landsbank A/S.

[47] Afgørelse vedrørende Betalingslovens § 63, stk. 1 om adgang til betalingskonti, der føres i kreditinstitutter—Arbejdernes Landsbank A/S 29.

activity, and lastly the bank did not want a payment institution as a client when its parent company is headquartered abroad in a country the bank classifies as high risk in terms of money laundering. The authority ordered the bank to change its terms to comply with the requirements of objectivity, non-discriminatory, and proportionality, which the bank adhered to.[48]

The cases illustrate the diverging interests of the credit institution, the payment institution, and the market for payment services.[49] From the point of view of the credit institution, it is to some degree being forced to offer its services to a client which it would otherwise not have engaged with. As long as the payment institution is complying with anti-money laundering regulations and the like, and the credit institution does not have evidence of incompliance, the credit institution does not have a strong case for rejecting access. This can be perceived as extensive interference with its freedom of contract. On the opposite side stand the interests of the payment institution, for whom it is crucial to have access to payment account services to be able to offer their services to customers. This also highlights why article 36 is so important when addressing the market failure of imperfect competition. Without the provision, it would be possible for incumbent institutions to effectively keep new entrants, only authorised as payment institutions, out of the market for payment services by depriving them of any payment account services.[50] Incumbent credit institutions, which also offer payment services, could effectively control the market.

By forcing credit institutions to give access to payment account services to payment institutions, the PSD2 effectively addresses the previously existing market failure.[51] It does so by applying firm-facing conduct of business rules targeted only at the market participants capable of utilising their pre-existing market power. With its article 36, the PSD2 manages to lower the practical entry barrier for new entrants providing payment services, which contributes to enhanced competition in the market. As these new entrants also tend to provide innovative solutions, and hereby ensures enhanced competition, the provision also advances the goal of furthering innovation within payment services. Finally, by enhancing competition through lower entry barriers, the provision also increases consumer protection by ensuring a wider selection of

[48] Afgørelse vedrørende betalingslovens § 63, stk. 1 om Sydbanks vilkår.

[49] The problem of credit institutions using AML requirements to decline requests for payment accounts is also critiqued by European Fintech Association, *Position Paper on the Revised Payment Services Directive 2* (European Fintech Association 2022).

[50] Gimigliano, 'Title 2 "Payment Service Providers", Chapter 2 "Common Provisions" (art 35-37) sect. F and G' 98.

[51] Remember that this provision, as mentioned above in section 3.2, is new and did not exist under the PSD1.

services, which also has a positive impact on ensuring fair pricing of the payment services in favour of payment service users.

These cases clearly show the importance of the adoption of article 36. By securing a right of access for payment institutions, effectively ensuring their ability to provide their services, the provision manages to break down a crucial entry barrier. The provision manages to enhance competition in the market for payment services, while at the same time creating a more level playing field and contributing towards more innovation in the market by helping new entrants into the market. In combination with the safeguarding requirement in article 10, it is safe to say that payment service users will undoubtedly be in a better position than they were previously.

3.3 The transfer of power from market participants to users

To make the payment services market more efficient and competitive, the EU legislator transferred the control of access to accounts from service providers to payment service users. Where dominant market participants could previously effectively control the market access of new entrants, this power has now been vested in the individual payment service user.[52] The previous situation was problematic, not only because of the negative impact on competition, but also because of the restrictions it placed on the payment account service user's rights. After entering into a contract with the account servicing PSP, the payment account service user assumes the right to use the payment account service to fulfil their (legal) payment needs. By not being in control of who can access the payment account, the service user's right is restricted without legal authority.

This also suggests that there existed multiple problems in this regard prior to the adoption of the PSD2. For one, incumbent institutions possessed sufficient market control to distort competition and restrict entrance to the market. Second, payment service users, here among many being consumers, could not effectively exert the rights connected to the acquisition of a payment account.

This section sets out to examine the failure of the payments market described in section 2, focusing on the transfer of power. To do this, first the new articles 66 and 67 of the PSD2, which implement the transfer of power to payment service users, will be examined. The inquiry will initially present the

[52] Donnelly, 'Payments in the digital market: Evaluating the contribution of Payment Services Directive II' 831.

content of the articles, including the regulatory goals implied by them, combining this with the measure's regulatory strategy and the impact this has on addressing the initial failure of market control and entry barriers.

3.3.1 Account access for third-party payment service providers

To address the issue of entry barriers for new third-party PSPs, the PSD2 adopted the new articles 66 and 67. The first requires account servicing PSPs to give access to customers' payment accounts upon request from the customer. This provision covers access for third-party providers providing Payment Initiation Services (PIS). Article 67 sets a similar requirement for account servicing PSPs to give access upon request from the customer, but this provision only covers third-party PSPs offering Account Information Services (AIS).

The two access provisions are separated into different provisions because of the services' differing functionalities. The PIS is an initiation of a payment transaction. The PIS initiates an agreed change to the balance of the service user's payment account, as requested by the payment service user. Provisions such as article 65, which obliges account servicing PSPs to confirm availability of funds on an account, are therefore also important in this regard.[53] The AIS, on the other hand, only accesses information about the payment account, such as balance amount and transactions. The services therefore have different impacts on the service user's payment account. The AIS is far less intrusive than the PIS in terms of balance effect and hence impacts the business of the account servicing PSP less. This is also why the wording of the two provisions differs. The following will therefore examine the content of each article separately, to identify the rights and obligations attached to the new provisions.

3.3.1.1 The payment initiation service

Article 66 covers payment initiation services, and sets out conditions, rights, and obligations for the payment service user, the account servicing PSP, and the PISP. The Directive defines a payment initiation service in article 4(15) as 'a service to initiate a payment order at the request of the payment service user with respect to a payment account held at another PSP.' The definition indicates the dependency of the PISP on the account servicing PSP—a relationship the provision sets out to regulate.

The first paragraph of the provision clearly states that a payer, whose account is accessible online, has the right to make use of a PISP to obtain PIS. The second paragraph then states the account servicing PSP's obligation to

[53] Brener, 'Payment Service Directive II and Its Implications' 112.

ensure the payer's right under the first paragraph. This includes performing actions specified in paragraph 4 of the article, the most interesting of which is litra c). This litra directly orders account servicing PSPs to treat all payment orders transmitted without any discrimination, except for the objective reasons which are listed in the provision. An obligation to treat all payment orders equally is essential to ensure a level playing field in the payment services market. Otherwise, the account servicing PSP could prioritise their own transactions, leaving third-party PSPs worse off and unable to guarantee the completion of transactions to customers. For a PSP, and its customers, this would be unacceptable. The measure directly attempts to prevent account servicing PSPs from taking anticompetitive measures against third-party PSPs.[54] This illustrates how the EU legislator has identified a problem in the market, a market failure, and has sought to mitigate the issue by addressing anticompetitive behaviour with an obligation to give access and perform requested transactions without discrimination, delay, or duress in any other form.

To create a balance in the relationship between account servicing PSPs and third-party PSPs, the article's third paragraph sets out conduct of business rules for the PISP to comply with. This comprises of a list of responsibilities for PISPs, of which litra a) is the most vital. Litra a) states that the PISP shall not at any time hold the payer's funds when providing their PIS.

The responsibilities of the PISP and the obligations of the account servicing PSP are on some points integrated. This is the case, for example, with the reciprocal obligation to communicate securely with one another when performing transactions and to provide necessary information related to the transactions. The PISP is also instructed to protect user-data and not collect, store, access, or use data for any purpose not directly related to the provision of its services. This is particularly important for consumer protection, as the protection of consumers' financial data is a key issue.

An important instrument applied with the provision's paragraph 5 is the conduct rule regulating the relationship between the PISP and the account servicing PSP, or more correctly perhaps, the lack of a need for any contractual relationship between the two. The paragraph mandates that the provision of the services shall not be dependent on the existence of a contractual relationship between the PISP and the account servicing PSP for that purpose. This makes it abundantly clear that no restrictions may be imposed by the account

[54] Gabriella Gimigliano, 'Chapter 9—Title IV, "Rights and obligations in relation to the provision and use of payment services", chapter 2 "Authorisation of payment transactions" (Arts 64-77)' in Gabriella Gimigliano and Marta Bozina Beroš (eds), *The Payment Services Directive 2—A Commentary* (Elgar Commentaries in Financial Law, Edward Elgar 2021) 158.

servicing PSP once the payment service user has requested and explicitly consented to the use of the service. The provision further underscores that the payment service user has full discretion in deciding who gets access to their account.

The key element to unlocking access for third-party PSPs is the payment service user's explicit consent. The right of usage for the payment service user in article 66(1) is connected to the obligation laid upon the account servicing PSP in article 66(2). The latter provision explicitly states that the obligation is triggered when the payer gives their explicit consent. To establish when the obligation is triggered, it is necessary to determine what constitutes explicit consent. The Directive's article 4 containing definitions relevant to the Directive does not include a definition of such explicit consent. PSD2 article 94(1) states that:

> the provision of information to individuals about the processing of personal data and the processing of such personal data and any other processing of personal data for the purposes of this Directive shall be carried out in accordance with Directive 95/46/EC, the national rules which transpose Directive 95/46/EC and with Regulation (EC) No 45/2001.

GDPR[55] article 94 states that these references should be construed as references to the GDPR and will hence be treated as such. Furthermore, the provision's second paragraph states that:

> payment service providers shall only access, process and retain personal data necessary for the provision of their payment services, with the explicit consent of the payment service user.

The direct references to the EU Data Protection rules would suggest that the term explicit consent should be understood in accordance with the GDPR's definition of consent.[56] Concerning explicit consent in article 66, based on the purpose of the provision, it can be deduced that explicit consent from the

[55] Regulation (EU) 2016/679 of the European Parliament and of the Council of 27 April 2016 on the protection of natural persons with regard to the processing of personal data and on the free movement of such data, and repealing Directive 95/46/EC (General Data Protection Regulation) [2016] OJ L 119/1.

[56] A further examination of the GDPR's definition of consent is outside the scope of this book and will not be entertained further here. European Banking Federation, *EBF response to European Commission Consultation on the review of the revised payment services Directive (PSD2)* (European Banking Federation 2022) 55 also emphasises the importance of clear consent terminology to secure consumer trust. For a deeper examination of 'consent' see Wolters and Jacobs, 'The security of access to accounts under the PSD2' 34.

payment service user has been given when the transaction with an amount and a given payee has been requested.

3.3.1.2 The account information service

The presence of third-party PSPs offering AIS called for a new provision in the regulatory framework. As identified in section 2, the initial market failure was one of imperfect competition, where incumbents made it difficult for new entrants to enter the market. Since the AISP is dependent on access to its customers' account information, held at the account servicing PSPs, also known as the incumbents, regulatory intervention was deemed necessary to address the failure and promote competition and innovation.

In the words of the PSD2, an account information service is 'an online service to provide consolidated information of one or more payment accounts held by the payment service user with either another payment service provider or with more than one payment service provider.'[57] The PSD2 ensures access to the necessary information for an AISP through the right of the payment service user to use its services. Article 67(1) requires Member States to ensure that a payment service user has the right to make use of services, enabling access to account information referred to in point (8) of Annex 1— the account information service. Similar to the rules on access for PISPs, article 67 is divided into obligations for the AISP in paragraph 2, and for the account servicing PSP in paragraph 3. As with article 66, the rules in article 67 (2) and (3) are conduct of business rules which aim to guide the behaviour of market participants in a certain direction.

The second paragraph directs the AISP's behaviour towards their clients by requiring explicit consent from the payment service user, and instructs them not to use, access, or store any data not necessary for the purpose of performing the service explicitly requested by the payment service user. This also underscores the power that has been given to the payment service user to control their use of payment services. Other litra of the second paragraph set out market-facing conduct rules, as they are security and communication requirements which the AISP must adhere to. Specifically, litra b) and c) govern the relationship between the AISP and the account servicing PSP regarding security credentials and communication. These provisions are also further supported by article 67 (3) litra a) and b), which compel the account servicing PSP to communicate securely and treat data requests without any discrimination, unless based on objective reasons. Even though article 67 initially places the

[57] Directive (EU) 2015/2366 (PSD2) art 4(16).

power to obtain access with the payment service user, the second and third paragraphs of the provision strictly regulate the permitted behaviour of the AISP and the account servicing PSP, only considering the payment service user when it comes to their explicit consent.

Of greatest importance for AISPs to ensure entry into the market is perhaps the fourth paragraph of article 67. This paragraph clearly states that the provision of account information services shall not be dependent on the existence of a contractual relationship between the AISP and the account servicing PSPs for that purpose. This is important as it removes any ambiguity as to whether account servicing PSPs could demand such a relationship in order to allow access to customers' account data. The provision makes it perfectly clear that any AISP with explicit consent from their payment service user has the right to access the requested information, irrespective of their relationship with the account servicing PSP.

Article 67 goes to great lengths to limit the access to, use of, storage, and sharing of financial data to protect the payment service user and their privacy. But with the current scope of the AIS, it becomes relatively easy for AISPs to sidestep the limits set out in the article by offering a broadly defined service.[58] This could indicate that while drafting the provision, with the goals of improving competition and innovation in the market for payment services, the balancing tools to ensure proper consumer protection might have been neglected slightly. This also raises the question as to whether it is responsible to place the control of access in the hands of the payment service users, who are ultimately consumers.

3.3.2 Impact on market participants

Articles 66 and 67 contribute to all three Directive goals. The goal of competition is pursued by transferring the power to accept or allow access to payment service users' payment accounts from the account servicing PSP—often being a credit institution—to the payment service user. This forces incumbent institutions to give access to new entrants upon request from the payment service user. The provisions allow for more service providers to enter the market, as they no longer depend on bilateral agreements with incumbents, but rather their ability to acquire customers. By increasing the number of service

[58] This problem is also highlighted by Gimigliano, 'Chapter 9—Title IV, "Rights and obligations in relation to the provision and use of payment services", chapter 2 "Authorisation of payment transactions" (Arts 64-77)' 161.

providers on the market, competition is expected to increase and become more efficient.[59]

The entrance of new service providers into the market for payment services also paves the way for two potential improvements in innovation in financial services. The first is the impact of new entrants, who often enter the market because of new innovative solutions they wish to offer on the market. This will naturally boost financial innovation. The other aspect is the increased competition. If there are more providers on the market, market participants will be incentivised to innovate their provision of services, in order to gain a greater market-share.[60] Essentially, both the expected market improvements stemming from increased competition and improved financial innovation advance the Directive's goal of consumer protection. But the transfer of power in the provisions also independently contributes to improving consumer protection. This happens because the payment service users, among which are many consumers, are given a nearly unrestricted choice of which service provider they want to use.

Examining the two provisions, it is clear that the goals of the Directive have influenced the content. The goal of competition is evident by allowing more service providers to enter the market, although to balance supply with demand, the crucial access to payment accounts is dependent on payment service users requesting such access. This also intertwines with the goal of consumer protection, as more choices and control of one's payment account are intended to improve consumer welfare. Lowering the entry barriers and making the market more accessible for new entrants also seeks to increase financial innovation, the third Directive goal. The preliminary works of the Commission and other EU institutions prior to the adoption of the PSD2 support the statement that these goals did indeed play a key role when drafting the Directive. This is a significant finding for legal scholarly work as it documents the interplay of law and economics when drafting legislation and hence highlights the importance of using economics in the analysis of law. What is now interesting to consider is the impact the Directive has had on market participants.

The primary market participants to consider in this context are the account servicing PSPs and the third-party PSPs providing either the PIS or the AIS. The former, who offer deposit accounts to their customers, will be authorised as credit institutions and are thus subject to a much more demanding and

[59] Wolters and Jacobs, 'The security of access to accounts under the PSD2' 31.

[60] For a similar perception cf. Iris H-Y Chiu, *Regulating the Crypto Economy: Business Transformations and Financialisation* (Hart Publishing 2021) 196.

scrutinising regulatory framework than institutions authorised as payment institutions under the PSD2. With articles 66 and 67, their freedom to conduct business was confined to a forced relationship with third-party PSPs. And this relationship was enforced without remuneration but instead entailed further costs to develop functional APIs to provide an interface in compliance with the access requirements of the provisions.[61]

On the opposite side of the playing field, we have the third-party PSPs who, due to the nature of their services, were unable to provide services to customers if the account servicing PSP refused access. On a free market, the will of the account holders—the payment service users—might have forced the account servicing PSPs to contract with the third-party PSPs in order to retain customers. With the regulatory intervention which articles 66 and 67 constitute, the legislator has attempted to level the playing field in advance. This measure does provide undeniable progress towards the goal of innovation on payment services by ensuring access for new entrants, but for the goal of competition the state of things is less clear. There is no doubt that ensuring access to payment accounts is vital for third-party PSPs, yet a full, free access upon the payment service user's request might be tipping the balance too much in favour of third-party PSPs.[62] To be able to understand the full motivations for the provisions, it is necessary to examine the position of payment service users further, as consumer protection plays a significant role in the regulatory framework for payment services.

3.3.3 Payment service users' biased decision-making

Payment service users can generally be separated into two categories, the payer, often a consumer, and the payee, often a merchant, although it is increasingly possible for them to be another consumer. The focus of the Directive is to increase consumer protection, and the focus in this section will therefore be on payment service users who are consumers. What is interesting in this case, where the payment service user has been granted the power to control access to their payment account, is that this access has been granted predominantly

[61] For a critique of the free access for third-party providers see Finans Danmark, *Finance Denmark's response to the Commissions consultation on the review of the revised Payment Services Directive (PSD2)* (2022) 2; European Banking Federation, *EBF response to European Commission Consultation on the review of the revised payment services Directive (PSD2)* 58; for a more descriptive process see Wolters and Jacobs, 'The security of access to accounts under the PSD2' 31.

[62] The professional organisation for credit institutions in Denmark also pointed to an imbalance and an unlevel playing field in Finans Danmark, *Finance Denmark's response to Targeted consultation on the review of the revised payment services Directive (PSD2)* (2022) 19 as well did European Banking Federation, *EBF response to European Commission Consultation on the review of the revised payment services Directive (PSD2)* 58.

to consumers. As we see in other areas, such as the GDPR, the trend is to grant consumers excessive influence and control over personal decision-making. When this control expands into the consumer's financial decision-making, other factors should be considered than simply improving consumer welfare. As presented in chapter 2, a sub-category of asymmetric information is the consumer's biased, individual decision-making, and when linked to financial decisions, the consumer's financial literacy becomes of high importance too.

The OECD defines financial literacy as 'a combination of awareness, knowledge, skill, attitude, and behaviour necessary to make sound financial decisions and ultimately achieve individual wellbeing.'[63] Consumers must have, and be aware of this, knowledge and understanding of financial concepts and risks, and the skills, motivation, and confidence to apply such knowledge and understanding in order to make effective decisions across a range of financial contexts, to improve their financial well-being in the short and long term, and to enable them to participate in economic life.[64] But whereas financial literacy includes elements of financial knowledge and skills to manage money, financial capabilities are also affected by mental capacity.[65] This is where financial capabilities and consumers' individual, biased decision-making intertwines. In neoclassical economic thinking man, or people, are rational when making decisions. This means that a person will make the decision that is most beneficial for themselves based on the available information. But for consumers, the general view is that they are not rational in decision-making. Instead, consumers hold biases that are individual to their personal experiences and preferences. Combining this with the average low financial literacy among consumers[66] does not necessarily suggest that the outcome of the transfer of power in articles 66 and 67 will be improved consumer welfare.

The primary subject of protection regarding consumers in relation to the access provisions in articles 66 and 67 is their financial data. To protect the payment service user's data, the articles go to great lengths to forbid the storage of sensitive payment data of the payment service user,[67] requesting any data other than those necessary to provide their services,[68] and the use, access, or storage of any data for purposes other than for the provision of their services as explicitly requested by the payment service user, in accordance with data protection

[63] OECD, *OECD/INFE Toolkit for Measuring Financial Literacy and Financial Inclusion* (2018) 4.

[64] OECD, *PISA 2018 Assessment and Analytical Framework* (2019).

[65] Andrea Lučić, Dajana Barbić and Marija Uzelac, 'Theoretical underpinnings of consumers' financial capability research' (2022) International Journal of Consumer Studies 1, 8.

[66] OECD, *OECD/INFE 2020 International Survey of Adult Financial Literacy* (2020) 7.

[67] Directive (EU) 2015/2366 (PSD2) art 66(3)(e).

[68] Directive (EU) 2015/2366 (PSD2) art 66(3)(f) and art 67(2)(e).

rules.[69][70] Although the Directive places these restrictions on the third-party PSPs, the limitations can be circumvented or modified depending on the design of the service offered by the third-party PSP.[71] The design and content of the access provisions show that even though consumer protection is of great importance to the legislator, the objective of market growth in payment services, supporting further competition and innovative developments, has taken priority.[72]

The ESAs have, in accordance with the founding regulations' article 9(1)(b), published a joint repository focusing on financial education and digitalisation initiatives of NCAs.[73] The authorities are required to take a leading role in promoting transparency, simplicity, and fairness in the market for consumer financial products and services across the internal market. This includes reviewing and coordinating financial literacy and education initiatives by the competent authorities. The initiatives are important steps toward improving financial literacy among consumers and enabling them to manage the powers granted to them by articles 66 and 67. The EBA is also aware of the challenge for regulators and supervisors which financial innovation developments represent, and how they could potentially undermine consumer protection, the level playing field, the integrity of the financial markets and the stability of the financial system.[74] Although the provisions could potentially improve financial inclusion, particularly in Member States with low financial inclusion, balancing with financial literacy among consumers seems to have been neglected in favour of supporting financial innovation. The limited ability of consumers to make sound financial decisions is not aligned with the extensive and intervening character of the power which they possess after the implementation of the PSD2, considering the impact they could have on the protection of their financial data.

4 Evaluation—Fair competition after PSD2?

When evaluating the regulatory measures applied to address and mitigate failures, it is necessary to revisit the framework within which the analysis is

[69] Directive (EU) 2015/2366 (PSD2) art 66(3)(g) and art 67(2)(f).
[70] Wolters and Jacobs, 'The security of access to accounts under the PSD2' 31.
[71] Wolters and Jacobs, 'The security of access to accounts under the PSD2' 32.
[72] Wolters and Jacobs, 'The security of access to accounts under the PSD2' 40.
[73] European Supervisory Authorities, *Joint ESAs thematic repository of national financial education initiatives on digitalisation—with a specific focus on cybersecurity, scams and fraud* (2022).
[74] European Banking Authority, *EBA Financial Education Report 2019/2020* (2020) 19.

situated. In section 2, two primary problems were identified. First, the market failure of inefficient competition explicitly manifesting itself in market control and unfair entry barriers. Secondly, the non-market failure of the legislative mismatch between the scope of the PSD1, causing third-party PSPs to not be covered by the Directive, and the innovative development in financial services driven by such third-party PSPs. The task for the PSD2 was thus to revise the regulatory framework to be flexible in scope, accounting for future innovative developments and inducing appropriate incentives to ensure efficient competition.

When evaluating the PSD2's management of the problems described, this must be done with the Directive's goals in mind, but the purposes of individual articles should also be considered. The goals of the PSD2 comprise effective competition, consumer protection, and improving conditions for innovation, but the primary objectives of the provisions treated in this chapter were competition, innovation, and creating a level playing field.

4.1 Freedom to conduct business

Before the regulatory intervention, which the PSD2 with its articles 35, 36, 66, and 67 constitutes, credit institutions and payment institutions were free to conduct business based on the parties' individual interests. This meant businesses were able to decide, among other things, their own risk profiles, who they were associated with, and the terms of cooperation with contractual parties. Unfortunately, it also resulted in a payment services market where credit institutions held and exercised market control. Being able to control entry into the market distorts competition and affects the development of the market negatively, both in terms of economic growth and innovation. This market failure justified a regulatory intervention to re-establish efficiency in the market for payment services. But did the intervention, in its efforts to level the playing field, in fact end up going too far in favour of third-party PSPs, creating a new form of unlevel playing field?

The access provided through article 35 to participate in payment systems is perhaps the least intrusive of the measures discussed in this chapter. The access does not entail building or sharing systems but instead secures a right to participate on equal terms with other payment institutions. This access must hence contain fair and objective participation terms that apply to all payment institutions participating in the payment system. What is being curtailed with this provision is the payment system owner's right to deny access based on subjective reasons or competitive considerations. This part of the provision, its first paragraph, does not seem to have caused trouble in practice, based on case numbers. Instead, the provision's second paragraph, the exemption rule, has caused unclarity in practice. Considering the circumstances of the *American Express* case,[75] it can hardly be argued that the exemption rule, and its limit of extent in the second sub-paragraph, is too intrusive on financial institutions' freedom to conduct business.

Article 36, on the other hand, reduces the freedom to conduct business in an entirely different manner than article 35. By setting strict limitations on justifiable reasons to deny access to a credit institution's payment account services, credit institutions see themselves as forced to contract with payment institutions which they would not otherwise have dealt with. This measure, interfering directly with how credit institutions conduct business, is of an intrusive character, yet it is also balanced by the ability to decline access for objective, non-discriminatory, and proportionate reasons.[76] As was presented above in section 3.2.1, reasons related to risk exposure were found to be proportionate in justifying a rejection, whereas other reasons such as the payment institution's reputation and assumptions about business plans and illegal behaviour were found to be discriminatory and not objective. This indicates that article 36 has created a more level playing field in practice, without being unreasonable to some market participants. As the cases presented in section 3.2.1 showed, credit institutions did try to force payment institutions into a disadvantageous position, being without a payment account service, and the regulatory intervention was therefore necessary to create fair competition in the market for payment services.

The most encumbering regulatory intervention is the addition of articles 66 and 67. Although it happens at the request of payment service users, the provisions give third-party PSPs the indispensable access to payment accounts that enables them to provide their services. But this access involves costs that are carried by credit institutions, such as developing a new API. On top of this, the credit institutions are expected to give the required access for free. The market control problem prior to the adoption of these articles was not ideal for ensuring a level playing field, but neither is the situation created with the provisions which gives preferential treatment to third-party PSPs that effectively reverses the unlevel playing field.

[75] Case C-643/16 *American Express*.

[76] Although European Fintech Association, *Position Paper on the Revised Payment Services Directive 2* does call for better access and points to credit institutions using AML to decline requests for payment accounts by payment institutions.

Considering the Directive's motivation to improve consumer welfare might nuance this discussion. The access to payment accounts ensures consumers have more choices in their selection of payment services, presumably at a better price, both of which generally improve consumer welfare. But spill-over effects might include higher prices for consumers on other services with their account servicing PSP, as a result of the costs connected to providing the interface necessary for access under articles 66 and 67. Adding the problem of consumers' individual, biased decision-making and (limited) financial literacy, using the consumer protection perspective to justify the intrusive character of the provisions is not convincing. It is one thing to point out a problem with current legislation, but without a viable solution, this holds little value.

When evaluating the problem caused by the measure the PSD2 applied to the initial market failure, it is important to keep in mind the goals of the Directive and how the current measure missed the mark. The primary concerns behind articles 66 and 67 are the goals of competition and innovation, but the Directive's goal of consumer protection must also be remembered. A solution proposed by a professional industry organisation[77] is to make it possible for all parties involved in enabling the services of articles 66 and 67 to be able to monetise these services. The current wording of the provisions, particularly article 66(4)(c) and article 67(3)(b), only requires the account servicing PSP to execute transactions and treat data requests without any discrimination, unless objective reasons apply. The former also highlights charges vis-à-vis payment orders transmitted directly by the payer. A black letter interpretation of these provisions does not limit the possibility of charging third-party PSPs a reasonable amount for providing the access, as long as this happens in an objective and non-discriminatory manner. A reasonable amount could be set by assessing the costs of maintaining the APIs in good order taking into account the number of service users and providers accessing the API. To ensure a level playing field, the EBA should use its powers delegated by the founding regulation article 9—to promote transparency, simplicity, and fairness in the market for consumer financial services—to establish guidelines for standardised monetization for all parties involved in maintaining APIs and access to payment accounts.

Recapitulating, while the provisions treated in this chapter restrict or change the way credit institutions can conduct business, it is only in the case of articles

[77] Finans Danmark, *Finance Denmark's response to the Commissions consultation on the review of the revised Payment Services Directive (PSD2) and a European organisation also supports a revision which allows all parties to monetize on this, see*; European Banking Federation, *EBF response to European Commission Consultation on the review of the revised payment services Directive (PSD2)* 3 and 58.

66 and 67 that the restrictions have altered the relationship between credit institutions and third-party PSPs too far, to one side's advantage. Fortunately, an interpretation of the current wording of the provisions does not rule out adopting standardised rules to level the playing field through fair possibilities to monetise for all participants.[78]

4.2 Transfer of power and consumer protection

A question which should be posed when considering the transfer of power inherent in articles 66 and 67 is, how far should we go in the quest to protect consumers? The spectrum ranges from giving consumers full autonomy to make their own decisions, including leaving them to collect and understand financial information entirely independently, to a full-on cotton wrapped protection scheme with no autonomy and no need for financial understanding. Neither extreme is desirable for society, but where is the perfect balance in between?

The PSD2 goes a long way to ensure the disclosure of information to consumers when using payment services, and articles 66 and 67 seek to protect the consumer's payment data. But this is also necessary when the provisions leave it to consumers to decide who gets access to their payment accounts. What essentially seems to need attention is the consumer's individual biased decision-making process and particularly improving financial literacy among consumers in the EU. This is a difficult matter to address, as the acceptance of any steps toward increasing financial knowledge and understanding among consumers is dependent on consumers being willing and aware of their need to improve financial literacy.[79] Recognising this difficulty, the primary measures applied so far in financial regulation have focused on disclosure rules.[80] The application of disclosure rules, mandating what information a service provider must share with its customers, is common in financial services and addresses the problem of collecting information. When a service provider is obliged to disclose information to the service user, the service user has been

[78] Although, the best solution might be to move the AIS, including art 67, to the Proposal for a Regulation of the European Parliament and of the Council on a framework for Financial Data Access and amending Regulations (EU) No 1093/2010, (EU) No 1094/2010, (EU) No 1095/2010 and (EU) 2022/2554 (COM(2023) 360 final) [2023].

[79] And as showcased in the European Banking Authority, *EBA Financial Education Report 2019/2020* the national competent authorities have taken different measures to address this problem.

[80] An example in the PSD2 is Title 3 entitled 'Transparency of Conditions and Information Requirements for Payment Services'. The provisions places information, or disclosure, requirements upon PSPs prior to contracting with payment service users.

supplied with the necessary information to base sound financial decision-making upon. But if the recipient of this information does not possess the capabilities to process the information adequately, or is biased instead of rational in their decision-making, the availability of the information alone cannot ensure sound financial decisions.

This is indeed where the initial question again becomes relevant to ask. Can or should government take further initiatives to protect consumers who are not able to process the disclosed information adequately to make sound financial decisions? When it comes to the EU's internal market for payment services, the issue is further complicated by the inability to solve the problem centrally. Not only because of the lack of competence delegation to, for example, the EBA, but also because of the different national languages and varying cultures present in the Member States. To address the problems. present in each Member States, it might be necessary to leave it to the NCAs to educate their consumers, which would be a disadvantage to the PSD2's objective of full harmonisation.

Legislation can only go so far towards creating a safe regulatory framework. By drafting a framework which seeks to ensure appropriate market conduct and disclosure of necessary information, the legislator has come a long way towards making sound financial decision-making possible for consumers. It is impossible to control the acts and decisions of each consumer, but to regulate the service providers in a manner that ensures safe, transparent, and fair market behaviour is possible. The PSD2 intervenes to correct the market failure of imperfect competition, to create a level playing field with fair competition and room for innovation, yet it still manages to take measures to protect consumers and improve consumer welfare. The answer to the question must therefore be that the PSD2 performs adequately to protect consumers.

4.3 Striking a balance

The legislator, with the provisions treated in this chapter, sets out to manage the market failure of imperfect competition, but also to redeem the non-market failure caused by the narrow scope of the PSD1 in light of the innovative development in payment services. The goals of the examined articles shared a common interest in improving competition and innovative growth in the EU payment services industry, which conduct of business rules had been used to varying degrees to achieve. But the Directive also seeks to generally improve consumer protection, which should be included in reflections on how these provisions perform in addressing the initial market and non-market failures.

Based on the findings in section 3, the legal intervention has successfully achieved the goal of improving competition on the market for payment services, as the articles enable more new providers to enter the market.[81] Although it can be argued, as above in section 4.1, that articles 66 and 67 in their current implementation have taken things a step too far, resulting in a less familiar form of unlevel playing field, where the credit institutions are the ones left at a disadvantage. However, it would be possible to address this problem through guidelines from the EBA on standardised rules for all participants to monetise the investments put into developing and maintaining APIs.[82] The efforts toward improving competition, particularly for third-party PSPs, but also small and medium sized PSPs, directly affect the goal of innovation. By lowering the entry barriers for new, innovative PSPs, the PSD2 accommodates more innovation in payment services.

The last goal of the PSD2, concerning consumer protection, has not taken a central position in these articles. The goal is particularly important to consider when discussing articles 66 and 67, as these ensure access to payment service users' payment accounts. Although the access can only be provided through the payment service user's request, there exists a concern that consumers do not possess sufficient financial knowledge and understanding, including the understanding of how their data is used and processed, to be able to make informed, sound decisions regarding this access. This is combined with the easily circumventable wording of article 67, whereby third-party PSPs can describe their services broadly enough to be able to access monetizable financial data on their users.[83]

Overall, it can be argued that in this case, with the management of imperfect competition addressed by articles 35, 36, 66, and 67, consumer protection has been given a lower priority in order to make room for innovative developments and growth in the EU market for payment services.[84] However, it should also be remembered that part of the driving force behind innovative development in financial services is the demand among consumers. The market is providing what is demanded, which is more personalised services that are tailored to fit the individual payment service user.

[81] Michał Polasik and others, 'The impact of Payment Services Directive 2 on the PayTech sector development in Europe' (2020) 178 Journal of Economic Behavior & Organization 385 also documents an increase in granted licenses after the implementation of PSD2.

[82] Perhaps similar to the data sharing schemes proposed in the Proposal for FiDA.

[83] Wolters and Jacobs, 'The security of access to accounts under the PSD2' 32f.

[84] Wolters and Jacobs, 'The security of access to accounts under the PSD2' 40.

6

FINANCIAL FRAUD AND THE PSD2

1 Introduction

Financial institutions are more prone to being exploited for money laundering purposes than non-financial companies.[1] As such, financial crime is a sector-wide problem for financial institutions. Limiting the scope to payment institutions, financial crime often covers money laundering, terrorist financing, and financial fraud.[2] These crimes are, if we exclude pure cash crimes, dependent on banking services, including payments. With the continuous developments in financial innovation, the risk of new ways to commit financial crimes appearing also rises.[3] The regulatory framework therefore needs to be flexible and visionary in order to prevent financial crime, and hard-hitting when sanctioning crime ex-post. By examining this topic from a law and economics angle, it is possible to analyse the issues, objectives, measures, and results from a perspective that accounts for economic rationale, societal feelings of justice, and the legal toolbox available.

This chapter explores the preventive measures, sanctions, and motivations that exist to fight financial crime on the EU internal market for payment services. The scope of the chapter has been limited to cover financial fraud only, as money laundering and terrorist financing could take up the space of an entire book alone.[4] Furthermore, the PSD2 does not contain provisions specifically addressing money laundering or terrorist financing, as the Directive in articles 5(1)(k), 19(1)(b), and 32(6) simply refers to required compliance with Directive (EU) 2015/849 (AMLD4).

[1] Bank for International Settlements, *AML and CFT in Banking—Executive Summary* (2021); Expert Group on Regulatory Obstacles to Financial Innovation (ROFIEG), *30 Recommendations on Regulation, Innovation and Finance* (2019) 11.

[2] Michael Levi, 'Financial Crimes' in Michael Tonry (ed), *The Oxford Handbook of Crime and Public Policy* (OUP 2009) 225 provides an overview of types of economic crime.

[3] Expert Group on Regulatory Obstacles to Financial Innovation (ROFIEG), *30 Recommendations on Regulation, Innovation and Finance* 10f; Levi, 'Financial Crimes' 238.

[4] Although it would have been interesting to investigate, for example, the relationship between the payment institution and the credit institution in relation to the payment institution's AML compliance, and their customers' AML compliance further, this will have to be pursued elsewhere.

EU Payment Services. Louise Damkjær Christensen, Oxford University Press. © Louise Damkjær Christensen 2025.
DOI: 10.1093/9780198949084.003.0006

Section 2 will explain the current penal and preventive measures, how financial crime is indeed a market failure, and how government could take action to address this issue. The third section examines the legal measures to prevent financial crime in the PSD2 and the relationship to the meta-goals of financial innovation, regulatory strategies, and providing the most efficient incentives through regulation. Section 4 will evaluate the prior two by discussing the appropriability of the measures applied to the described market failure.

2 Financial fraud as an externality

In a utopian market, providers can set the prices of their products, produce them, and sell them to customers without worrying about how others might utilise or abuse their product for personal gain, while also harming societal interests.[5] In the real world, providers of financial services have long been ordered to comply with certain requirements to prevent financial crimes such as fraud and money laundering. There is no doubt in financial regulation that the problem of financial fraud is a sector-wide problem. This also explains why it is considered a meta-goal of financial regulation to prevent financial crime.[6]

Financial fraud is a sub-category of the overarching category of financial crime. Financial fraud occurs when someone takes money, or other assets, from a person through deception or criminal activity. From the perspective of payment services, financial fraud can be committed either by the person entitled to use the payment instrument, or by a third-party. In the first-party situation, the payment service user exploits their payment instrument, for example through an overdraft on a credit card which was not contractual. The primary victim of such crime is the PSP or credit institution suffering the loss inflicted by the payment service user. With third-party fraud, the payment service user is instead the primary victim defrauded of money or other assets.

With the developments in financial innovation, particularly new solutions for providing payment services, increased attention to the goal of preventing financial crime becomes necessary. With more opportunities to defraud consumers of their funds, the requirements to security measures in payment solutions must be more strict. Payment institutions can and should play an active role in applying preventive measures to protect against financial crime.

[5] Levi, 'Financial Crimes' 226 describes the economic and societal damage caused by financial crime further.

[6] As was discussed in more detail in chapter 3.

From the perspective of a payment institution providing payment services, when determining the price of their services, the objective of preventing financial crime is not calculated into the equation as it does not contribute to profit maximisation for the company. Financial crime is the utilisation of financial services, often for personal gain at the expense of others, but the financial institution is not necessarily directly affected. The institution might see an impact on its share price or reputation if proper precautions against financial crime have not been taken, but these are external factors which the institution cannot account for in its calculation of product prices. In a free market, prior to regulatory intervention, financial crime can therefore best be categorised as an externality. Since the consequences of financial crime impact society negatively, it is a negative externality which government wishes to diminish.

On the free market, there is no incentive for payment institutions to voluntarily—and free of charge to the end user—prevent financial crime, as it does not affect their income directly. Government therefore needs to create sufficient incentive to motivate payment institutions to take adequate precautions, for example through regulation which internalises the costs. When the market develops and creates new ways for criminals to utilise the financial system for criminal behaviour, government can be required to take further initiatives to prevent financial crime. Subsection 2.1 will explain this relationship between financial fraud and financial innovation further.

Within criminal law, the deterrence theory tries to change behaviour through laws and punishment, ie we sanction to mould behaviour in a societally desired manner. This can be combined with the societal desire to punish the unwanted behaviour performed by criminals. As such, the criminal sanction can have both a preventive and penal effect.[7] From an economic perspective we assume that persons, natural as well as legal, are rational decision makers that decide what to do based on what is most valuable to them. This means that if government wish to use less of a good or avoid a certain behaviour, government make it more costly to choose that option or make it cheaper to behave in another, desirable way.[8] These would most likely be perceived as

[7] Alison S Burke and others, *SOU-CCJ230 Introduction to the American Criminal Justice System* (Open Oregon Educational Resources 2019) section 1.8 on the crime control model and section 5.5 on the neoclassical criminology theory; Elena Maculan and Alicia Gil Gil, 'The Rationale and Purposes of Criminal Law and Punishment in Transitional Contexts' (2020) 40 Oxford Journal of Legal Studies 132 section 3.

[8] Robert Cooter and Thomas Ulen, *Law and Economics* (6th edn, Berkeley Law Books 2016) 460f; Steven Shavell, 'The Optimal Structure of Law Enforcement' (1993) 36 Journal of Law and Economics 255.

preventive measures. Ex-post government would sanction financial fraud severely enough to discourage the behaviour.

As such, financial fraud is inefficient because effort is being put into protecting and stealing property. These efforts could have been used more efficiently elsewhere for value creation.[9] When an objective, such as to avoid or prevent financial crime, is of extremely high importance to society, it is based on both a problem of economic inefficiency and the need to create safety for citizens. Here, government can decide to implement preventive (ex-ante) measures in combination with ex post sanctions. The second subsection, 2.2, will explain the relationship between ex-ante and ex-post regulatory measures further, and discuss their interdependent relationship.

2.1 Financial fraud and financial innovation

Financial services have long been impacted by a continual increase in financial innovation.[10] This has resulted in increasing digital solutions for users of financial services. For the payment services market, this can be illustrated with the addition of the PIS and the AIS, which depend ultimately on the connection to an Application Programming Interface (API).[11] The development in financial innovation fits well into the European Commission's strategy for the EU retail payment services market,[12] and although financial innovation is creating more applications, opportunities,[13] and choices for payment service users, it also brings about an increased risk of financial crime and threats to consumer welfare in general.[14]

In many ways, financial innovation has led to a digitalisation of financial services, making payment services either internet based, card based, or phone (app) based. This changes the interface for service users when the payment is conducted online or via smartphone, as the 'salesperson' is removed from the equation. The 'salesperson' would previously embody an amount of trust

[9] Shavell, 'The Optimal Structure of Law Enforcement'.

[10] EY, *Global FinTech Adoption Index 2019* (2019); Peter Yeoh, 'Innovations in Financial Services: Regulatory Implications' (2016) 37 Business Law Review 190.

[11] The increased activity in open banking and the relationship to its broader 'sibling' is also addressed in Sarah Lamont, *Open Banking Walked so Open Finance Could Run* (Fintech Prime Time 2024).

[12] European Commission, *The Retail Payments Strategy* (European Commission 2020).

[13] Dirk A Zetzsche and others, 'From FinTech to TechFin: The Regulatory Challenges of Data-Driven Finance' (2018) 14 New York University Journal of Law & Business 393, 416.

[14] Zetzsche and others, 'From FinTech to TechFin: The Regulatory Challenges of Data-Driven Finance' 427; European Banking Authority, *EBA Guidelines on ICT and security risk management* (2019) 3 and 30.

for the user and provide required information for the payment service user to make well-informed financial decisions. Added to this issue is the increase in financial data connected to the individual payment service user.[15] When using digital payment services, the user gives access to their financial data. To process their request, the provider uses and creates further data about the user. These data can be utilised to optimise marketing, advice, and product supply, but can also be exploited for criminal offences such as financial fraud or identity theft. Essentially, working towards realising the goal of improving innovative development in financial services also entails a classic market failure, externalities. How the PSD2 has addressed this failure will be examined in section 3.1.[16]

Most of the measures mentioned so far are ex-ante initiatives to prevent financial crime, but the regulatory framework also needs to manage the situation where the crime has been committed and a payment service user might have lost funds. In such situations, it is necessary to balance the interests of the PSP, any account servicing PSP, and the payment service user claiming to be the victim of a financial crime. How the regulatory framework tackles this situation will be examined further in section 3.2.

To summarise, even though financial innovation is a Directive-specific goal of the PSD2, it also involves issues in relation to preventing financial crime, which is a meta-goal of financial regulation. As there are generally two dominating tendencies when it comes to combatting financial crime, the following section 2.2 will discuss strategies of using sanctions and precautions.

2.2 Sanctions or prevention?

It is very important when drafting legislation to consider which tools or regulatory strategies to apply. Prior to drafting a new or revised regulatory framework, it should be decided what the framework's purpose is. For the PSD2, this has been defined to be the improvement of competition, consumer protection, and innovation.[17] To achieve these goals, it is then necessary to consider which regulatory strategies to apply, and which risks inherent to the market

[15] Zetzsche and others, 'From FinTech to TechFin: The Regulatory Challenges of Data-Driven Finance' 430 on the increased aggregation of data.

[16] European Commission, *Green Paper: Towards an integrated European market for card, internet and mobile payments* (COM(2011) 941 final) (2012) 3 also mentions improved security and safety of payments as an objective for a revised Directive.

[17] European Commission, 'FAQ: Making Electronic Payments and Online Banking Safer and Easier for Consumers' (2019) <https://ec.europa.eu/commission/presscorner/detail/en/qanda_19_5555> accessed 16 June 2022.

must be prevented. Preventive measures and sanctions relate particularly to the latter part of taking precautions against risks. Before delving into the considerations necessary when choosing between sanctions and precautions, it is useful to outline what, in the present context, is understood by sanctions and precautions.

In the context of financial fraud, sanctions not only cover criminal or penal sanctions, such as imprisonment or fines imposed by a court of law, but also encompass administrative sanctions, such as fines imposed by national competent authorities (NCAs).[18] The NCA will often have a repertoire of available sanctions when enforcing current law. If a misdemeanour is not severe enough to trigger a fine, other enforcement actions could include 'naming and shaming', injunctions, or prohibitions. Precautions, or preventive measures, on the other hand cover a wide array of actions or options. Preventive measures can be divided into business branches, and as the focus here is limited to payment institutions, the precautions outlined will cover this sector only.

The preventive measures applied are often not intended to protect the individual payment institution but instead aim to protecting payment service users and society in general. The individual payment service user could be exposed to theft of banking data or identity theft, resulting in personal financial losses. Society, or perhaps more precisely the government's treasure chest, would also suffer loss of income from taxes if money laundering is not prevented.

As these descriptions suggest, there is an important distinction to be made between sanctions and precautions. Maintaining this distinction between prevention and sanctions is also important when aiming towards creating more efficient law enforcement.[19] Where sanctions are formed in a general manner, preventive measures are drafted with the aim to prevent more specific actions. A sanction in criminal law could be applied to any crime which in general terms fulfils the conditions described in the provision, whereas preventive measures must be more specific to be administrable in practice. This will also be illustrated in section 3 where specific preventive measures will be examined.

When considering how to draft a regulatory framework, it should not be taken for granted that payment institutions will take an efficient amount of precaution. As is known within economic theories of tort law, incentives are necessary to ensure an efficient amount of precaution. This serves the purpose to internalise externalities.[20] When the PSP does not directly see an impact on

[18] There is of course also the dimension of civil or private sanctions but these fall outside the scope of the subject treated here.

[19] Shavell, 'The Optimal Structure of Law Enforcement' 255.

[20] Cooter and Ulen, *Law and Economics* 189; Shavell, 'The Optimal Structure of Law Enforcement' 271.

businesses turnover if their customers experience financial fraud it is, as described in subsection 2.1, an externality. This also means that there is no direct economic incentive for payment institutions to take the efficient amount of precaution. The preventive measures are per se public goods, as everyone can use them, for example by going through Know-Your-Customer requirements prior to becoming a customer with a payment institution, but your use of them will not pre-empt others from using them as well. To make sure that payment institutions have an efficient amount of precaution to protect against financial fraud, government must create incentives for payment institutions to implement and apply the needed measures. This can be resolved through regulation.

For regulation and supervisory authorities' enforcement thereof to be effective, sanctions are required. The sanctions should address who is responsible, what type of sanctions to apply, and whether informal settlement should be an option.[21] A particularly important feature of sanctions is the range applicable for supervisory authorities and their match with the severity of the breach of compliance.[22] There must be proportionality between the undesired behaviour and the applicable sanction, but this match must also meet the economic requirements relevant for preventive measures. If it is cheaper for the party to pay a fine for breaching a rule than to comply with that rule, the sanction is inefficient. As such, both preventive measures and sanctions must be drafted with economic incentives in mind, to ensure effective enforcement of the regulatory framework.

When discussing the application of sanctions and precautions, it should not be a question of which to apply to a given area, but instead it is a matter of creating the right balance between the two.[23] Such a balance should incentivise payment institutions to take the efficient amount of precaution, ie the sanction must be more costly than the costs of taking precautions.[24] Preventive measures protect the financial system and society, but the sanctions criminals can expect are equally important to efficiently incentivise them to not commit crime.[25] These considerations are important to remember when examining a regulatory framework with a meta-goal of preventing financial crime. The

[21] Iain MacNeil, 'Enforcement and Sanctioning' in Niamh Moloney, Eilís Ferran and Jennifer Payne (eds), *The Oxford Handbook of Financial Regulation* (OUP 2015) 295f.

[22] MacNeil, 'Enforcement and Sanctioning' 296.

[23] Maculan and Gil Gil, 'The Rationale and Purposes of Criminal Law and Punishment in Transitional Contexts' section 3.A.2 on the importance of prevention; Shavell, 'The Optimal Structure of Law Enforcement'.

[24] Cooter and Ulen, *Law and Economics* 460f; Burke and others, *SOU-CCJ230 Introduction to the American Criminal Justice System* section 5.5 describes this from a criminology perspective.

[25] Levi, 'Financial Crimes' 241; Shavell, 'The Optimal Structure of Law Enforcement' 274f on the problem with this balance in criminal law.

considerations will therefore be included in section 3 below where specific measures to prevent financial crime in payment services will be examined. The regulatory intervention and the considerations on sanctions and precautions will also contribute to the discussion in the fourth section.

3 Regulatory measures to prevent financial crime

The key issue with financial crime is the person committing the criminal act. With financial fraud, this person is rarely the payment institution, but instead someone taking advantage of the payment service's existence to commit their devious actions. This causes a problem for the legislator, as their tools to adjust behaviour can scarcely control the person committing the criminal act. For this, they have the option of criminal sanctions. While the legislator can incentivise criminals not to commit these unwarranted actions through penal sanctions, the toolbox is considerably larger when looking at preventive measures and financial institutions. With the current supervisory architecture, even more possibilities arise for society to keep financial crime in check.[26]

This section examines the measures applied to ensure safe and secure payment services. First, the Directive's measures to manage security risks, for example the SCA requirements for authentication, will be scrutinised to show how regulation is addressing the developments in financial innovation on the payment services market. This part constitutes an examination of selected preventive measures in the Directive. The second part of the examination will investigate the ex-post measures in the PSD2. As such, the section examines what happens when it all goes wrong. This will show the current relationship between ex-ante preventive measures and ex-post sanctions or reactions, including an examination of the liability rules ex-post the criminal offence in the case of financial fraud and of the sanctions applicable to persons who do not comply with the rules set out in the regulatory framework.

3.1 Preventing financial fraud

With increased innovation and focus on security aspects of digitalised payment services, the PSD2 introduced a new addition to the previous regulatory framework. Title IV, Chapter 5, consisting of articles 95–98, is entirely new to

[26] Initiatives within so-called RegTech and SupTech have been particularly popular in recent years.

the PSD2. The expansion is largely due to the inclusion of third-party PSPs, which calls for new precautions to deal with operational and security risks.[27] These measures all share a focus on preventing abuse of the financial system and protection of payment service users. To deal with the growing risks related to financial innovation, the chapter addresses the problem from three angles.

The first tool to manage the risks is article 95, which prompts Member States to ensure that PSPs establish a framework with mitigation measures and control mechanisms to manage the operational and security risks related to the services they provide. This framework includes an obligation for PSPs to establish and maintain effective incident management procedures which must include the detection and classification of major operational and security incidents.

The second paragraph of article 95 proceeds from the first paragraph to require PSPs to provide updated and comprehensive assessments of their operational and security risks relating to their provision of payment services to the NCA, on at least an annual basis. This reporting requirement also includes an assessment of the adequacy of the mitigation measures and control mechanisms the PSP has implemented in response to the risks relating to their provision of payment services.

While the two first paragraphs impose requirements upon the PSPs, paragraphs 3 to 5 contain requirements for the EBA, which serve to support the adoption and implementation of the first two paragraphs. The EBA is instructed to issue guidelines in accordance with article 16 of its founding regulation,[28] on the establishment, implementation, and monitoring of the security measures. These guidelines must, when requested by the Commission, be developed into draft regulatory technical standards, which the Commission in article 95(4) has been delegated competence to adopt. Lastly, the EBA is instructed to promote cooperation on the area between the NCAs and the ECB, including the sharing of information.

Another area where security and protection of payment service users play an instrumental role is in relation to the protection of data. The Directive's article 94(1) allows processing of personal data by payment systems and PSPs when this is necessary to safeguard the prevention, investigation, and detection of

[27] Ruth Wandhöfer, 'Title IV "Rights and Obligations in Relation to the Provision and Use of Payment Services", Chapter 5 "Operational and Security Risks and Authentication" (Arts 95-98)' in Gabriella Gimigliano and Marta Bozina Beroš (eds), *The Payment Services Directive 2—A Commentary* (Elgar Commentaries in Financial Law, Edward Elgar Publishing 2021) 189.

[28] Regulation (EU) No 1093/2010 of the European Parliament and of the Council of 24 November 2010 establishing a European Supervisory Authority (European Banking Authority), amending Decision No 716/2009/EC and repealing Commission Decision 2009/78/EC [2010] OJ L 331/12.

payment fraud. This must of course be carried out in accordance with the rules on data protection in the GDPR.[29] Prior to adopting the Directive, the European Data Protection Supervisor issued an opinion on a draft for the Directive.[30] Here, the authority stressed the need for further data protection initiatives in the Directive, which to a great extent influenced changes to the draft, including the final wording of this article.[31] The provision addresses the issue of financial fraud specifically, and aims to prevent future fraud by setting up mechanisms to detect it. As such, there is a welcome interplay between article 94 and the mechanisms set up in article 95.

The second paragraph of article 94 further stresses that PSPs are only to access, process, and retain personal data necessary for the provision of their payment services, and only with the explicit consent of their payment service users. The wording of this paragraph, from a black letter interpretation, allows the PSP to define their payment services in a rather wide scope to allow for wider access to data, processing of such data, and retainment of it.[32] From a teleological interpretation, with the goal of increased consumer protection in mind, it would not be possible to exploit the provision to harvest financial data from payment service users. Unfortunately, the actual wording of a provision is traditionally given greater weight when deciding on the correct interpretation. The lack of consumer protection in relation to article 94(2), and the wide scope it allows for PSPs to access financial data of payment service users, is unfortunate and does not seem to be balanced by other means of protection.

Where article 95 instructs PSPs to establish and use a system to detect and manage risks, article 96 treats the process when an incident occurs. In the case of a major operational or security incident, PSPs must notify their NCA without undue delay. If this incident might also have an impact on the financial interests of the PSP's payment service users, the users must also be informed about both the incident and the measures they can take to mitigate its effects.

[29] Regulation (EU) 2016/679 of the European Parliament and of the Council of 27 April 2016 on the protection of natural persons with regard to the processing of personal data and on the free movement of such data, and repealing Directive 95/46/EC (General Data Protection Regulation) [2016] OJ L 119/1.

[30] European Data Protection Supervisor, *Executive Summary of the Opinion of the European Data Protection Supervisor on a Proposal for a Directive of the European Parliament and of the Council on payment services in the internal market amending Directives 2002/65/EC, 2006/48/EC and 2009/110/EC and repealing Directive 2007/64/EC, and for a Regulation of the European Parliament and of the Council on interchange fees for card-based payment* transactions (2014/C 38/07) (Official Journal of the European Union 2014 C38 14 2014).

[31] Gloria González Fuster, 'EU Data Protection and Future Payment Services' in Gabriella Gimigliano (ed), *Bitcoin and Mobile Payments* (Palgrave Macmillan 2016) 186.

[32] González Fuster, 'EU Data Protection and Future Payment Services' 189; Pieter T J Wolters and Bart P F Jacobs, 'The security of access to accounts under the PSD2' (2019) 35 Computer Law & Security Review 29.

When an NCA receives such a notification, it must forward this information about the incident without undue delay to the EBA and ECB, and if necessary to relevant authorities in the Member State. Other NCAs will be notified if the EBA and ECB find it of relevance, in cooperation with the notifying NCA. The ECB must also assess the incident's potential to cause issues relevant to the payment system and notify the European System of Central Banks where relevant. PSPs are also required to provide statistical data on fraud relating to different means of payment to their NCAs, who are to share this data in aggregated form with the EBA and ECB.

The collection of data on fraud makes it possible to follow the developments in financial fraud across Member States and provides insight into the impact of regulatory measures applied to fight financial crime. As with the previous article, the EBA is instructed to issue guidelines in accordance with the founding regulation's article 16. PSD2 article 96(3) instructs the EBA to issue guidelines, first to PSPs on the classification of major incidents and the content etc. expected for notifying such incidents, and secondly to NCAs on the criteria for how to assess the relevance of the incident and the details required for the incident reports. This represents a centralisation of the power to decide what constitutes an incident and how these are to be reported. As such, it removes discretion from Member States and centralises it to ensure harmonised implementation of these security provisions across the EU.

Articles 95 and 96 are both divided into two functions. First, each provision instructs PSPs on requirements for their management of operational and security risks. Each provision then instructs supervisory authorities on the expected handling of incidents, and delegates power to the EBA to issue guidelines and regulatory technical standards. Both provisions seek to improve the general security of increasingly digital payment services. This contributes to improved quality of payment services, but establishing and implementing such procedures and mechanisms is also costly for the PSPs. Inflicting these requirements upon PSPs, and particularly new entrants, can bring about two independent consequences. For one, the prices for payment services could be affected, as the total costs of providing payment services rise, causing the price equilibrium to increase. Rising prices do not contribute positively to consumer welfare. The second consequence relates to the Directive's goal of improving conditions for innovation. Raising the bar on requirements for the PSPs management of operational and security risks also raises the bar for new entrants wanting to participate in the market.

The seemingly disharmonious relationship between innovation and security illustrates an important balance which the Directive must take due care of. By requiring a specific standard, as is done with articles 95 and 96, the legislator ensures that even new innovative providers comply with certain security standards which are essential to maintaining a safe payment services market. As such, it can be said that in this situation, security is more important than the freedom which new entrants can innovate within.

Where articles 95 and 96 address security concerns in a more general manner, article 97 addresses the issue very specifically and formalises payment security requirements into law.[33] The provision sets requirements for strong customer authentication for the use of payment services. Furthermore, as an addition to the substantive requirements in article 97, article 98 delegates the EBA to draft regulatory standards related to strong customer authentication. This combination of provisions and their content and potential impact deserves further examination in the following subsection 3.1.1.

3.1.1 Strong customer authentication

In its efforts to protect payment service users, and especially consumers, from becoming the victims of financial crime, the PSD2 applies strict rules on authentication. This is done by obligating PSPs to develop and implement strong customer authentication (SCA). Authentication is a procedure which allows the PSP to verify the identity of a payment service user or the validity of the use of a specific payment instrument and the use of the user's personalised security credentials.[34] Strong customer authentication is an independent authentication based on the use of two or more elements categorised as knowledge (something only the payment service user knows),[35] possession (something only the payment service user possesses),[36] and inherence (something the payment service user is).[37] What makes the authentication strong is the independence, meaning that the breach of one element does not compromise the reliability of the others, and it is designed in such a way as to protect the confidentiality of the authentication data.[38]

[33] European Banking Authority, *Opinion of the European Banking Authority on the implementation of the RTS on SCA and CSC* (2018) 7, para 30.

[34] Directive (EU) 2015/2366 of the European Parliament and of the Council of 25 November 2015 on payment services in the internal market, amending Directives 2002/65/EC, 2009/110/EC and 2013/36/EU and Regulation (EU) No 1093/2010, and repealing Directive 2007/64/EC [2015] OJ L 337/35 art 4(29).

[35] For example, a password or PIN code.

[36] For example, a payment card, a mobile phone, or a one-time password sent via short messaging system (SMS).

[37] These include biometrics such as fingerprint, voice recognition, facial recognition, iris, pulse, and even behavioural characteristics.

[38] Directive (EU) 2015/2366 (PSD2) art 4(30).

To clarify what constitutes an SCA, the EBA, in their opinion of 13 June 2018,[39] stated that the two elements must belong to two different categories in order to conform with the requirements set out by the Directive. Opinions from the EBA are soft law instruments. The one in question here has been drafted with reference to the EBA Regulation's article 29(1)(a), prompting them to play an active role in building a common Union supervisory culture and consistent supervisory practices, and the recipients here are the NCAs. If this opinion were to be considered to make the rules under the PSD2 more strict, its status as a soft law instrument would be problematic.[40] Instead, if we perceive the opinion as an interpretative measure that simply clarifies the content and intention of existing legal rules, there is no issue. Perceiving the instrument in this way is also in best concord with its legal foundation, being to play an active role in building common and consistent supervisory practices across the Union.

The question of what constitutes the three independent elements was tested in a case before the Danish Financial Board of Appeal,[41] where a payer had been the victim of financial fraud, but the PSP declined to cover the loss.[42] The Board of Appeal argued that the use of credit card data and a text message code both belong to the same category, possession. The authentication process was therefore found to not comply with the SCA requirements, and the PSP was liable for the loss incurred by the payment service user. Of specific interest in relation to opinions issued by the EBA, the Financial Board of Appeal used an opinion issued by the EBA in 2019[43] to interpret the understanding and contents of the required security elements of an SCA.

By going to such lengths about the definition and content of authentication, the PSD2 adds significant new measures towards improving protection against

[39] European Banking Authority, *Opinion of the European Banking Authority on the implementation of the RTS on SCA and CSC* para 33.

[40] This was also discussed in chapter 2, section 3.2.

[41] 165/2020 *Indsigelse mod at hæfte for misbrug af betalingskort i forbindelse med phishing. Spørgsmål om, hvorledes der var sket anvendelse af engangskode sendt via SMS* [2020] Det finansielle ankenævn (Danish Financial Board of Appeal).

[42] The Financial Board of Appeal also previously decided on similar matters in cases 88/2019 *Indsigelse mod korttransaktion efter modtagelse af falsk e-mail og indtastning af oplysninger på falsk hjemmeside. Modtagelse af 3D Secure sms, der alene angav en talkode.* [2019] Det finansielle ankenævn (Danish Financial Board of Appeal); 137/2019 *Indsigelse mod korttransaktion vedrørende et køb hos en udenlandsk internetforretning gennemført ved brug af 3D Secure/Verified by Visa* [2019] Det finansielle ankenævn (Danish Financial Board of Appeal); 94/2019 *Indsigelse mod korttransaktioner vedrørende køb hos to udenlandske internetforretninger gennemført ved brug af 3D Secure/Verified by Visa* [2019] Det finansielle ankenævn (Danish Financial Board of Appeal); 144/2018 *Indsigelse mod transaktion, der blev genenmført som en '3D Secure' betaling.* [2018] Det finansielle ankenævn (Danish Financial Board of Appeal); 243/2019 *Indsigelse mod transaktioner gennemført ved 3D Secure* [2019] Det finansielle ankenævn (Danish Financial Board of Appeal).

[43] European Banking Authority, *EBA Guidelines on ICT and security risk management.*

operational and security risks.[44] Its predecessor, the PSD1, only contained two articles referring to the term 'Authentication'—the definition in article 4(19) and article 59. The first defined authentication as a procedure which allows the PSP to verify the use of a specific payment instrument, including its personalised security features. Article 59 addressed the provision of evidence in the case of a user denying the authorisation of an executed payment transaction, or the incorrect execution of a transaction. Neither defined the content or process of authentication.[45]

Furthermore, the PSD1 did not contain any provisions specifically on the operational and security risks related to payment services. The addition of Title IV, Chapter 5 of the PSD2 should be seen in relation to the development in financial services, with innovation playing a significant part in the evolution of new services, specifically the AIS and the PIS. As described above in section 2.1, the addition of new innovative services has made it possible to remove the physical, in-branch 'salesperson', enabling internet and mobile banking activities. The remote factor also applies to other payment services, stressing the importance of greater attention to PSPs' handling of these risks.

To deal with the authentication process, PSD2's article 97 (1) places the obligation on all Member States to ensure that PSPs apply strong customer authentication, where the payer a) accesses its payment account online, b) initiates an electronic payment transaction, or c) carries out any action through a remote channel which may imply a risk of payment fraud or other abuses. While litra a) and b) cover the general scope of the application, litra c) catches any exceptions if they imply a risk of financial crime.

The second paragraph of article 97 further specifies that the PSP in their SCA must include elements which dynamically link the payment transaction to a specific amount and a specific payee. This measure aims to ensure certainty for payers, so that they can be certain of the amount transferred and the recipient of the amount in non-proximal, remote situations such as e-commerce.[46] This paragraph naturally serves to improve consumer protection in payments by securing transparency and disclosure of relevant available information for all remote payment transactions.

[44] Mary Donnelly, 'Payments in the digital market: Evaluating the contribution of Payment Services Directive II' (2016) 32 Computer Law & Security Review 836.

[45] Wandhöfer, 'Title IV "Rights and Obligations in Relation to the Provision and Use of Payment Services", Chapter 5 "Operational and Security Risks and Authentication" (Arts 95-98)' 190.

[46] Wandhöfer, 'Title IV "Rights and Obligations in Relation to the Provision and Use of Payment Services", Chapter 5 "Operational and Security Risks and Authentication" (Arts 95-98)' 199.

The provision's third paragraph places the obligation to ensure adequate security measures to protect the confidentiality and integrity of payment service users' personalised security credentials upon the PSP. This stresses the importance of confidentiality and integrity of the payment service user's credentials, and should be read in the context of articles 66 and 67 which require account servicing PSPs to provide facilities to communicate securely with PISPs and AISPs.[47] Furthermore, articles 66 and 67 force the account servicing PSPs to allow access to all payment accounts that are accessible online when this is necessary for the third-party provider to provide their services.[48] Such access must be accompanied by a reliance on the authentication procedures provided by the account servicing PSP for the AISP and PISP being in accordance with article 97(5).

The article's fifth paragraph contributes to improving working and start-up conditions for new innovative entrants by exempting them from the requirement of issuing their own authentication procedures and credentials.[49] This enables them to act as light intermediaries who can facilitate value-adding services without having to cater to all payment service users and without opening additional accounts.[50] The provision improves circumstances for new innovative entrants, who can keep compliance costs down, as well as for payers requesting a payment initiation from a merchant via the merchant's PISP, without having to on-board or apply other disincentivising requirements. Though these aspects are positive and contribute towards two of the Directive's goals, the third goal, competition, has not necessarily been affected positively. The measure does level the playing field from the new entrants' point of view, if this entrant is a third-party PSP, but from the perspective of incumbent institutions it has the opposite effect. The provision burdens account servicing PSPs further by placing obligations upon them, not only on their own behalf, but also in regard to third-party providers, which are their direct competitors. This skews the playing field and favours one category of PSPs over another. The fairness of this will be discussed further in section 4.

Finally, article 97(4) emphasises that PISPs are also obligated to comply with the second and third paragraph, and AISPs to comply with the first and

[47] Directive (EU) 2015/2366 (PSD2) art 66(3)(b) for PISP and art 67(2)(b) for AISP.

[48] This was also treated in detail in chapter 5.

[49] Commission delegated Regulation (EU) 2018/389 of 27 November 2017 supplementing Directive (EU) 2015/2366 of the European Parliament and of the Council with regard to regulatory technical standards for strong customer authentication and common and secure open standards of communication [2017] arts 30(2) and 33(5).

[50] Wandhöfer, 'Title IV "Rights and Obligations in Relation to the Provision and Use of Payment Services", Chapter 5 "Operational and Security Risks and Authentication" (Arts 95-98)' 201.

third paragraph. This serves to clarify that even when the payer acts with a PISP or AISP as intermediary, it is not possible to evade the requirement for applying SCA.[51] As such, the provision can be perceived as a means for the legislator to avoid evasion of the SCA requirement through creative interpretation of the provision's first paragraph. Considering the definition of a PSP in article 4(11) as '*a body referred to in art. 1(1) or a natural or legal person benefitting from an exemption pursuant to art. 32 or 33*', it should be clear that both the PISP and the AISP are covered by the term 'PSP' as referred to in article 97(1). Nonetheless, the legislator has taken initiative to curb the interpretative opportunities in order to secure safe payments for all payment service users. This also contributes to protecting the payments market from the increased risks of financial innovation by ensuring sector wide application of safety measures such as the SCA.

To fill in the practical content of article 97, the Directive delegates competence in article 98(4) and (5) to the EBA to create, review, and update a regulatory technical standard (RTS) setting out the rules for SCA and common and secure open standards of communication (CSC). The further criteria that this RTS must take into consideration is listed in paragraphs 1–3 of the provision. This resulted in the adoption of the RTS on SCA and CSC by the European Commission on 27 November 2017,[52] which introduce detailed requirements and exemptions. With the adoption by the European Commission, the RTS drafted by the EBA becomes binding for all Member States.

Of particular interest for the topic treated here is the RTS' specification of the contents of article 97(1). Article 10 of the RTS allows account servicing PSPs to not require SCA when a payment service user wants to access their payment account online through an AISP.[53] The exemption is voluntary for account servicing PSPs to implement, causing issues for some AISPs. The issue arises because when the AISP has to apply SCA every time a payment service user accesses the service, it is more burdensome and poses a barrier to use, which also makes for differing user rules depending on the payment service user's account servicing PSP. As such, making the exemption voluntary leaves it to the discretion of incumbent institutions to decide whether to make room for AISPs, ie new innovative providers, or if they wish to raise the bar of entry.

[51] Wandhöfer, 'Title IV "Rights and Obligations in Relation to the Provision and Use of Payment Services", Chapter 5 "Operational and Security Risks and Authentication" (Arts 95-98)' 200.

[52] RTS 2018/389 on SCA and CSC.

[53] Wandhöfer, 'Title IV "Rights and Obligations in Relation to the Provision and Use of Payment Services", Chapter 5 "Operational and Security Risks and Authentication" (Arts 95-98)' 202 for a more detailed specification of the provision.

Among the more interesting provisions in the RTS filling in rules regarding article 97(1)(b) —the payer initiating a payment—are the rules on contactless and low-value payments in articles 11 and 16.[54] The provisions make it possible to execute payment transactions without SCA if they stay below a given amount and below a cumulative number of consecutive transactions. This applies to both in-store usage and online purchases (remote), but the values allowed without SCA are lower for online transactions than for in-store purchases. The exemption improves accessibility and ease-of-use for payers when initiating transactions. Considering the number of payers using payment services who are consumers, the exemption improves the overall consumer welfare by improving the service accompanying a payment service. Although the ease-of-use for payers is increased with this measure, it also raises the possibility of abuse as possession of the payment instrument, for example a credit card, is sufficient to initiate transactions.

Another exemption to the use of SCA can be found in the RTS' articles 18, 19, and 20, which allow PSPs to not use SCA when they conclude that a remote payment transaction is low risk. This exemption is dependent on the PSP using transaction risk analysis, which naturally adds costs to the provider's total cost of providing their services, making it more affordable to providers who are able to benefit from economies of scale. To be allowed to apply the exemption the PSP must have basis points of fraud below certain levels, have complied with certain procedural requirements in terms of informing the regulator that they intend to make use of the exemption, and to have implemented transaction risk analysis as a real-time monitoring mechanism. By making the exemption conditional on the use of transaction risk analysis in real-time, the provision shows a balance which takes into account the respective interests of the PSP and the payment service user, while also including considerations on the meta-goal of preventing financial crime.

The last group relating to article 97(1)(c) concerns payment service users carrying out any action through a remote channel which may involve a risk of fraud. This part is especially interesting for the topic of this chapter as to how the PSD2 addresses the problem of financial crime in payment services. The wording of the provision is general, unlike its two preceding provisions, and entails a wide scope of application. Litra c) is a catch-all provision and can be perceived as the safety net below the other provisions, picking up everything

[54] Wandhöfer, 'Title IV "Rights and Obligations in Relation to the Provision and Use of Payment Services", Chapter 5 "Operational and Security Risks and Authentication" (Arts 95-98)' 203 for a full walk-through of all provisions relating to the payer initiating a payment.

that falls through. This safety-net ensures that no PSP can interpret the safety provisions in a way to evade the requirements established to ensure safe and secure payments, and as such, the provision is a necessity in the work towards preventing financial crime.

3.1.2 The delegation of competence

The provisions of the PSD2 Title IV, Chapter 5 contain several different delegations of competence to the EBA to issue guidelines and RTSs. The contents of these delegations vary and the specificities of the delegations particularly have different forms. This can entail different consequences in terms of discretion left to the EBA and NCAs, and can have an instructive effect on the final products if the delegations become too rigid. The fluctuating degree of discretion calls for a further examination of the delegation provisions in Title IV, Chapter 5 of the PSD2.

The first delegation concerns article 95(3), which instructs the EBA to issue guidelines in accordance with article 16 of its founding regulation.[55] Article 16 directs the EBA to issue guidelines and recommendations with the purpose of establishing consistent, efficient, and effective supervisory practices within the European System of Financial Supervision. The guidelines and recommendations can be addressed to competent authorities, as well as to financial institutions, who are required to make every effort to comply with the guidelines and recommendations or otherwise explain why they are non-compliant. Article 95(3) states that the EBA, in close cooperation with the ECB and consulting all relevant stakeholders to reflect all interests involved, shall issue guidelines with regard to the establishment, implementation, and monitoring of the security measures, including certification processes where relevant. The provision does not specify an addressee, but considering the content, the natural recipient of the guidelines would be PSPs.[56] The delegation gives the EBA great discretion with regards to the further content of the guidelines, as the provision does not entail further specifications other than that the guidelines must address the establishment, establishing and implementing security measures, and the monitoring of security measures. Paragraph 4 of article 95 continues by delegating to the EBA the power to develop draft RTSs based on the experience acquired in the application of the guidelines, which the Commission has delegated power to adopt in accordance with articles 10-14 of the EBA Regulation.

[55] EBA Regulation no 1093/2010.

[56] The current version of the guidelines, European Banking Authority, *EBA Guidelines on ICT and security risk management*, also mentions PSPs as their primary recipient at 11.

Where article 95 left the field wide open for the EBA to further define the contents of the guidelines, article 96(3) goes a bit further into detail on the expectations for the guidelines, which are also to be issued in accordance with the EBA Regulation's article 16. As with the instructions in article 95(3), article 96(3) instructs the EBA to issue the guidelines in close cooperation with the ECB, consulting all relevant stakeholders to reflect all interests involved. The recipients of the guidelines have been separated into two groups with further, specified, intended content. The first group is PSPs, whose guidelines must detail the classification of major incidents, including the content, format, standard notification templates, and procedures for notifying such incidents. The second group is competent authorities whose guidelines must define the criteria on how to assess the relevance of the incident, and the details of the incident reports to be shared with other domestic authorities. Paragraph 5 further states that the guidelines must take into account standards or other specifications developed and published by the European Union Agency for Network and Information Security for sectors pursuing activities other than payment service provision. Although this delegation of competence to the EBA contains two specific recipient groups, the general wording of the provisions is similar to the general style used in article 95(3). Like the preceding article, article 96 gives discretion to the EBA to develop suitable guidelines for the payment services market.

Compared to the two preceding delegations the situation with articles 97 and 98 is rather different. For one thing, the delegation has been moved to article 98, making article 97 the substantive rules for market participants to comply with whilst article 98 delegates power to the EBA to further detail the content and expectations set out in article 97 in RTSs, in accordance with article 10 of the EBA Regulation.[57] Again, the draft shall be developed in close cooperation with the ECB and must include a consultation with all relevant stakeholders to reflect all interests involved. The expectations of the RTS are fleshed out over the course of three paragraphs.[58]

The first paragraph identifies the areas of article 97 that the EBA is to specify. This includes the requirements of SCA, the exemptions from applying SCA, which security measures must be complied with for the purpose of protecting the confidentiality and integrity of the payment service users' personalised security credentials, and the requirements for CSC for the purpose of

[57] EBA Regulation no 1093/2010.

[58] Wandhöfer, 'Title IV "Rights and Obligations in Relation to the Provision and Use of Payment Services", Chapter 5 "Operational and Security Risks and Authentication" (Arts 95-98)' 201f.

identification, authentication, notification, and information, and requirements for the implementation of security measures.

The second paragraph could be considered more unusual as it defines the purpose or rationale of the draft RTS. According to article 98(2), the RTS must include the following considerations: '*(a) ensure an appropriate level of security for payment service users and payment service providers, through the adoption of effective and risk-based requirements, (b) ensure the safety of payment service users' funds and personal data, (c) secure and maintain fair competition among all payment service providers, (d) ensure technology and business-model neutrality, and (e) allow for the development of user-friendly, accessible and innovative means of payment*'.

Further specification of the guiding criteria for the content of the RTS is made in paragraph three, which states the criteria which the exemptions from applying SCA must be based on. The paragraph makes it mandatory to base the exemptions on the level of risk involved in the service provided, the amount or/and the recurrence of the transaction, and the payment channel used for the execution of the transaction. As such, little discretion has been left to the EBA with regards to the content, purpose, or eligible criteria to develop the draft RTS.

Granted, the delegation in article 98 is with regards to a draft RTS, whereas the delegations in articles 95 and 96, in the first instance, is only as regards guidelines which are of lower value in the legal hierarchy. The power to draft the RTS is delegated pursuant to TFEU article 290, and will, once adopted by the Commission, have binding force across the Union. The guidelines are of soft law character and are not binding, but through article 16 of the EBA Regulation, Member States and their NCAs are required to provide best efforts towards compliance. This would seemingly justify greater detail in the provision delegating power to draft RTSs, compared to those regarding guidelines.

Article 290, which enables the Commission to be delegated power to adopt RTSs,[59] calls for the delegation in a legislative act to clarify the objectives, content, and scope of the RTSs, but how confined does this have to be? Other RTSs draft delegations in the PSD2 include articles 15, 28, and 29, of which only the delegation in article 29 has some degree of confinement. As such, there would seem to be no legal reason to differentiate the discretion left to the EBA when drafting RTSs. Whether this can be reasoned with a varying degree of care or

[59] The delegation to draft such RTSs which the Commission can adopt is made under the legislative act, here PSD2, with reference to the EBA Regulation art 10 which is adopted by the European Parliament and the Council.

with conflicts in the process of drafting specific provisions is also unknown, but it does spark the question whether this is problematic for the confidence placed in the EU institutions to ensure quality regulation which contributes towards a harmonised internal market.[60]

3.1.3 Consumer duties

Although many of the preventive measures applied by the PSD2 have the PSP as their addressee, the Directive also addresses the payment service user in order to protect their funds.[61] As such, the Directive applies conduct rules on the payment service user—where the Directive expects the payer to often be a consumer—to mould their behaviour in the desired manner. Unlike the moulding mentioned above in section 2, the purpose here is not to prevent criminal activity committed by the payment service user, but to protect them from becoming the victim of financial crime. The following will further examine the duties placed upon consumers in the PSD2, and the relationship with the Directive's goals.

The obligations of the payment service user when using a payment instrument and the personalised security credentials can be found in the Directive's article 69.[62] The provision states that it is the duty of a payment service user, entitled to use a payment instrument, to use the payment instrument in accordance with the terms governing the issuance and use of the payment instrument, and to notify the PSP without undue delay on becoming aware of the loss, theft, misappropriation, or unauthorised use of the payment instrument.

According to the provision's second paragraph, it is furthermore the duty of the payment service user to take all reasonable steps to keep their personalised security credentials safe. The Directive's article 4(1)(31) defines personalised security credentials as personalised features provided by the PSP to a payment service user for the purposes of authentication. The issuance of the personalised security credentials is an obligation placed on the PSP by article 70(1)(a), which also entails an obligation, without prejudice to the one placed on the payment service user in article 69, to make sure that the information is not accessible to other parties. The personalised security credentials are key to performing the strong customer authentication treated in section 3.1.1, which was

[60] Donnelly, 'Payments in the digital market: Evaluating the contribution of Payment Services Directive II' 839 argues that the increase in evolvement of EBA for guidelines, recommendations, and RTSs is an attempt to increase supervisory harmonisation across Member states.

[61] Directive (EU) 2015/2366 (PSD2) recital 69.

[62] Donnelly, 'Payments in the digital market: Evaluating the contribution of Payment Services Directive II' 833 on the provision's relationship with its predecessor.

put in place to maximise the preventive measure against financial fraud and abuse of payment services.

The question of interest is, how much care is enough for a consumer to fulfil their obligations in article 69? The Directive's recital 72 offers some guidance on this question, although it is ultimately up to the individual Member State's national law. The recital mentions that negligent conduct implies a breach of the duty of care, and gross negligence involves a significant degree of carelessness. This would be the case if the pin-code to a credit card was written on a post-it note placed on the credit card, or if the security credentials used for a payment service app were kept on the back of the phone. The key element here is that the duty is breached when the credentials are placed beside the payment instrument in a manner that is open and easily detectable by third parties. From this, it can also be concluded that by not writing down or in any way sharing the personalised security credentials, the payment service user protects themselves significantly from any accusations of negligence.

In a case decided by the Danish Financial Board of Appeal,[63] the complainant claimed that their credit card had been abused and the app on their phone authorising the transaction had been hacked. The credit institution, which was the PSP, maintained that the complainant had acted with gross negligence, as the payment had been authorised using the personalised security credentials and the transaction was executed using strong customer authentication. When the payment was to be authorised using the mobile app, a message is shown with the request, naming the payee and the amount. By authorising the payment without checking that the information was correct or initiated by the payer, the payer became liable for the transaction value and had to bear the loss personally because of gross negligence.

The case illustrates what happens when the payment service user has undoubtedly not observed the duty of care placed upon them by article 69(2), but it also shows the risks connected to innovation and new payment solutions. The negligent behaviour of not checking that the payee and amount is correct when authorising via the mobile app would not have been possible if innovation had not created the solution. The innovation places higher demands on consumers and their financial and technical literacy. The SCA was designed to protect payment service users from the fraudulent behaviour displayed in the case by the third-party abusing the payment service configuration, but not

[63] 83/2022 *Indsigelse mod korttransaktion, der blev gennemført som en 3D Secure betaling ved godkendelse i NemID-nøgleapp.* [2022] Det finansielle ankenævn (Danish Financial Board of Appeal).

even the SCA can protect consumers from authorising a payment transaction without checking that the payee and amount are correct.

The recitals of the PSD2 clearly state that the obligations placed on payment service users are to protect consumers from becoming victims of fraud and unauthorised access to payment accounts.[64] However, it is an unusual measure to directly address consumers as a regulatory tool,[65] because consumers are considered more difficult to address effectively. For example, the supervisory authorities do not have tools to supervise whether consumers observe their duties, this is left for courts or tribunals to decide when the damage is done, as was the situation with the Danish case mentioned above.

As such, the new developments in payment services, largely due to increased innovation, have raised the bar of what a consumer must be capable of to manage their personal finances. But the obligations in article 69 are also necessary to create incentive for consumers to protect their funds. If there were no incentives, moral hazard would be a likely problem, as the consumer would have their funds recovered whether they protect their payment instruments and personalised security credentials or not. This would not be reasonable for the parties which would have to pay the costs of such a system, be it the payment institutions or society in general through national guarantees. The increased expectations on consumers, and hence the change in consumer protection, are necessary to accommodate innovation and competition on the market for payment services, and constitute a balance created by the regulator to accommodate all participants and all goals.

3.2 Ex-post measures—What happens when it all goes wrong?

From the perspective of economics and efficiency, prevention can only carry society to a certain point, from which it becomes inefficient in terms of costs to go further, compared to the costs of financial crime. When financial crime does occur, it is important that the regulatory framework is equipped with suitable response options. The response must address the interests of the parties affected or injured by the criminal act. The first person who comes to mind when dealing with financial fraud is the payment service user who is being defrauded of their money. The PSD2 handles this situation with provisions on liability for

[64] Directive (EU) 2015/2366 (PSD2) recital 69.

[65] John Armour and others, *Principles of Financial Regulation* (OUP 2016) 76 where financial education is used as a user (or consumer) oriented tool, but the actual obligations are placed on, eg, supervisory authorities to provide such education.

unauthorised transactions which cover articles 71–74. The further contents of these articles will be examined in subsection 3.2.1. The analysis will investigate the Directive's ability to further its goals of competition, innovation, and consumer protection and balance these with preventing financial crime.

The second group of interests to cultivate belongs to society in general. Sanctions can serve multiple purposes,[66] two of which are deterrence from committing crime and retribution. The latter is important for society's sense of justice.[67] When a person commits a crime, it is important to restore the balance that has been skewed by the criminal act. This can be done through sanctions upon the person or company who commits a criminal act or does not comply with the agreed regulatory framework. The second subsection, 3.2.2, will examine the options provided in the PSD2 to sanction non-compliance. Sanctioning criminal acts entails elements of criminal law and is therefore outside the scope of the subject treated in this book.

3.2.1 Who is liable in the case of financial fraud?

Where a payment service user has been defrauded of money through a payment service, there can be three or four participants involved in the situation.[68] First, we have the payment service user who has suffered a monetary loss. Secondly, we have the criminal committing the crime. Thirdly, we have the PSP, and if the PSP is a PISP we also have a fourth player, the account servicing PSP. The question is, who is liable for the loss incurred by the payment service user? The obvious answer is the criminal who is responsible for the loss occurring, but given the nature of crime this is rarely an option. Due to the scope of the subject treated here, this is also where we remove the criminal from the equation and focus on the three remaining participants.

Before delving deeper into the rules provided by the PSD2 to solve this issue, it is worth outlining the financial interests of the participants and the Directive, and how these might be in conflict. The payment service user is interested in recovering the lost amount of money. The PSP, whether this is a PISP or an account servicing PSP, is interested in limiting their monetary loss as much as possible. In a regulation-free market this would result in the PSP not covering any part of the payment service user's loss. The Directive

[66] Maculan and Gil Gil, 'The Rationale and Purposes of Criminal Law and Punishment in Transitional Contexts' section 3.

[67] Maculan and Gil Gil, 'The Rationale and Purposes of Criminal Law and Punishment in Transitional Contexts' section 3.A.1.

[68] Alan Brener, 'Payment Service Directive II and Its Implications' in T. Lynn and others (eds), *Disrupting Finance* (Palgrave Pivot, Cham. 2019) 108 also highlights the lack of clarity on liability in PSD1.

aims to improve consumer protection, which includes a situation where a consumer has suffered a monetary loss due to being the victim of financial crime. At the same time, the Directive also aims to ensure fair competition and a level playing field, while improving conditions for innovation to thrive. This means that the Directive cannot place full liability on either the payment service user or the possible PSPs, as this would be in conflict with one or more goals of the Directive. To balance the goals of the Directive and the interests of the parties, the Directive applies articles 71–74[69] to create a regulatory framework which can resolve the conflicts of interest in the case of financial fraud using payment services.[70]

The step in the process after the crime has been committed is for the payment service user to notify the PSP of the unauthorised payment transaction. The PSP must be notified without undue delay after the payment service user becomes aware of the transaction, and no later than 13 months after the debit date.[71]

PSD2 article 71(1) gives the payment service user the right to have an unauthorised payment transaction rectified. This means that the PSP must restore the user's payment account to the state it was in before the unauthorised transaction, which includes not only replacing the missing funds but also any interest or fees for overdraft etc.[72] The deadline for notifying the PSP is set to be as short as possible, to reduce the risks and consequences of unauthorised transactions.[73] This also serves other interests as well. For one, if the response of the payment service user is rapid, potential interest which will have to be rectified will also be of less monetary value, which is in the interest of the rectifying PSP. Another reason relates to stopping further misuse of the payment instrument which has been misused for unauthorised transactions, including increasing the likelihood of identifying the person who committed the crime.

When the payment service user notifies the PSP of the unauthorised payment transaction, submitting their claim for rectification, the PSP will naturally want to ensure that the payment service user has not acted with gross

[69] These provisions also handle cases of incorrectly executed payment transaction but due to the subject being treated in this chapter focus is only on unauthorised payment transactions.

[70] Marte Eidsand Kjørven, 'Who Pays When Things Go Wrong? Online Financial Fraud and Consumer Protection in Scandinavia and Europe' (2020) European Business Law Review 77, 88f also provides an overview of the liability regime of the PSD2.

[71] Directive (EU) 2015/2366 (PSD2) art 71(1).

[72] Gabriella Gimigliano, 'Chapter 9vTitle IV, "Rights and obligations in relation to the provision and use of payment services", chapter 2 "Authorisation of payment transactions" (Arts 64-77)' in Gabriella Gimigliano and Marta Bozina Beroš (eds), *The Payment Services Directive 2—A Commentary* (Elgar Commentaries in Financial Law, Edward Elgar 2021) 150.

[73] Directive (EU) 2015/2366 (PSD2) recital 70.

negligence. To protect the payment service user from its assumed stronger opponent, the PSP, the Directive states in article 72(1) that the burden of proof for authorisation of the payment transaction is placed on the PSP.[74] The PSP is required to provide evidence to prove that payment transactions were authenticated, accurately recorded, entered in the accounts, and not affected by a technical breakdown or some other deficiency of the service provided.

Article 72(2) goes further in favour of the payment service user, as it states that where a payment service user denies having authorised an executed payment transaction, the use of a payment instrument which is recorded by the PSP in accordance with article 72(1), is not sufficient in itself to prove either that the payment transaction was authorised by the payer, or that the payer acted fraudulently or failed with intent or gross negligence to fulfil their obligations under article 69. Fraud or gross negligence requires further evidence to be proved, which must be provided by the PSP. Where there is a strong suspicion that an unauthorised transaction is the result of fraudulent behaviour by the payment service user, and this is based on objective grounds, the PSP should, depending on national laws, be able to conduct further investigations within a reasonable time. However, if these investigations do not confirm such a suspicion, the payment service user's account must be rectified, with a credit value date no later than the date when the lost amount was debited.[75] To assess whether a payment service user has acted negligently when using a payment instrument, we return to the obligations placed on the payment service user in article 69.

The obligation in article 69(2), to take all reasonable steps to keep their personalised security credentials safe, is of particular importance when dealing with negligence in relation to unauthorised payment transactions.[76] As discussed above in section 3.1.3, the Directive offers some guidance to assess negligence but also refers to national law. To incentivise the payment service user to observe the duties in article 69, the limit which the user can at most be liable for, when these duties have been observed, has been set at EUR 50.00, with the purpose of ensuring a harmonised and high level of user protection within the EU.[77] As previously concluded, the bar is set relatively low for the payment

[74] Donnelly, 'Payments in the digital market: Evaluating the contribution of Payment Services Directive II' 835; Maria Raquel Guimarães and Reinhard Steennot, 'Allocation of Liability in Case of Payment Fraud: Who Bears the Risk of Innovation? A Comparison of Belgian and Portuguese Law in the Context of PSD2' (2022) European Review of Private Law 29. 56; Kjørven, 'Who Pays When Things Go Wrong? Online Financial Fraud and Consumer Protection in Scandinavia and Europe' 89.

[75] Directive (EU) 2015/2366 (PSD2) recital 71.

[76] Kjørven, 'Who Pays When Things Go Wrong? Online Financial Fraud and Consumer Protection in Scandinavia and Europe' 94.

[77] Directive (EU) 2015/2366 (PSD2) recital 71.

service user to be able to avoid accusations of negligence, making it difficult for the PSP to provide the required evidence to support a suspicion of negligence.

The PSP's liability is described in article 73, which correlates with the notification of unauthorised transactions in article 71.[78] When notified, the PSP must refund the payer the amount of the unauthorised transaction immediately, and never later than the following business day, except for cases with reasonable grounds for suspecting fraud. As established in article 71, the payer has the right to have their payment account rectified, which means that the PSP must return the payment account to the state it would have been in had the unauthorised transaction not taken place.

The rules on liability for PSPs place the burden of financial crime on the PSP instead of the immediate victim, the payment service user. This can be justified with reference to the strong position of the financial institution compared to its counterpart, the payment service user, who is often a consumer. The financial institution is expected to be much better able to sustain the financial burden of the loss than the average consumer, and this statement can be supported with reference to the extensive regulations on capital requirements and financial soundness applicable to financial institutions.

Although the PSP is expected to be better equipped to bear the financial losses inflicted by financial fraud, the payer can also be liable to varying degrees. The liability of the payment service user is regulated by article 74. In cases where the payer has acted with gross negligence or intent, the payer is solely liable for the amount lost.[79] This is also the case where the payer has not observed their duties under article 69 with gross negligence[80] or intent. Where the payment instrument has been lost, stolen, or misappropriated, the payer will be liable for up to EUR 50.00 of the loss. This does not apply if the payer has not acted fraudulently and the loss, theft, or misappropriation of the payment instruments was not detectable to the payer prior to the payment transaction, or if the loss was caused by acts or lack of action by employees, agents, or branches of the PSP. In the latter cases, the payer will bear no liability.

As provided for in the Directive's recitals,[81] the Directive aims to provide a high degree of consumer protection. Although it cannot be read from the

[78] Donnelly, 'Payments in the digital market: Evaluating the contribution of Payment Services Directive II' 834 for more on primary liability.

[79] Kjørven, 'Who Pays When Things Go Wrong? Online Financial Fraud and Consumer Protection in Scandinavia and Europe' 92 on the term, and importance of, gross negligence under the PSD2.

[80] Although it is possible for national law to adopt limits to liability in cases of gross negligence as is the case, for example, in the Danish Payments Act § 100(4).

[81] Particularly recital 72, this is also supported by Guimarães and Steennot, 'Allocation of Liability in Case of Payment Fraud: Who Bears the Risk of Innovation? A Comparison of Belgian and Portuguese Law in the Context of PSD2' 50.

examined provisions, the Directive does not allow derogation from the provisions when the payment service user is a consumer. All terms and conditions which limit the payer's right of rectification, impede notification of unauthorised transactions, or in any way worsen the positions of a consumer, are to be considered null and void. This further underlines the protection provided by the PSD2 for consumers against losses resulting from financial crime.

The protection of consumers continues to be an overarching goal when the payment transaction involves a PISP. Article 73(2) states that when a payment transaction is initiated through a PISP, the account servicing PSP must still provide rectification immediately to the payer. The provision makes it clear that the inter-partes relationship between the PISP and the account servicing PSP does not concern the payment service user, which is to be treated in the same manner whether a third-party provider has been used or not. This is also reiterated in the recitals, which continuously highlight the importance of unrestricted access for payment service users to use third-party PSPs.[82]

While the payment service user has been granted a right of rectification directly through the account servicing PSP, the PISP bears the burden of evidence in article 72(1) within its sphere of competence. This contributes to balancing the relationship between the account servicing PSP and the PISP, so both bear their share regarding the provision of evidence and the ultimate coverage of the loss resulting from the unauthorised payment transaction.

The Directive also emphasises the importance of PSPs applying SCA on payment transactions, as article 74(2) places full liability on PSPs if they do not require SCA, except for cases of fraudulent behaviour by the payer.[83] This provision serves as an incentive to motivate all PSPs to implement and apply SCA on all payment transactions, to avoid covering the full cost of losses due to unauthorised payment transactions. In a case decided by the Danish Financial Board of Appeal,[84] it was questioned whether the SCA applied by the PSP fulfilled the requirements set out in the Directive. The Board of Appeal found that the authentication process only contained one of the three elements, where two elements is the minimum requirement. As the SCA process did not comply with the SCA requirements, the PSP was found liable for the entire lost amount.

In all aspects of liability for unauthorised payment transactions, the PSD2 takes an approach which favours or protects the ordinary consumer, the payer.

[82] Directive (EU) 2015/2366 (PSD2) recitals 69 and 73.

[83] Guimarães and Steennot, 'Allocation of Liability in Case of Payment Fraud: Who Bears the Risk of Innovation? A Comparison of Belgian and Portuguese Law in the Context of PSD2' 59.

[84] 165/2020 Det finansielle ankenævn.

Only in cases of gross negligence or fraudulent behaviour will the payer be liable for the incurred loss. These protective measures serve not only to enhance consumer protection, but also to incentivise PSPs to implement and apply preventive measures in their provision of payment services. Although it might be difficult to calculate the potential costs of not doing so, the outlook of being liable for losses due to financial fraud serves as an incentive to bear the costs of preventive measures such as SCA. While protecting consumers, the PSD2 also manages to address its goal of competition by making sure payment service users' use of third-party PSPs such as a PISP is not hindered. This also contributes to improving the working conditions for new and innovative service providers, while still balancing this improvement with the shared liability in cases of unauthorised payment transactions.

3.2.2 Sanctions in case of non-compliance

The purpose of the PSD2 and the competences vested in the EU are limited to certain areas decided solely by the participating Member States. Criminal sanctions as such are not directly included in these competences.[85] Hence, the PSD2 is not equipped with sanctioning provisions in a traditional criminal law understanding. Instead, the Directive holds a provision on withdrawal of authorisation in article 13. This should be perceived as the ultimate sanction for any payment institution that wishes to provide payment services in a Member State.

Here, the focus will be on whenit can be applied in circumstances where the payment institution has acted in a manner which is not in line with the meta-goal of preventing financial crime. In this regard, the provision's first paragraph, litra d), presents itself as an applicable measure. The provision reads:

> (if the payment institution) would constitute a threat to the stability of or the trust in the payment system by continuing its payment services business.

If the PSP continuously proves unable to implement and apply the preventive measures treated in this chapter, it constitutes a threat to the security of payment service users. This can have a negative impact on the trust of consumers

[85] Jacob Öberg, *Limits to EU Powers—A case study of EU regulatory criminal law* (Hart Studies in European Criminal Law, Hart Publishing 2017) 85f and 119f go into depth with EU criminal law and the extent to which EU holds the competence to sanction.

in the payments system and could potentially damage the integrity of the financial system in general.

Withdrawing an authorisation can have consequences for more parties than the payment institution in question. The decision to withdraw an authorisation must be based on the individual, relevant circumstances. The measure is, naturally, a last resort remedy which must be used with proportionality and considering all interests at stake.[86] The decision is made by the NCA who is most often also responsible for the supervision of the payment institution. When deciding on withdrawing an authorisation, consideration should be given to the potential consequences for financial stability, the loss of value for the payment institution and the market, and the impact on the real economy.[87]

In a situation where the payment institution was unable to meet the requirements to ensure safe payments, it would presumably be in the interest of financial stability to withdraw the authorisation, so the market avoids a (further) loss of trust in payment solutions. On the other side is the payment institution and the loss of value if it can no longer provide its services. Unfortunate as it may be for the individual payment institution, the PSD2 sets out clear rules for obtaining authorisation and the requirements to ensure safe payments, and by not complying with the ruleset it would seem only reasonable to withdraw the authorisation.

Although the PSD2 does not contain many options to sanction misbehaviour such as financial fraud, it goes a long way to protect the payment service user in cases of financial fraud. While the focus in the PSD2 has been to restore the loss incurred by the payer, with the aim of providing strong protection for consumers, retributive measures to sanction the criminal act and maintain the societal feeling of justice will have to be found elsewhere.

4 Evaluating the prevention of financial fraud

The examination of preventive measures in the PSD2 has shown an emphasis on the Directive's goal of consumer protection, in spite of the primary objective, the meta-goal, being to prevent financial crime. The provisions examined in section 3 focus on setting minimum standards for security measures

[86] Although the report is focusing on AML/CFT, the same interests and considerations regards payment institutions and systemic risks are presented in European Banking Authority, *Joint ESAs Report on the withdrawal of authorisation for serious breaches of AML/CFT rules* (2022) 57.

[87] European Banking Authority, *Joint ESAs Report on the withdrawal of authorisation for serious breaches of AML/CFT rules* 58.

in the provision of payment services, and on the implementation of risk procedures and incident reporting to manage the individual PSP's risk profile in regard to financial crime. These contribute to giving supervisory authorities the tools to supervise and measure criminal activity on the market. This is necessary to enable authorities to intervene with new measures to maintain the safety of payment solutions.

The discussion in the following subsections will address, first, how the PSD2 deals with the problem of financial crime, and in particular the potential increase in opportunities followed by innovation. The second subsection, 4.2, will take a further look at the Directive's ability to balance its goals internally, and with the meta-goal of preventing financial crime.

4.1 The PSD2's management of the threat of financial fraud

With innovation threatening to heighten the risk of financial crime in the payment services market, it would be expected that the PSD2 sought to mitigate and address this risk. The most novel measure examined above, in section 3.1.1, was the requirement for PSPs to apply strong customer authentication (SCA). The initial purpose of SCA was to make payments more secure, hence addressing the increased risk of financial crimes in payment services. And although the measure certainly does aid the meta-goal of preventing financial crime, the work of drafting and implementing the subsequent RTS on SCA and CSC[88] was mired in conflicting interests. This, though, should come as no surprise considering the list of requirements posed to the EBA in drafting the RTS.

PSD2 article 98(2) lists five requirements which can hardly be expected to be fulfilled without conflicts. According to the provision, the RTS must ensure an appropriate level of security for payment service users and PSPs through the adoption of effective and risk-based requirements. This speaks directly to the topic of this chapter and the meta-goal of preventing financial crime. This focus is continued with litra b), which demands that the safety of payment service users' funds and personal data is ensured, both of which are significant parts of financial fraud. But then the requirements change direction to ensure and maintain fair competition among all PSPs. This complements the Directive's goal of improving competition and levelling the playing field, especially by accentuating that this goes for all PSPs, making it impossible to neglect PSPs authorised or registered under the exemption rules in articles 32 and

[88] RTS 2018/389 on SCA and CSC.

33. The goal of improved competition is further supported by litra d), which sets out to ensure technology and business-model neutrality. This can also be interpreted as a means of improving the conditions for innovation, which is further supported in litra e), by requiring allowance for the development of user-friendly, accessible, and innovative means of payment. The challenge for the EBA was to balance the goal of improved conditions for, and further development of, innovation in financial services, while addressing the increased risks of financial crime and protecting payment service users.

As described in section 2, the innovative development in financial services leads to new or increased risks of financial crime. But such development also raises the possibility of utilising new innovations to improve the safety of payments and security of payment systems. With the addition of Title IV, Chapter 5 on Operational and Security Risks and Authentication, the PSD2 takes an important step in the fight against financial crime. In particular, article 97 on authentication and the RTS on SCA and CSC increase the security and safety of payments in the European Union, in terms of the legal framework at least. Implementation and compliance in practice among PSPs is outside the scope of the European legislator. Instead, the EBA has been trusted with powers to, generally, create and foster convergent supervisory practices, while NCAs are responsible for ensuring compliance among licensed and registered PSPs in their Member State. In terms of actual numbers on fraud, these have improved since the adoption of the PSD2, indicating less cases of financial fraud.[89] This is partly due to the implementation of SCA, but other factors such as the GDPR also make it more difficult for fraudsters to commit financial fraud.[90]

The provision also posed the challenge of balancing the opposed interests of account servicing PSPs and third-party providers. With article 97(4), the Directive sought to place the same rules upon account servicing PSPs as on third-party PSPs, but with article 97(5), the balance is slightly changed in favour of the third-party PSPs, who are able to rely on the authentication procedures provided by the account servicing PSP. This places an obligation on account servicing PSPs to share the security benefits of their authentication procedures with someone who did not take part in paying for the development of such procedures or systems.[91] To meet this obligation, many account servicing PSPs implemented a dedicated interface in the form of an API. Given

[89] NETS, *European Fraud Report—Payments Industry Challenges* (2019).

[90] NETS, *European Fraud Report—Payments Industry Challenges* 41.

[91] This is also critiqued by Finans Danmark, *Finance Denmark's response to Targeted consultation on the review of the revised payment services Directive (PSD2)* (2022); European Banking Federation, *EBF response to European Commission Consultation on the review of the revised payment services Directive (PSD2)* (European Banking Federation 2022).

the uncertainty of an API's quality, and this being rated differently between the providers, the account servicing PSPs, the consumers, and the third-party PSPs, the latter group had the initial RTS draft amended to condition the use of a dedicated interface on implementing a contingency mechanism.[92] This would tilt the balance even further in favour of third-party providers, and at the request of account servicing PSPs, an exemption to a contingency mechanism was included in the RTS article 33(6). By amending the RTS to include the exemption for account servicing PSPs that provide a dedicated interface, the balance set in the PSD2 was restored.

The preference for using APIs for the dedicated interface that enables the third-party PSPs to essentially provide their services, is at odds with the demands set out in PSD2 article 98(2) litra d) and e). This is particularly surprising, as two of the Directive's goals are competition and innovation. By favouring one technology over others, technology-neutrality is not ensured. Secondly, the use of APIs also limits the ability of third-party PSPs to innovate when developing user-friendly, accessible, and innovative means of payment.[93]

The possible distortion of competition between account servicing PSPs and third-party PSPs is further illustrated by the difficulties that using APIs in practice has led to. This caused the EBA to issue an Opinion[94] clarifying, among other things, when the account servicing PSP is setting an obstacle for the use by a third-party PSP, which is also acting in defiance of articles 66 and 67 of the PSD2 when the third-party PSP is a PISP or an AISP. Essentially, third-party providers are dependent on account servicing PSPs and their APIs to be able to provide their services to customers—services which must be migrated and customised to fit into the account servicing PSPs' API. This clearly strikes to the issue of improving competition and innovation in payment services, leaving especially third-party PSPs behind in preference to using a specific technology to apply SCA.[95]

The resistance to standardising the use of an API as the gateway to payment accounts held with account servicing PSPs is peculiar considering the call for standardisation in the Commission's Impact Assessment.[96] Here, the lack of

[92] Wandhöfer, 'Title IV "Rights and Obligations in Relation to the Provision and Use of Payment Services", Chapter 5 "Operational and Security Risks and Authentication" (Arts 95-98)' 205.

[93] Wandhöfer, 'Title IV "Rights and Obligations in Relation to the Provision and Use of Payment Services", Chapter 5 "Operational and Security Risks and Authentication" (Arts 95-98)' 202.

[94] European Banking Authority, *Opinion of the European Banking Authority on obstacles under Article 32(3) of the RTS on SCA and CSC* (2020).

[95] European Fintech Association, *Position Paper on the Revised Payment Services Directive 2* (European Fintech Association 2022) also calls for less strict requirements for third-party PSPs and other options than SCA to provide secure payments.

[96] European Commission, *Commission Staff Working Document Impact Assessment* SWD (2013) 288 final (2013) 120.

standards and interoperability was criticised as one of the key obstacles to mobile payments, a statement supported by numerous studies.[97] While the studies on standardisation clearly favour it, the reactions among PSPs to this specific process of designing such standards calls for a revision of the standard. The requirements set in article 98 might have been too extensive and conflicting to enable the EBA to draft a standard that aligns the most important goals of regulation, without creating obstacles to competition and innovation. When revising the provision, the legislator should consider what the end-goal should be, and which routes to that goal are acceptable.

Although the PSD2, in article 96, requires PSPs to report incidents and provide annual statistical data on fraud related to different means of payment to their NCAs, it can be questioned whether this is sufficient to effectively combat financial crime. It does provide each PSP, their NCA, the EBA, and the ECB with data on incidents and annual statistical data, which in its aggregated form could be useful to further prevent financial crime. But to effectively combat fraud, all information must be collected, processed, and shared between all PSPs, NCAs, the EBA, and the ECB. While financial innovation is creating more opportunities to commit financial crime, it is also improving the opportunities to prevent financial crime. On a customer-by-customer basis, this could prevent banks or PSPs from onboarding a customer who was declined or terminated at another payment institution due to money laundering activities or other fraudulent behaviour, if they were allowed to share this data internally in the sector. In conclusion though, the PSD2 does go a long way towards improving the payment services market's ability to prevent financial crime, which leaves the regulator in a good position when revising the Directive.

4.2 Balancing the directive goals in preventing financial crime

Preventing financial crime is a meta-goal of financial regulation in general. The issue is present across different sectors of the financial markets.[98] The

[97] Niina Mallat and Virpi Kristiina Tuunainen, 'Exploring Merchant Adoption of Mobile Payments: An Empirical Study' (2008) 6 e-Service Journal 24; Carlo RW De Meijer and Jonathan Bye, 'The Increasing Adoption of Mobile Payments in Europe—and Remaining Challenges to Growth' (2011) 5 Journal of Payments Strategy & Systems 273.

[98] This is, for example, evident in Bank for International Settlements, *AML and CFT in Banking—Executive Summary*; Expert Group on Regulatory Obstacles to Financial Innovation (ROFIEG), *30 Recommendations on Regulation, Innovation and Finance* 11.

PSD2's goal of innovation creates an interesting conflict with the meta-goal of preventing financial crime. On one side, innovation also opens up new ways for criminals to misuse the new solutions or procedures created through innovation. But on the other side, innovation also enables new possibilities to prevent financial crime. This is, for example, the case with the implementation of SCA in the PSD2.

The SCA requirement serves to ensure safe payment services, protecting payment service users from becoming victims of unauthorised transactions. As such, SCA is a measure which addresses the meta-goal of preventing financial crime directly, but it also comes with a cost for all PSPs that have to develop and implement SCA. This can be particularly burdensome on new, innovative PSPs.[99]

The SCA requirement sets the same minimum standard for authentication requirements for all PSPs, which contributes to levelling the playing field and fair competition on the market. Although the RTS on SCA and CSC[100] does provide for exemptions, particularly for smaller PSPs like third-party providers, this does not, in the bigger picture, pose a problem when one considers the costs associated with not applying SCA in terms of liability.

Where the RTS does pose a problem for the goals of competition and innovation though is in its preference for the API technology chosen by the account servicing PSPs which places these payment institutions in a stronger position than their competitors, the third-party PSPs, who are dependent on the access to accounts through a secure gateway. If the APIs fail, even momentarily, it could have damaging consequences for the reputation of not the responsible account servicing PSP but the third-party provider which a payment service user is trying to use. As discussed in the previous subsection, 4.1, the API problem reflects the diverging interests of the market participants, and the EBA as the mediating party responsible for drafting a suitable RTS can only do so much to reflect all relevant interests.

The meta-goal of preventing financial crime and the Directive's goal of improving consumer protection go hand-in-hand. When the Directive applies measures to prevent financial fraud, particularly where the payment service user's funds are the target, this also contributes to making payment services safer by lowering the risk of fraud when a consumer uses a payment service.

[99] Although, as pointed out by European Banking Federation, *EBF response to European Commission Consultation on the review of the revised payment services Directive (PSD2)* 62 the burden on account servicing PSPs is also considerable, especially taking into account the exemptions made in the RTS for third-party PSPs.

[100] RTS 2018/389 on SCA and CSC.

The quality parameter of consumer welfare can therefore be said to have improved with the requirements set forth in the PSD2 to improve the security of payment services. Although the Directive does, in article 69, place obligations on the payment service user, this is done in a proportionate and just manner, where only gross negligence or intentional fraudulent behaviour will be punished through the liability rules.

Targeting consumers with obligations can be difficult to manage or monitor for the supervisory authorities, as it is near impossible to supervise their compliance. The Directive handles this issue through the evidence rules in article 72, placing the primary burden of proof on the PSPs, who should hold the relevant data in their systems.

The liability rules for unauthorised payment transactions clearly show an emphasis on ensuring high levels of consumer protection in cases of financial fraud.[101] Giving the payer a right to have their account rectified by the account servicing PSP in all cases where a strong suspicion of first-party fraud is not present, serves as protection for consumers who are victims of financial crime. Expanding this right to cover all cases, irrespective of what kind of PSP was used, also contributes to the goals of competition and innovation. Innovation is improved as it is not the third-party PSP (which in the case of PISPs never touches the client's funds), who is the first point of contact for the rectification. This is balanced by the obligation to convey evidence within their competence and cover their part of the loss based on the evidence. Making the rectification process easy for consumers also contributes to making their choices of PSP more free, and increases the chances of them using PSPs other than their account servicing PSP.

One aspect where the Directive can hardly be said to manage the interests of consumers well is regarding data protection. In particular, the wording of article 94(2), in combination with the freedom to define services for account information services, opens the way for broad access to, processing of, and retainment of, financial data belonging to the payment service user. This problem has two interesting perspectives. The first is the inherent desire of the EU to protect consumers' data. The other is the consumer's constant desire for custom-made or tailored solutions that matches their specific needs. The latter is rather unlikely if the first is also ensured. Whether EU citizens most desire the former or the latter is for them to decide, but the EU must in any case make any contact with such data safe and secure for consumers.

[101] Which is also evident in the wording of recital 73 in Directive (EU) 2015/2366 (PSD2).

Recapitulating on the failures presented in the beginning of this chapter and the measures applied by the PSD2 to manage the failure of financial crime, the findings show a potent force to prevent financial crime in payment services. As such, the Directive manages to internalise the externality of financial crime with the implemented liability regime. The Directive also contains novelties in the form of SCA and much stronger obligations for PSPs in terms of managing security risks and incidents, which is evidence of the Directive's intention to address and manage the failure of financial crime. As discussed, the PSD2 manages to address the failure in line with the Directive-specific goals, while also working towards the meta-goal of preventing financial crime in the financial markets. While there are issues in terms of balancing the interests of market participants in practice, as seen in the RTS on SCA and CSC, and the interests of consumers in relation to their financial data, these will be manageable when the time comes to revise the PSD2, hopefully in a more technology neutral version.

7

THE FUTURE OF EU PAYMENT SERVICES

1 Introduction

The present, or what is, is crucial to consider what ought to be, or in the case perhaps what could be the future of EU payment services. While the previous chapters have examined provisions of the PSD2 and how they address market and non-market failures, this chapter seeks to build on top of that to provide perspectives on the possible future of the regulation of EU payment services and how it interacts with innovative developments in the market.

Understanding the failures prior to regulatory intervention and the measures applied enables a discussion of how well the Directive has addressed the failures and managed the accommodation of increased innovation. This knowledge also makes it possible to envision possible scenarios for how to continue developing regulation in order to shape a prosperous payment services market in the future. As such, the framework presented in chapter 3 makes for a great tool to access current regulation and build upon this to provide suggestions for policy decisions to support the future developments.

The purpose of this chapter is to summarise the findings of the analysis in the three previous chapters, discuss the findings, and conclude on where this leaves the future of innovation and regulation in EU payment services. In the following, section 2 will discuss the findings in relation to how the PSD2 has managed the identified market and non-market failures. Then section 3 will discuss the Directive's ability to accommodate innovation in payment services. This includes reflections on how the Directive's goals and the meta-goals were balanced, and considerations on regulatory strategies. At last section 4 will consider the future of EU payment services including considerations of current proposals to revise the PSD2.

EU Payment Services. Louise Damkjær Christensen, Oxford University Press.
DOI: 10.1093/9780198949084.003.0007

2 The market and non-market failures of the PSD2

The findings of chapters 4–6 will be presented and discussed in the following subsections. This serves the purpose of drawing conclusions on the PSD2's ability to regulate the EU payment services market in a way which takes into account the existing market and non-market failures. If the Directive were to simply ignore the existing problems, it would hardly be efficient as a regulatory tool. Instead, highlighting how the PSD2 manages to interact with existing issues serves as evidence as to whether the Directive is on the right path in terms of improving the EU payment services market.

The structure in the following subsections 2.1–2.3 is based on chapters 4–6 of this book, to follow the normal life cycle of a business providing payments services, but also the natural structure of financial regulation which starts with the authorisation and continues to matters of fair competition, and ends, for this book's scope, with the measures applied to prevent financial crime in payment services. The last subsection, 2.4, will discuss and conclude on the Directive's management of failures.

2.1 Excluding providers from the regulatory scope

The first non-market failure, concerning the exclusion of some providers from the regulatory scope, appeared in both chapter 4 and 5, but here it will be discussed in relation to the licensing regime. The failure was an internality caused by technological development making existing regulation outdated. The scope of the PSD1 excluded third-party PSPs from being covered by the regulatory framework. This led to more than one market failure, as will be discussed further later in this section. First, the focus will be on how PSD2 managed to address the problem of unregulated PSPs caused by the regulatory framework being too narrow.

The first measure the legislator used was an extension of the Directive's scope. By including third-party PSPs, particularly in the forms of AISPs and PISPs, the PSD2 ensured that all PSPs were obligated to comply with the same rules. This measure improved competition in the market, as different rules for the same services had a distortive effect on competition, but the accommodation of these new providers did not stop at a widened scope. To improve conditions for innovative providers, modifications were also made to other parts of the Directive, in particular to the licensing regime, as dealt with in chapter 4.

The licensing regime's exceptions in article 5(2) and (3) and the exemption in article 33 target third-party PSPs specifically. The first two provisions ensure the safety of payment service users who choose to use these providers by ensuring that they have the ability to cover potential liability. This increases consumer protection by making the greater number of choices safer to choose and improving the quality of the service by ensuring the PSP's ability to cover liability claims in cases of unauthorised transactions or unauthorised access to account information.

The exemption in article 33 significantly lowers the entry barriers for AISPs when the PSP only delivers the AIS. This exemption contributes to the Directive's goal of innovation but also creates risks in terms of competition and consumer protection; having some PSPs only complying with a lower standard of regulation distorts competition. To make up for this, the Directive limits the exemption to AISPs, creating a level playing field for this group of PSPs who are not directly in competition with other PSPs which provide payment initiation services or execute payment transactions. Only PSPs that offer both the AIS and other payment services are directly affected by this competitive disadvantage, but these providers also hold the advantage of being able to offer multiple services to their customers, placing them in a stronger position in the market. As such, the exemption does not impact their welfare significantly.

When third-party PSPs were placed outside the scope of the regulatory framework, there was a risk of moral hazard in the relationship between consumers and third-party PSPs. Given the consumer group's generally low financial literacy, it cannot be expected that consumers understand the significance of third-party PSPs not being regulated under the same framework as account servicing PSPs. It could not be assumed that consumers understood that the liability, data processing, and execution of transaction rules they knew from their relationships with account servicing PSPs did not apply automatically to third-party PSPs prior to PSD2. It was therefore also in the interest of consumers to have third-party PSPs covered by the Directive even if this caused the price of their services to rise.

Another market failure derived from the exclusion of third-party PSPs was systemic risks. Systemic stability, being a public good, must be produced by financial institutions, as it is crucial for society to function. By creating a suboptimal situation, where some PSPs were unregulated while others had to comply with the burdensome rules of the PSD1, the regulator put the stability of the system at risk. Although systemic risk is classified as a market failure, it was the regulatory intervention in the form of the PSD1 which caused third-party PSPs to be excluded from the scope of regulation at the EU level.

Placing requirements on only a selected group of PSPs also creates problems in relation to the Directive's goals of competition and consumer protection. For competition, giving competitors different rules to comply with has a distortive effect when this is not based on proportional and objectively reasoned decisions by the regulator. For example, the exemption in article 32 for PSPs with a transaction volume below a certain threshold places less requirements on them, but this is justified by their small-scale business. The exemption is further balanced by restricting the exempted PSPs to operating in their home Member State. This is also an example of how the PSD2 addresses the differences in PSPs, making room for smaller providers while still balancing this with the goal of ensuring fair competition.

As already discussed above, consumer protection was enhanced by including third-party PSPs in the scope of the PSD2. By making sure that payment services can only be provided after obtaining authorisation, the regulator ensured that all providers satisfy the same standards, hence offering adequate consumer protection. This essentially addresses both the failure of information asymmetry and moral hazard and mitigates the systemic risks.

In conclusion, the EU legislator manages the initial non-market failure and the derived market failures through regulatory intervention—the PSD2. The interventions examined in this book's chapter 4, the licensing regime and the widened scope of the Directive, address the failures while balancing the Directive-specific goals. The goal of innovation stands out more than the other two, as the authorisation rules provide specific measures to further accommodate new and smaller entrants that only offer the newly added payment services—the AIS and PIS. Unfortunately, the Directive risks creating the same internality as its predecessor by leaving new innovations such as payments using cryptocurrencies out of its scope. This leaves the cryptocurrency payments sector outside the scope of regulation, creating risks to financial stability and consumer welfare comparable to those from third-party PSPs previously.[1]

[1] Iris H Y Chiu, 'A New Era in Fintech Payment Innovations? A Perspective from the Institutions and Regulation of Payment Systems' (2017) 9 Law, Innovation and Technology 190 229; Louise Damkjær Christensen, 'Crypto payments – a danger to consumer protection?' (2022) 16 Law and Financial Markets Review 197; European Fintech Association, *Position Paper on the Revised Payment Services Directive 2* (European Fintech Association 2022) also call for this problem to be addressed by the EU legislator.

2.2 Market control and entry barriers

Imperfect competition in the form of market control resulting in incumbent institutions being able to create entry barriers was the key market failure discussed in chapter 5. Imperfect competition naturally collides with the Directive's goal of fair and efficient competition, but it also impedes the Directive's two other goals. Without competition, it is unlikely that prices for services will reflect decreasing costs of provision. The other three consumer welfare parameters—quality, service, and choice—are also expected to decline when providers are not exposed to efficient competition. The legislative measures examined in the chapter contributed to all three Directive goals to varying extents.

With PSD2 articles 35 and 36, the goals of competition and innovation were addressed by allowing new entrants to participate in payment systems and to hold payment accounts at credit institutions. The right to a payment account is crucial for any business not based on customers paying in cash only. Article 36 in particular—providing payment accounts in credit institutions—is interesting from the perspective of fair competition. While it clearly promotes innovation, it could also be perceived as having a distortive effect on competition to force credit institutions—which also provide payment services—to provide payment account access for their direct competition. Faced with such a dilemma, where two goals actively conflict, the legislator must consider the problem from various angles.

Starting with one of this book's fundamental areas of focus, the legislator has to consider whether the market itself can correct this market failure. As the failure involves competing market participants which have to negotiate and contract with each other, it is hardly realistic to expect the market to correct this failure on its own, as this would entail incumbent institutions damaging their own market share by letting new competitors onto the market. Perceiving the problem as being solely a lack of access to essential payment accounts, the regulator holds the necessary tool to correct this failure, and as the market cannot do this, the intervention would be justified. But the situation also entails further aspects to consider before deciding to intervene with regulation.

With the measure applied by the EU legislator, essentially forcing credit institutions to provide payment accounts to payment institutions, the effects on innovation and competition and the chosen balance between the two goals are worth noting. The conditions for innovation and innovative PSPs are improved significantly by securing them access to payment accounts at credit institutions. Meanwhile, the impact on competition is two-sided. Firstly, for new entrants which have previously been disadvantaged when entering the market for payment services, the situation has improved considerably. This levels the playing field, as all PSPs now have access to payment accounts, which are crucial in order to deliver payment services. But from the perspective of incumbent institutions, particularly the credit institutions, this measure removes, or perhaps more correctly restricts,[2] the competitive advantage they held over non-bank PSPs prior to the PSD2. The restriction also limits the right of credit institutions to choose whom they do business with, as they can no longer reject competitor PSPs based on them being direct competition. The law now forces them to invite their competitors inside.

The following question can therefore be posed: is this situation fair? The image of Lady Justice and her scales weighing the situation comes to mind. The situation prior to the PSD2, with incumbent institutions essentially dictating market entry, was not fair to any participant and did not serve any of the Directive's goals. Lady Justice's scales could be said to have 'hit the floor' on one side. The situation post PSD2, with regulation restricting the private actor's freedom in the market, might be less fair to incumbent institutions, but this is levelled up by how it serves all three of the Directive's goals. In essence, the goal of innovation has been found to be of greater importance than the credit institution's right to choose who to conduct business with. As such, Lady Justice's scales have been tipped in favour of accommodating innovation and efficient competition.

Another measure examined in chapter 5 was the access to payment accounts held with an account servicing PSP when the payment service user requested such access for a third-party PSP. Articles 66 and 67 placed this power to decide which providers get access in the hands of consumers. Prior to the PSD2, that power had been in the hands of the credit institutions acting as the account servicing PSPs. Prior to the PSD2, third-party PSPs were dependent on entering into bilateral agreements with credit institutions in order to provide their services to consumers. The measure applied by the PSD2, enforcing a specific conduct of behaviour onto the relationship between third-party PSPs and account servicing PSPs, impacts all three Directive goals.

Provided that the payment service user requests the access to their payment account (seen as constituting consent), the provisions impact the goal of innovation considerably by ensuring essential access for AISPs and PISPs.

[2] As there still remains the possibility to reject the request for a payment account if it is reasoned on objective, non-discriminating, and proportional grounds, restricting their freedom is the most appropriate phrase.

Without this access they could not provide their services. But the access also has consequences for the goal of competition. At first glance, allowing third-party PSPs to have the essential access they need would not seem to harm account servicing PSPs any more than the measure in article 36, but when this access is examined more closely the picture changes. New and important details emerge.

For account servicing PSPs to provide this access they have to develop, implement, and maintain an API. As with anything in business, this does not come without costs.[3] The API is expensive for the account servicing PSP and does not inherently contribute any value to the institution directly. Instead, it creates value for competitors and for consumers who can enjoy the increased variety of services and choice of providers. And these are important values for the payment services market. But is it fair to place all the costs of an API on the credit institutions without any form of remuneration, when it creates no direct value for them?

It is recommended that the relevant authorities establish standards on the price of access for third-party providers, to create a more even burden of costs between AISP, PISP, and account servicing PSPs.

The goal of consumer protection is also impacted by these two provisions. As discussed in chapter 5, the financial literacy among consumers could be improved.[4] This causes concern when the legislator places the power of access in the hands of consumers. As was argued in chapter 5, consumers cannot be expected to be sufficiently able to understand and process the information provided by PSPs in order to make sound financial decisions. Particularly the access to financial data granted to AISPs is problematic, as the provider, depending on their definition of their service, gets access to, processes, and potentially shares pseudo-anonymised data about the consumer to target tailored options for the consumer. The sophistication of consumers does call for these customised options, but the mechanism conflicts with the GDPR and the EU's desire to protect citizens' data. Perhaps the root of the problem is also the solution; the EU wants consumers to own their data, through this ownership the consumer can choose to sell or share the data with the AISP. If the EU wants

[3] Also see the critique on this in Finans Danmark, *Finance Denmark's response to Targeted consultation on the review of the revised payment services Directive (PSD2)* (2022); European Banking Federation, *EBF response to European Commission Consultation on the review of the revised payment services Directive (PSD2)* (European Banking Federation 2022) both criticising the lack of value creation for account servicing PSPs who must bear the full cost of establishing access through APIs.

[4] European Banking Authority, *EBA Financial Education Report 2019/2020* (2020); OECD, *OECD/INFE 2020 International Survey of Adult Financial Literacy* (2020).

personal ownership over data, should it then be dictating what consumers can do with their own data?

With the consumer effectively owning their own data, they are free to allow third-parties, such as an AISP, to access and use it. The role of the regulator is therefore not to restrict the consumer in giving such access to data, but to guide them in making sound decisions using this freedom. But how much should the regulator attempt to help consumers? The economic theory which this book's framework is built upon provides an answer to this question.

The problem with consumers' ability to make sound financial decisions can essentially be boiled down to the market failure of asymmetric information and consumers' individual, biased decision-making. The role, or justification, of the regulator's intervention can therefore be stretched as far as is necessary to restore the efficiency of the market. This means that the regulator can intervene only as far as the measures applied mitigate the failure of consumer's decision-making process without damaging other efficiencies of the market. If a non-market failure is caused by the intervention, the regulator has gone too far in their intervention.

The regulator often applies disclosure rules when aiming to ensure sufficient information for consumers prior to making financial decisions, but this entails two problems. The first problem is the risk of information overload, where too much information is made available to the consumer, resulting in them not taking the time to become familiar with it. The information can also be of such a nature that the average consumer cannot be expected to process it correctly.[5] The focus could instead be recommended to be on the material disclosed to consumers. For example by requiring PSPs to supplement the rather voluminous and incomprehensible current material with a simple document stating the exact consequences of consenting to give access to payment accounts in plain and simple language.[6] Intervening on the complexity of the material disclosed to consumers also passes the test of efficient intervention, as it does not involve severe or unfair problems for other market parties, but contributes to making the information flow more efficient.

Concluding on the PSD2's ability to address the market failure of market control, the measures analysed in chapter 5—articles 35, 36, 66, and 67—primarily

[5] As the Danish Financial Supervisory Authority also points out in a 2009 decision, *Lov om investeringsforeninger og specialforeninger samt andre kollektive investeringsordninger m.v. § 18—Påtale—Jyske Invest* [2009], the expectations of an average consumer must be fairly low.

[6] For example: 'By consenting to this we will access the data on your payment account and process it in order to deliver a financial overview to you. We will also share the data with our partners to obtain offers tailored to your needs.'

applied conduct of business rules to change the distorting, anti-competitive behaviour of some market participants. The provisions clearly conform with the Directive's goals of competition and innovation. The goal of consumer protection on the other hand is, regarding articles 35 and 36, affected indirectly, but with articles 66 and 67 the choices for consumers to use different PSPs is improved, while also entailing a risk that consumers make unsound decisions about providing access to their financial data. The provisions also mirror macro-prudential intentions by the regulator which shows a desire to ensure systemic stability by including more PSPs under the regulatory framework, while securing their relationship to the system through micro-prudential rules ensuring financial soundness in all payment institutions.

2.3 Financial fraud in an innovative market

While innovation has been the driver of development in payment services, it has also been a driver in the development of new and more complicated ways for criminals to commit financial fraud. To protect the payment services market, and other financial markets, from financial crime, technological innovation has also contributed new ways to secure payments and access payment services. As examined in chapter 6, one way the PSD2 has addressed the market failure of financial crime in payment services is through the implementation of secure customer authentication. SCA serves as a prevention mechanism, protecting payment service users from financial fraud.

The underlying technology of SCA constitutes the complicated matter of this regulatory intervention. As such, the measure is efficient in addressing the issue of financial fraud as long as the payment service user observes the obligation in article 69 to protect their personalised security credentials, which are key in the SCA process. SCA prevents—or at least makes it a lot more difficult for criminals to commit—financial fraud via payment services. But the measure also entails complicated technological requirements which proved troublesome for PSPs to implement prior to the original deadline.[7] The SCA process was also costly for the PSPs to develop, implement, and now maintain. This was a cost placed solely on PSPs.

[7] According to European Banking Authority, *EBA report on the data provided by PSPs on their readiness to apply strong customer authentication for e-commerce card-based payment transactions* (European Banking Authority 2021) the EU PSPs were still not at 100% as of June 2021.

In the case of SCA, its impact on prevention of financial fraud has been measured by the EBA.[8] Although not all PSPs are yet fully compliant with the SCA process, the report from the EBA shows a decrease in fraud since the rolling implementation of SCA. Between the end of June 2020 and April 2021, the average percentage value of fraudulent transactions fell from 0.12% to 0.06% among issuers, and from 0.17% to 0.10% among acquirers reporting.[9] The report shows a positive impact on the rates of financial crime in payment services, which is attributed to the implementation of SCA. Even though the regulator has implemented an efficient tool to prevent financial crime, which is also a meta-goal of financial regulation, it should be questioned whether it is fair to place the entire burden of costs related to the development, implementation, and maintenance on the PSP.

Placing requirements and obligations upon financial institutions in order to prevent financial crime has more or less become the norm. This is, for example, also the case with preventive measures against money laundering, where financial institutions in particular must comply with extensive rulesets and regulations to avoid sanctions. From an efficiency perspective, placing these requirements on credit institutions is a solid solution, as most financial activities at some point transfer through a credit institution, for example by placing cash on an account, transferring money between accounts, or defrauding an account holder. As such, the regulator places requirements and the accompanying costs on financial institutions to prevent financial crime, and in the case of non-compliance or insufficient compliance in a financial institution, the regulator can issue a fine for the financial institution to pay to the local government or authority.

Although this might be the most efficient method of prevention, it can hardly be considered fair to expect financial institutions to bear the costs themselves. In essence, the price for some people to be better off is for financial institutions to be worse off, making Pareto optimality impossible. Considering the potential spill-over on the financial institutions' prices, ie financial institutions raising their prices to cover the rising costs, the prevention mechanism could be considered Kaldor-Hicks efficient if the improvement for society is valued higher than the loss for financial institutions, assuming that society also accepts the negative impact on consumer welfare in the form of rising prices. In conclusion, the regulator accepts the rising prices and their impact

[8] European Banking Authority, *EBA report on the data provided by PSPs on their readiness to apply strong customer authentication for e-commerce card-based payment transactions*.

[9] European Banking Authority, *EBA report on the data provided by PSPs on their readiness to apply strong customer authentication for e-commerce card-based payment transactions* 9.

on consumer welfare because the preventive effects against financial crime are more valuable.

The PSD2 also addressed the problem that arises when financial fraud has happened—the question of liability. The rules on liability in the case of unauthorised transactions clearly protected the consumer from suffering the loss of fraud, for example through the right to rectification from the account servicing PSP, even if a third-party PSP had been used. The Directive's goal of fair competition was also visible in the liability rules, as responsibility was divided between account servicing PSPs and third-party PSPs in accordance with their respective capabilities to document and provide evidence for the unauthorised transaction. A reliable liability regime is important in order to maintain consumer trust in financial institutions in cases of financial fraud. The PSD2's liability rules provide a suitable measure to manage the failure of financial crime ex-post concerning the loss suffered by the victim of the crime.

Although proportionate sanctions are essential in efficient enforcement of the regulatory framework, the role of financial regulation must be clearly separated from the role of criminal law. Sanctioning financial crime, ie the criminal committing the crime, must be covered by criminal law. The financial regulation can, and should, only sanction the situation where a financial institution or service user has not taken sufficient precaution to prevent the crime from happening. For payment institutions, the sanction is liability in the case of fraud, or in the worst-case withdrawal of authorisation.

For the payment service user, the application of conduct rules holds a different kind of importance. The supervisory authority has no real opportunity to monitor the consumer's compliance, but article 69 is necessary to avoid moral hazard among consumers. If there was no liability for consumers in cases of third-party fraud, there would be no incentive for consumers to protect their personalised security credentials. As such, the Directive manages to balance the different needs of the parties in a manner which contributes to both consumer protection and fair competition.

In conclusion, the PSD2 manages to address important aspects in preventing financial crime, where SCA and the liability rules have been found to make the greatest impact on the goals of the Directive and the meta-goal of preventing financial crime. It holds value to regulators, and society, to prevent financial crime as it impacts the financial system's integrity and consumer trust negatively when financial crime thrives. Preventive measures therefore also contribute to systemic stability, underlining the importance of a safe payments system in the EU.

2.4 The PSD2's management of failures

Across all three cases analysed in chapters 4–6, one theme has been the main driver of both failures and regulatory developments: innovation. Innovation in the provision of payment services triggered the internality of the PSD1 having too narrow a scope. Innovation introduced new types of payment services and providers, causing the market to fail in the form of imperfect competition. And innovation opened new ways for criminals to commit financial crime. But after regulatory intervention, innovation also contributed to improved consumer welfare, more secure payment solutions, and enhanced possibilities for monitoring transactions to detect and prevent financial crime.

The management of market and non-market failures has showed a balanced consideration of all three of the Directive's goals without jeopardising meta-goals of financial regulation. To a substantial extent, the Directive has managed to balance goals adequately when addressing failures, but the Directive does cause concern on two points which will be presented in the following.

Firstly, the Directive falls short of fully handling innovation in a similar fashion to its predecessor. Payments in cryptocurrency are gaining traction,[10] but the PSD2's definition of funds does not cover cryptocurrencies; hence these payments are not covered by the Directive. This exclusion holds the potential to cause systemic risks and poses a direct threat to consumer protection in particular.[11] It can only be recommended that the legislator considers including payments in cryptocurrencies when revising the PSD2.

The second point relates to the freedoms or rights entrusted with consumers, especially in articles 66 and 67. As has been discussed in this thesis, the consumer generally does not possess sufficient ability to collect information, understand the relevant consequences, and make sound decisions on financial matters. The consumer's individual, biased decision-making poses a problem when deciding on personal finance options. This leaves the question of how much the regulator should help the consumer make the 'right' decisions. The

[10] ECB Crypto-Assets Task Force, *Crypto-Assets: Implications for financial stability, monetary policy, and payments and market infrastructures* (European Central Bank 2019); Fabio Panetta, *For a few cryptos more: the Wild West of crypto finance* (European Central Bank 2022); Charles X, 'Cryptocurrency Payment Gateway Development—Best Crypto Development Solutions' (*Finextra*, 2021) <https://www.finextra.com/blogposting/20872/cryptocurrency-payment-gateway-development--best-crypto-development-solutions> accessed 18 August 2022; PYMNTS, 'PYMNTS Intelligence: The Promise of Faster Transactions Using Blockchain Technology' (*PYMNTS.com*, 2022) <https://www.pymnts.com/blockchain/2022/pymnts-intelligence-the-promise-of-faster-transactions-using-blockchain-technology/> accessed 18 August 2022.

[11] This exclusion is also critiqued by Mary Donnelly, 'Payments in the digital market: Evaluating the contribution of Payment Services Directive II' (2016) 32 Computer Law & Security Review. 837; Christensen, 'Crypto payments – a danger to consumer protection?'.

term 'right' is used because the consumer does after all, in light of the GDPR, own their personal data, making them the sole person able to decide what is right for them personally. It would be contrary to the intentions of consumer ownership of personal data for the EU regulator to decide what the consumer should do with their own data. The sophistication of modern consumers tends to demand tailored or custom solutions. These necessitate the provider having access to and being able to process the consumer's financial data to know what the consumer needs. When revising the PSD2, it would be advisable for the legislator to consider its position on this matter carefully, to ensure a harmonised position across different legal areas and even across the financial market.

3 Accommodating innovation in payment services

The scope of this book was not only to examine the regulation covering the EU payment services but also to inquire into the regulation's ability to accommodate innovation in payment services. This section will therefore summarise the book's findings on this aspect and discuss the impact of innovation on the regulation of payment services.

As was touched upon in the above section 2.4, innovation has been a driver for both market and non-market failures, and for developing new initiatives in regulation. Generally, it can be said that regulatory adjustments are necessary to accommodate innovation if the change caused by innovation poses a new risk, or if it creates a new possibility that regulation needs to or should accommodate being implemented in the market. In causing failures on the payment services market, innovation created the needed justification for government to intervene in the market according to economic theory. But innovation also brought new opportunities which held the potential to improve multiple functions of the market. Accommodation for innovation and prevention of failures was therefore simultaneously necessary.

To accommodate the possibilities financial innovations have created, the PSD2 secured new providers and services access to the market. As previously explained, this market access consisted of widening the scope of the Directive and including third-party PSPs in the licensing regime, creating the exemption for AISPs in article 33, ensuring access to payment systems for all payment institutions with article 35, providing access to payment accounts in credit institutions for all payment institutions in article 36, and finally the special provisions in articles 66 and 67 placing the power of access in the hands of consumers. But has the regulator with these provisions treated innovation too generously?

New risks also arose with the development in financial innovation, particularly the risk of financial crime, which was examined in this book. Chapter 6 dealt with the PSD2's new regime to make payment transactions and the use of payment services safer. These improvements to the safety and security of payments were also driven by innovation enabling new solutions. Although untapped potential still exists, for example data sharing across payment institutions to prevent financial crime, these can readily be explored in the upcoming revision of the PSD2.[12]

While safety is a risk the PSD2 has taken sufficient care of, the provisions granting access to the market for innovations also had to balance the Directive's other goals. Most of the provisions generally contributed to creating a level playing field and hence improved competition, but some provisions could be argued to have taken it a step too far in the name of innovation. As discussed in chapter 5, articles 66 and 67 provide access to a payment service user's payment account when the payment service user requests such access. In order to enable this access, the account servicing PSP must develop, implement, and maintain a gateway, an API, for third-party PSPs to access the account data through. This is expected to be provided by the account servicing PSP without any payment for access or option for remuneration. The provisions therefore effectively place costs on some PSPs, while enabling other PSPs to monetise the asset created by the costs. In this case, the regulator has gone too far in accommodating innovation, as it bears unjust consequences for other market participants, in essence distorting competition. It would therefore be recommended that the regulator considers standardising the terms of access through these mandatory gateways to re-establish a level playing field.

Even regulators find it challenging to keep up with and understand innovations in financial services. It would therefore be unreasonable to expect consumers to fully comprehend the consequences of all new innovations and possibilities. Giving them the power to grant access to their payment accounts and their financial data was a decision which correlates with the policy of the GDPR, for citizens to own their own data, but it does cause concern in relation to consumer protection. The choice parameter of consumer welfare is no doubt improved, as the consumer is ensured more choices, which is also assumed to

[12] Financial Action Task Force (FATF), *Partnering in the Fight Against Financial Crime: Data Protection, Technology and Private Sector Information Sharing* (2022) highlights private sector information sharing as an important measure in the fight against financial crime.

have a positive impact on price.[13] With other supporting provisions examined in the foregoing chapters, the parameters of quality and service cannot be expected to be impacted negatively either. Instead, the concern comes from the market failure of the consumer's biased, individual decision-making.

The PSD2 places the power to decide on access to account information in the hands of consumers, and also provides disclosure provisions, making the PSPs responsible of enlightening the consumer before going into a contract. But these disclosure provisions also risk overloading consumers with information, being often delivered in a terminology incomprehensible to the average consumer. It would therefore be recommended that a revision of the PSD2 considers new ways of improving financial literacy among consumers, for example through requirements on the comprehensibility of disclosed information.

The PSD2's goal of innovation also has to be in alignment with the meta-goals of financial regulation. This is achieved when the measures supporting the goal of innovation do not detract from the meta-goals. As two of the meta-goals are also Directive-specific goals, the goal of innovation holds the same potential to harm these as already discussed. The meta-goal of preventing financial crime has already been treated specifically in chapter 6, which showed that promoting both prevention and innovation is a delicate balance.

Based on the findings of this book, which are also supported by several statements posted by the EU Commission[14] promoting and accommodating innovation in financial markets is of high priority. Although there are plenty of compelling reasons for this position, innovation also comes with risks. Whereas the primary goal of financial regulation since the Global Financial Crisis has been the promotion of financial stability, the findings suggest that innovation is moving in to take top priority. This could be of concern if the regulator does not impose sufficiently strong incentives for all financial institutions to produce stability. It is of utmost importance that the regulator continuously maintains strong macro-prudential policies to ensure the safety and

[13] Although one could argue that there is a risk of consumers paying for either more than they need or for the same service with more than one provider.

[14] European Commission, *Commission Staff Working Document Impact Assessment* SWD (2013) 288 final (2013); European Commission, *Communication from the Commission to the European Parliament, the Council, the European Economic and Social Committee and the Committee of the Regions on a Retail Payments Strategy for the* EU (COM (2020) 592 final) (2020); European Commission, *Communication from the Commission: FinTech Action plan: For a more competitive and innovative European financial sector* (COM (2018) 109 final) (2018); European Commission, 'FAQ: Making Electronic Payments and Online Banking Safer and Easier for Consumers' 2019. <https://ec.europa.eu/commission/presscorner/detail/en/qanda_19_5555> accessed 16 June 2022; European Commission, *Payment services: Consumers to benefit from cheaper, safer and more innovate electronic payments* (European Commission 2018); European Commission, *The Retail Payments Strategy* (European Commission 2020).

integrity of the financial system. Innovation in payment services could potentially improve several of the meta-goals of financial regulation, but the risks it involves are important to contain. It can therefore only be recommended that the regulator does not promote innovation for the sake of innovation but does so in accordance with appropriate micro-prudential requirements to ensure the individual institution's stability, and with a macro-prudential policy which manages a safe relationship between the individual institution and the system as a whole.

In conclusion, the findings of this book have shown that the PSD2 accommodates the innovative development in payment services in multiple ways, and at times perhaps too much. This was shown with the examined provisions in chapter 5, where articles 35, 36, 66, and 67 contribute to improved competition, but the latter two articles favour third-party PSPs, while not allowing account servicing PSPs to monetise the forced investment and continuous costs they incur to provide the access required by law. In other aspects, the Directive manages to utilise innovation to improve the safety and security of payment services, as was examined in chapter 6. Implementing the SCA requirement also included a practical problem, as some PSPs were not able to implement SCA in due time. Innovation is not free; it comes at a monetary cost and requires continuous investments from each payment institution. Although the PSD2 goes a long way to accommodate innovation, while protecting the meta-goals of financial regulation, there are still things to consider for the regulator when revising the Directive, to improve the balance between innovation and financial stability.

4 Looking ahead

When pondering about the future of EU payment services, it is important to remember both the current issues that need to be addressed and to make room for the potential developments in the market. In the following, the problems and potentials identified in previous chapters of this book will be transformed to recommendations for future revisions of the PSD2. Although the EU Commission has already in June 2023 proposed a new third Payment Services Directive (PSD3),[15] Payment Services Regulation (PSR),[16] and Regulation on

[15] Proposal for a Directive of the European Parliament and of the Council on payment services and electronic money services in the Internal Market amending Directive 98/26/EC and repealing Directives 2015/2366/EU and 2009/110/EC (COM(2023) 366 final) [2023].

[16] Proposal for a Regulation of the European Parliament and of the Council on payment services in the internal market and amending Regulation (EU) No 1093/2010 (COM(2023) 367 final) [2023].

Financial Data Access (FiDA),[17] these will not be the primary subject here, as they merely constitute proposals.[18] Instead, reference will be made to the proposals when relevant.

Innovation have showed in the past to present a challenge to payment services regulation, as the PSD1 became outdated rather quickly, partly due to its narrow scope excluding third-party PSPs. Interestingly, innovation is here both the driver of the failure in the PSD1 as well as the driver of prosperous developments in the payment services market. The PSD2 presents a licensing regime tailored to also suit new payment institutions with the exemption provisions in articles 32 and 33, and particular requirements fitted for AISPs and PISPs in article 5(2) and (3)[19] to exempt them from the own funds requirements in articles 8 and 9(1). With this, the PSD2 created one licensing regime for all PSPs, which is essential to sustain systemic stability and fair competition. While the Directive clearly does accommodate innovation, the definition of 'funds' in article 4(25) effectively excludes cryptocurrency payments from the scope of the Directive, potentially causing the same failures as the widened scope set out to mitigate.[20] In a revision of the PSD2, the legislator ought to consider whether it is wise to continue upholding two different regimes for payment services, a difference in treatment solely based on the value the legislator, and not the payment service user, places in the currency.

In terms of competition, the PSD2's article 35, securing access to payment services for all PSPs, is a strong element of EU payment services regulation which ensures that all providers have a chance to make their payments business sustainable.[21] Adding the more fundamental right provided in article 36, the access to payment account services at credit institutions, makes for even stronger possibilities for new entrants to compete with existing PSPs. Though, this provision could be considered rather unfair for account servicing PSPs, as it restricts their freedom of contract, it is a necessary evil to ensure equal access to provide payment services in the EU.

Articles 66 and 67 have given third-party PSPs an advantage over their account servicing PSP competitors, as the latter group have been forced to give access without any option for remuneration despite having to pay for the costs

[17] Proposal for a Regulation of the European Parliament and of the Council on a framework for Financial Data Access and amending Regulations (EU) No 1093/2010, (EU) No 1094/2010, (EU) No 1095/2010 and (EU) 2022/2554 (COM(2023) 360 final) [2023].

[18] At the time of finalising this manuscript.

[19] These special requirements also look to be modified slightly in the proposed PSD3 as practice has shown that the special insurance can be very difficult to obtain prior to gaining authorisation.

[20] Christensen, 'Crypto payments – a danger to consumer protection?' also explains the dangers this pose to particularly consumers, even when paying with a well-known cryptocurrency such as bitcoin.

[21] Though, the proposed PSR does introduce an even more strict application of the provision.

related to providing access for their competitors. This can be considered a rather unjust configuration of the PSD2, though there might be hope a more level playing field in the future as the FiDA proposal entails a new solution, where market participants share the costs via membership in data access schemes.[22] This would prove to be a more sustainable long term solution, though payment account data are being kept outside the scope of the regulation for now.[23] While this could be promising for account servicing PSPs in the very long term, it could also come to impact the interpretation of the access obtained via article 67, as it can be argued that the AIS should only be interpreted narrowly as payment account data, ie leaving other deposit accounts, loans etc. at the same institution outside of the scope.[24] This would leave AISPs in a more restricted position in terms of how they design their service and the costs related to providing it, than what is the case under the PSD2, though it would provide for a more balanced payment services market.

In terms of creating safer payments, the PSD2 introduced an entire chapter to improve the safety and security of payment services. Although innovation was the driver of a need to improve security of payments, it also served as the means to improve this aspect with the new opportunities which APIs and SCA give rise to. Over the course of implementing SCA, statistics on fraud in payments have shown a decline, providing proof of the effect of implementing this safety measure. While a decrease in financial fraud is positive, examining the implementation of SCA in practice through the EBA's guidelines and RTSs showed a tendency to favour the technology of APIs. This preferential treatment is not in alignment with the EU Commission's agenda of promoting technology neutrality. Furthermore, account servicing PSPs have been required to develop and maintain APIs, which entails burdensome costs for these PSPs, but not for the others, without due reasoning. Such differential treatment does not provide the desired level playing field in the market for payment services.

With the focus on providing access to payment account data, the PSD2 has enabled Open Banking within the EU,[25] which entail important elements to build upon moving forward towards the desired Open Finance era.[26] As such,

[22] Proposal for FiDA art 10.

[23] Directorate-General for Financial Stability Financial Services and Capital Markets Union, *Financial data access and payments package* (European Commission 2023).

[24] Louise Damkjær Christensen, 'The New Financial Information Service – Changing the Market of Information Services for the Better?' (2024) 35 European Business Law Review 905 also examines the potential conflicts between the proposals.

[25] Francesco De Pascalis and Alan Brener, *Open Banking—Global development and regulation* (Routledge International Studies in Money and Banking, Routledge 2024) provides a thorough understanding of the Open Banking concept from multiple global perspectives.

[26] Francesco De Pascalis, 'The Journey to Open Finance: Learning from the Open Banking Movement' (2022) 33 European Business Law Review 397.

the lessons learned from implementing the PSD2 can be utilised to create even better conditions and solutions for a wider range of service areas with Open Finance. Though, as can be seen from the problems related to consumers and their ability to make informed financial decisions, the protection of consumers ought to be of utmost priority to avoid consumers being taken advantage. With Open Banking, as will also be the case for Open Finance, there exist a risk of data brokers harvesting consumers' financial data with the purpose of reselling them to create adverse financial products targeted that group of consumers, without their informed consent. To ensure continued consumer confidence in financial services, it is therefore important to shape the rules in a way that protects financial data belonging to consumers.

In summary, the PSD2 accommodates many of the developments present in financial innovation and utilises some of these to improve the safety of payment services. The financial markets are highly impacted by innovation, which the EU regulator has adopted as, what could almost be interpreted as, a new goal of financial regulation where in some situations, at least in the PSD2, innovation seems to have been weighed higher than other goals of financial regulation. For example, with the free access to payment account data incurring rising costs for account servicing PSPs with no option to monetise on their investments. This calls for considerations on creating standards for pricing access to payment accounts via APIs. Furthermore, the limited financial literacy of consumers is not in harmony with the continuously increasing level of ability needed for navigating the innovative market for payment services, which calls for rethinking how financial institutions disclose information to consumers.

With the Directive's article 107 in mind, which calls for full harmonisation in Member States when implementing the Directive, it makes immense sense that the EU Commission has proposed in its revision of the PSD2, a new PSD3 and a regulation in the form of the proposed PSR. The regulation will ensure full harmonisation on the material aspects of the current PSD2, only keeping Member State dependent matters in the proposed PSD3, in particular the rules concerning authorisation.[27]

As the work of this book testaments, there still exists some areas of potential problems for the future of EU Payment Services, but it is also worth acknowledging the PSD2's management of market and non-market failures and its efforts in accommodating financial innovation. It should be kept in mind that it

[27] This split into a directive and a regulation is also well-known within financial regulation as it is also the case with MiFID-MiFIR and CRR-CRD.

is not regulation's job to create a zero failure environment but an environment where failure can be managed so that it does not endanger the stability of the financial system and create market dislocation.[28] The PSD2 provides a regulatory framework where failures have been dealt with to varying degrees of satisfaction. Considering regulation's ever impossible task of keeping up with innovation and the EU Commission's launched proposals for a revision of the Directive, the regulatory efforts have been sufficient for now.

[28] Ross Cranston and others, *Principles of Banking Law* (3rd edn, OUP 2017) 28.

Bibliography

Books

Alexander K, *Principles of Banking Regulation* (CUP 2019)

Andenæs M and Chiu I H-Y, *The Foundations and Future of Financial Regulation—Governance for Responsibility* (Routledge Taylor & Francis Group 2014)

Armour J and others, *Principles of Financial Regulation* (OUP 2016)

Begg D, Fischer S, and Dornbusch R, *Economics* (6th edn, McGraw-Hill Publishing Company 2000)

Bork RH, *The Antitrust Paradox—A Policy at War with Itself* (Basic Books Inc. 1978)

Burke AS and others, *SOU-CCJ230 Introduction to the American Criminal Justice System* (Open Oregon Educational Resources 2019)

Buttigieg E, *Competition Law: Safeguarding the Consumer Interest*, vol 40 (International Competition Law Series, Kluwer Law International 2009)

Casanova J and Savoie M (eds), *Payment Services—Law and Practice* (Edward Elgar Publishing 2022)

Chiu I H-Y, *Regulating the Crypto Economy: Business Transformations and Financialisation* (Hart Publishing 2021)

Chiu I H-Y and Deipenbrock G (eds), *Routledge Handbook of Financial Technology and Law* (Routledge 2021)

Coase RH, *The Firm, the Market and the Law* (University of Chicago Press 1990)

Cooter R and Ulen T, *Law and Economics* (6th edn, Berkeley Law Books 2016)

Costa M and Peers S, *Steiner & Woods EU Law* (14th edn, OUP 2020)

Cowen T (ed), *The Theory of Market Failure—A Critical Examination* (George Mason University Press 1988)

Cranston R and others, *Principles of Banking Law* (3rd edn, OUP 2017)

De Pascalis F and Brener A, *Open Banking—Global Development and Regulation* (Routledge International Studies in Money and Banking, Routledge 2024)

Dau-Schmidt KG and Ulen TS, *Law and Economics Anthology* (Anderson Publishing Co. 1998)

Gimigliano G and Beroš MB (eds), *The Payment Services Directive 2—A Commentary* (Elgar Commentaries in Financial Law, Edward Elgar Publishing 2021)

Goodhart CAE, *The Regulatory Response to the Financial Crisis* (Edward Elgar Publishing 2009)

Hayek FAv, *The Road to Serfdom* (Routledge 1944)

Hayek FAv, *Denationalisation of Money* (The Institute of Economic Affairs 1976)

Hayne P, *The Economic Way of Thinking* (6th edn, Macmillan 1991)

Keynes JM, *The General Theory of Employment, Interest, and Money* (Palgrave Macmillan 2018 (original 1936))

Kohn M, *Financial Institutions and Markets* (2nd edn, OUP 2004)

Madir J (ed), *FinTech Law and Regulation* (Elgar Financial Law and Practice, 2nd edn, Edward Elgar Publishing 2021)

Marx K, *Das Kapital* (Gustav Kiepenheuer Verlag AG 1932 (original 1867))

Moloney N, *The Age of ESMA: Governing EU Financial Markets* (Hart Publishing 2018)

Moloney N, Ferran E, and Payne J (eds), *The Oxford Handbook of Financial Regulation* (OUP 2015)

Öberg J, *Limits to EU Powers—A Case Study of EU Regulatory Criminal Law* (Hart Studies in European Criminal Law, Hart Publishing 2017)

Pigou AC, *The Economics of Welfare* (MacMillan and Co. 1921)

Pistor K, *The Code of Capital: How the Law Creates Wealth and Inequality* (Princeton University Press 2019)

Ross A, *Om ret og retfærdighed* (Nyt Nordisk Forlag 1953)

Ross A, *On Law and Justice* (OUP 2019)

Pindyck RS and Rubinfield DL, *Microeconomics* (8th edn, Pearson 2013)

Schumpeter JA, *The Theory of Economic Development: An Inquiry into Profits, Capital, Credit, Interest, and the Business Cycle* (Harvard University Press 1934)

Smith A, *An Inquiry into the Nature and Causes of the Wealth of Nations* (George Routledge and Sons 1890 (original 1776))

Book chapters

Brener A, 'Payment Service Directive II and Its Implications' in Lynn T and others (eds), *Disrupting Finance* (Palgrave Pivot, Cham 2019)

Brener A, 'EU payment services regulation and international developments' in Chiu IH-Y and Deipenbrock G (eds), *Routledge Handbook of Financial Technology and Law* (Routledge 2021)

Corvese CG, 'Title 2 "Payment Service Providers", chapter 1 "Payment Institutions", section 1 "General Rules" (art. 5-18), section 2 "Other Requirements" (art. 19-21)' in Gimigliano G and Beroš MB (eds), *The Payment Services Directive—A Commentary* (Edward Elgar Publishing 2021)

Crotty J, 'The Realism of Assumptions Does Matter—Why Keynes-Minsky Theory Nust Replace Efficient Market Theory as the Guide to Financial Regulation Policy' in Wolfson MH and Epstein GA (eds), *The Handbook of the Political Economy of Financial Crises* (OUP 2013)

Divissenko N, 'Title 2 Payment Service Providers, Chapter 2 Common Provisions (arts 35-37)' in Gimigliano G and Beroš MB (eds), *The Payment Services Directive 2 A Commentary* (Elgar Commentaries in Financial Law, 2021)

Geva B, 'Title 1 "Subject Matter, Scope and Definitions" (arts 1-4)' in Gimigliano G and Beroš MB (eds), *The Payment Services Directive 2—A Commentary* (Edward Elgar Publishing 2021)

Gimigliano G, 'Chapter 9—Title IV, "Rights and obligations in relation to the provision and use of payment services", chapter 2 "Authorisation of payment transactions" (Arts 64-77)' in Gimigliano G and Beroš MB (eds), *The Payment Services Directive 2—A Commentary* (Elgar Commentaries in Financial Law, Edward Elgar 2021)

Gimigliano G, 'Title 2 "Payment Service Providers", Chapter 2 "Common Provisions" (art 35-37) sect. F and G' in Gimigliano G and Beroš MB (eds), *The Payment Services Directive 2—A Commentary* (Elgar Commentaries in Financial Law, Edward Elgar Publishing 2021)

González Fuster G, 'EU Data Protection and Future Payment Services' in Gimigliano G (ed), *Bitcoin and Mobile Payments* (Palgrave Macmillan UK 2016)

Heath J, 'A Market Failures Approach to Business Ethics' in *Morality, Competition, and the Firm: The Market Failures Approach to Business Ethics* (OUP 2014)

Kleiman MAR and Teles SM, 'Market and Non-Market Failures' in Moran M, Rein M, and Goodin RE (eds), *The Oxford Handbook of Public Policy* (OUP 2006)

Lastra R, 'Systemic Risk and Macro-Prudential Supervision' in Moloney N, Ferran E, and Payne J (eds), *The Oxford Handbook of Financial Regulation* (OUP 2015)

Levi M, 'Financial Crimes' in Tonry M (ed), *The Oxford Handbook of Crime and Public Policy* (OUP 2009)

MacNeil I, 'Enforcement and Sanctioning' in Moloney N, Ferran E, and Payne J (eds), *The Oxford Handbook of Financial Regulation* (OUP 2015)

Minto A, 'Law and Economics: Theory, Methodology and Policy Application' in Risvig Hamer C and Schaumburg-Müller S (eds), *Juraens Verden Metoder, Retskilder og Discipliner* (DJØF Forlag 2020)

Partnoy F, 'Financial Systems, Crises, and Regulation' in Moloney N, Ferran E, and Payne J (eds), *The Oxford Handbook of Financial Regulation* (OUP 2015)

Phang S-Y, 'Market Failures' in *Housing Finance Systems: Market Failures and Government Failures* (Palgrave Macmillan UK 2013)

Schaumburg-Müller S and Viskum B, 'Retspolitik og metode' in Risvig Hamer C and Schaumburg-Müller S (eds), *Juraens Verden Metoder, Retskilder og Discipliner* (DJØF Forlag 2020)

Skovmand Rasmussen N, 'Den retlige prøvelse af henstillinger og retningslinjer i EU-kapitalmarkedsret' in Jul Clausen N and others (eds), *Festskrift til Hans Viggo Godsk Pedersen* (2017)

Tuch AF, 'Conduct of Business Regulation' in Moloney N, Ferran E, and Payne J (eds), *The Oxford Handbook of Financial Regulation* (OUP 2015)

Veljanovski C, 'Economic Approaches to Regulation' in Baldwin R, Cave M, and Lodge M (eds), *The Oxford Handbook of Regulation* (OUP 2010)

Wandhöfer R, 'Title IV "Rights and Obligations in Relation to the Provision and Use of Payment Services", Chapter 5 "Operational and Security Risks and Authentication" (Arts 95-98)' in Gimigliano G and Beroš MB (eds), *The Payment Services Directive 2—A Commentary* (Elgar Commentaries in Financial Law, Edward Elgar Publishing 2021)

Journal articles

Akerlof GA, 'The Market for "Lemons": Quality Uncertainty and the Market Mechanism' (1970) 84 The Quarterly Journal of Economics 488

Barroso M and Laborda J, 'Digital transformation and the emergence of the Fintech sector: Systematic literature review' (2022) 2 Digital Business 100028

Basaran B and Bagheri M, 'The Relevance of "Trust and Confidence" in Financial Markets to the Information Production Role of Banks' (2020) 11 European Journal of Risk Regulation 650

Bator FM, 'The Anatomy of Market Failure' (1958) 72 The Quarterly Journal of Economics 351

Blunden C, 'Between Market Failures and Justice Failures: Trade-Offs Between Efficiency and Equality in Business Ethics: JBE' (2022) 178 Journal of Business Ethics 647

Borgogno O and Colangelo G, 'Consumer Inertia and Competition-sensitive Data Governance: The Case of Open Banking' (2020) 9(4) Journal of European Consumer and Market Law 143

Chiu IH-Y, 'A New Era in Fintech Payment Innovations? A Perspective from the Institutions and Regulation of Payment Systems' (2017) 9 Law, Innovation and Technology 190

Christensen LD, 'Crypto payments – a danger to consumer protection?' (2022) 16 Law and Financial Markets Review 197

Christensen LD, 'The New Financial Information Service – Changing the Market of Information Services for the Better?' (2024) 35 European Business Law Review 905

Claessens S, 'Competition in the Financial Sector: Overview of Competition Policies' (2009) 09 IMF Working Papers

De Meijer CRW and Bye J, 'The increasing adoption of mobile payments in Europe — and remaining challenges to growth' (2011) 5 Journal of Payments Strategy & Systems 273

De Pascalis F, 'The Journey to Open Finance: Learning from the Open Banking Movement' (2022) 33 European Business Law Review 397

Diamond D and Dybvig P, 'Bank Runs, Deposit Insurance, and Liquidity' (1983) 91 Journal of Political Economy 401

Dollery B and Wallis J, 'The Theory of Market Failure and Policy Making in Contemporary Local Government' (2001) 2001–6 Working Paper Series in Economics at University of New England

Donnelly M, 'Payments in the digital market: Evaluating the contribution of Payment Services Directive II' (2016) 32 Computer Law & Security Review 827–39

Ferretti F, 'Open Banking: Gordian Legal Knots in the Uncomfortable Cohabitation between the PSD2 and the GDPR' (2022) 30 European Review of Private Law 73

Gong R and Page F, 'Shadow Banks and Systemic Risks' (2016) SRC Discussion Paper

Greenwald BC and Stiglitz JE, 'Externalities in Economies with Imperfect Information and Incomplete Markets' (1986) 101 The Quarterly Journal of Economics 229

Guimarães MR and Steennot R, 'Allocation of Liability in Case of Payment Fraud: Who Bears the Risk of Innovation? A Comparison of Belgian and Portuguese Law in the Context of PSD2' (2022) 30(1) European Review of Private Law 29

Hansen T, 'The Role of Trust in Financial Customer-seller Relationships Before and After the Financial Crisis' (2014) 13 Journal of Consumer Behaviour 442

Hayek FAv, 'The Use of Knowledge in Society' (1945) 35 The American Economic Review 519

Kaplow L, 'Rules Versus Standards: An Economic Analysis' (1992) 42 Duke Law Journal 557

Kjørven ME, 'Who Pays When Things Go Wrong? Online Financial Fraud and Consumer Protection in Scandinavia and Europe' (2020) 31(1) European Business Law Review 77

Lando H, 'A Pragmatic View of Fairness and Social Welfare in the Analysis of Law' (2020) 20 CBS Law Research Paper Series

Lastra RM, 'Defining Forward Looking, Judgement-based Supervision' (2013) 14 Journal of Banking Regulation 221

Le Grand J, 'The Theory of Government Failure' (1991) 21 British Journal of Political Science 423

Lučić A, Barbić D, and Uzelac M, 'Theoretical underpinnings of consumers' financial capability research' (2022) International Journal of Consumer Studies 1

Maculan E and Gil Gil A, 'The Rationale and Purposes of Criminal Law and Punishment in Transitional Contexts' (2020) 40 Oxford Journal of Legal Studies 132

Mallat N and Tuunainen VK, 'Exploring Merchant Adoption of Mobile Payments: An Empirical Study' (2008) 6 e-Service Journal 24

Pinotti P, 'Trust, Regulation and Market Failures' (2012) 94 The Review of Economics and Statistics 650

Polasik M and others, 'The impact of Payment Services Directive 2 on the PayTech sector development in Europe' (2020) 178 Journal of Economic Behavior & Organization 385

Repullo R and Suarez J, 'The Procyclical Effects of Bank Capital Regulation' (2013) 26 The Review of Financial Studies 452

Romānova I and others, 'The Payment Services Directive 2 and Competitiveness: The Perspective of European Fintech Companies' (2018) XXI European Research Studies Journal 5

Rose K, 'Regulating the Externality of Money Laundering—Halfway there' (2019) No 19-12 CBS Law Research Paper Series

Shavell S, 'The Optimal Structure of Law Enforcement' (1993) 36 Journal of Law and Economics 255

Stigler GJ, 'The Theory of Economic Regulation' (1971) 2 The Bell Journal of Economics and Management Science 3

Stigler GJ, 'Free Riders and Collective Action: An Appendix to Theories of Economic Regulation' (1974) 5 The Bell Journal of Economics and Management Science 359

Tirole J, 'Market Failures and Public Policy' (2015) 105 The American Economic Review 1665

Wolf Jr. C, '"Non-Market" Failures and Market Failures' (1978) The Rand Paper Series

Wolf Jr. C, 'A Theory of "Non-Market Failure": Framework for Implementation Analysis' (1978) The Rand Paper Series

Wolters PTJ and Jacobs BPF, 'The security of access to accounts under the PSD2' (2019) 35 Computer Law & Security Review 29

Yeoh P, 'Innovations in Financial Services: Regulatory Implications' (2016) 37 Business Law Review 190

Zetzsche DA and others, 'From FinTech to TechFin: The Regulatory Challenges of Data-Driven Finance' (2018) 14 New York University Journal of Law & Business 393

EU documents and reports

Directorate-General for Financial Stability Financial Services and Capital Markets Union, *Revised rules for payment services in the EU—Summary of Directive (EU) 2015/2366 on EU-wide payment services* (2016)

Financial data access and payments package (European Commission 2023)

ECB Crypto-Assets Task Force, *Crypto-Assets: Implications for financial stability, monetary policy, and payments and market infrastructures* (European Central Bank 2019)

European Banking Authority, *EBA report on the data provided by PSPs on their readiness to apply strong customer authentication for e-commerce card-based payment transactions* (European Banking Authority 2021)

Joint ESAs Report on the withdrawal of authorisation for serious breaches of AML/CFT rules (European Banking Authority 2022)

EBA Financial Education Report 2019/2020 (2020)

European Banking Authority, European Securities and Markets Authority and European Insurance and Occupational Pensions Authority, *Joint Report: FinTech: Regulatory sandboxes and innovation hubs* (2019)

European Commission, *Completing the Internal Market* (COM(85)310 final) (1985)

European Commission, *Green Paper: Towards an integrated European market for card, internet and mobile payments* (COM(2011) 941 final) (2012)

European Commission, *Commission Staff Working Document Impact Assessment* (SWD(2013) 288 final) (2013)

European Commission, *Summary of contributions to the 'Public Consultation on FinTech: a more competitive and innovative European financial sector'* (2017)

European Commission, *Payment Services Directive: Frequently Asked Questions* (https://ec.europa.eu/commission/presscorner/detail/en/MEMO_15_5793 2018)

European Commission, *Payment services: Consumers to benefit from cheaper, safer and more innovate electronic payments* (European Commission 2018)

European Commission, *The Retail Payments Strategy* (European Commission 2020)

European Data Protection Supervisor, *Executive Summary of the Opinion of the European Data Protection Supervisor on a Proposal for a Directive of the European Parliament and of the Council on payment services in the internal market amending Directives 2002/65/EC, 2006/48/EC and 2009/110/EC and repealing Directive 2007/64/EC, and for a Regulation of the European Parliament and of the Council on interchange fees for card-based payment transactions (2014/C 38/07)* (Official Journal of the European Union 2014 C38 14 2014)

European Banking Federation, *EBF response to European Commission Consultation on the review of the revised payment services Directive (PSD2)* (European Banking Federation 2022)

European Fintech Association, *Position Paper on the Revised Payment Services Directive 2* (European Fintech Association 2022)

European Supervisory Authorities, *Joint ESAs thematic repository of national financial education initiatives on digitalisation—with a specific focus on cybersecurity, scams and fraud* (2022)

Expert Group on Regulatory Obstacles to Financial Innovation (ROFIEG), *30 Recommendations on Regulation, Innovation and Finance* (2019)

Finans Danmark, *Finance Denmark's response to Targeted consultation on the review of the revised payment services Directive (PSD2)* (2022)

Finans Danmark, *Finance Denmark's response to the Commissions consultation on the review of the revised Payment Services Directive (PSD2)* (2022)

Proposal for a Directive of the European Parliament and of the Council on payment services and electronic money services in the Internal Market amending Directive 98/26/EC and repealing Directives 2015/2366/EU and 2009/110/EC (COM(2023) 366 final)

Proposal for a Regulation of the European Parliament and of the Council on a framework for Financial Data Access and amending Regulations (EU) No 1093/2010 (EU) No 1094/2010, (EU) No 1095/2010 and (EU) 2022/2554 (COM(2023) 360 final)

Proposal for a Regulation of the European Parliament and of the Council on payment services in the internal market and amending Regulation (EU) No 1093/2010 (COM(2023) 367 final)

Other documents and reports

Bank for International Settlements, *AML and CFT in banking—Executive Summary* (2021)

Basel Committee on Banking Supervision, *Sound Practices: Implications of fintech developments for banks and bank supervisors* (2018)

Bourreau M, Krämer J and Buiten M, *Interoperability in Digital Markets* (CERRE 2022)

EY, *Global FinTech Adoption Index 2019* (2019)

Financial Action Task Force (FATF), *Partnering in the Fight Against Financial Crime: Data Protection, Technology and Private Sector Information Sharing* (2022)

Financial Stability Board, *Financial Stability Implications from FinTech: Supervisory and Regulatory Issues that Merit Authorities' Attention* (2017)

Finanstilsynet (Danish Financial Supervisory Authority), *Temaundersøgelse om betalings—og e-pengeinstitutters sikring af brugermidler* (2023)

Konkurrence—og Forbrugerstyrelsen (Danish competition and consumer authority), *Betalingsrapport 2024* (2024)

Nakamoto S, *Bitcoin: A Peer-to-Peer Electronic Cash System* (White Paper, 2008)

NETS, *European Fraud Report—Payments Industry Challenges* (2019)

OECD, *Regulatory Policy and Governance* (2011)

OECD, *Consumer vulnerability in the digital age* (OECD Digital Economy Papers No 355, 2023)

OECD/INFE Toolkit for Measuring Financial Literacy and Financial Inclusion (2018)

OECD/INFE 2020 International Survey of Adult Financial Literacy (2020)

PISA 2018 Assessment and Analytical Framework (2019)

Websites and newspapers

'Public Consultation on FinTech: a more competitive and innovative European financial sector' (2017) <https://ec.europa.eu/info/consultations/finance-2017-fintech_en> accessed 11 October 2021

'FAQ: Making Electronic Payments and Online Banking Safer and Easier for Consumers' (2019) <https://ec.europa.eu/commission/presscorner/detail/en/qanda_19_5555> accessed 16 June 2022

Browne R, 'Wirecard scandal hits UK consumers as online banking apps freeze accounts' (*CNBC*, 2020) <https://www.cnbc.com/2020/06/29/wirecard-scandal-hits-users-of-uk-fintech-apps-curve-anna-and-pockit.html> accessed 8 October 2021

European Banking Authority, 'The Single Rulebook' (*European Banking Authority*, <https://www.eba.europa.eu/regulation-and-policy/single-rulebook> accessed 16 December 2022

European Commission, 'Payment Services' <https://ec.europa.eu/info/business-economy-euro/banking-and-finance/consumer-finance-and-payments/payment-services/payment-services_en> accessed 10 February 2022

Financial Conduct Authority, 'Regulatory Sandbox' (2022) <https://www.fca.org.uk/firms/innovation/regulatory-sandbox> accessed 27 October 2022

Lamont S, *Open Banking Walked so Open Finance Could Run* (Fintech Prime Time 2024)

McKendry I, 'ISIL May Be Using Bitcon, Fincen's Calvery Says' *American Banker* (16 November 2015) Law and Regulation <https://www.americanbanker.com/news/isil-may-be-using-bitcoin-fincens-calvery-says> accessed 24th April 2022

Open Banking Limited, 'The Open Banking Standard' (2024) <https://standards.openbanking.org.uk/> accessed 8 July 2024

Oxvig M and Højlund S, 'Direktør kaster nyt lys over betalingskonkurs: Kunders penge var formentlig ikke godt nok beskyttet' (*JP/Politikens Hus A/S*, 2022) <https://finanswatch.dk/Finansnyt/Fintech/article13576760.ece> accessed 6 January 2022

Oxvig M and Højlund S, 'Kurator undersøger om regler for betalingsinstitutter er overholdt i konkursramt selskab' (*JP/Politikens Hus A/S*, 2022) <https://finanswatch.dk/article13575248.ece?utm_campaign=FinansWatch%20Morgen&utm_content=2022-01-14&utm_medium=email&utm_source=finanswatch> accessed 14 January 2022

Panetta F, *For a Few Cryptos More: The Wild West of Crypto Finance* (European Central Bank 2022)

PYMNTS, 'PYMNTS Intelligence: The Promise of Faster Transactions Using Blockchain Technology' (*PYMNTS.com*, 2022) <https://www.pymnts.com/blockchain/2022/pymnts-intelligence-the-promise-of-faster-transactions-using-blockchain-technology/> accessed 18 August 2022

Yuniar RW, 'Bitcoin, PayPal Used to Finance Terrorism, Indonesian Agency Says' *The Wall Street Journal* (10 January 2017) World—Asia <https://www.wsj.com/articles/bitcoin-paypal-used-to-finance-terrorism-indonesian-agency-says-1483964198> accessed 24th April 2022

X C, 'Cryptocurrency Payment Gateway Development—Best Crypto Development Solutions' (*Finextra,* 2021) <https://www.finextra.com/blogposting/20872/cryptocurrency-payment-gateway-development--best-crypto-development-solutions> accessed 18 August 2022

Index

For the benefit of digital users, indexed terms that span two pages (e.g., 52–53) may, on occasion, appear on only one of those pages.